Praise for *Confessing and Believing*

"This is a survival handbook for those venturing to explore life in all its risk and excitement. The author knows the heights and depths of the terrain, and opens them up to the reader with warmth, humor, and deep insight."

—Judith Wolfe, University of St. Andrews

"The Apostles' Creed is a theological statement, but it is theology that arises from and finds its home in the life of the church. That same intersection might describe this wise, learned, and engaging reflection on the Creed. Trevor Hart is one of our most gifted theologians. But in these pages he also addresses the whole church as a skilled pastor, with great clarity, warmth, and wit."

—Steven R. Guthrie, Belmont University

"Trevor Hart's exposition breathes new life into this ancient creed, essentially a distillation of the story of Scripture, and shows that it is at once the Christian's belief system, worship hymn, and dramatic script. That this book began as a series of sermons serves as a reminder that the best theology serves the church as a guide to faith's search for understanding."

—Kevin J. Vanhoozer, Trinity Evangelical Divinity School

Trevor Hart is an unusual writer. Being both a seasoned academic theologian and a working pastor, he brings to his treatment of the Apostles' Creed the critical eye of the scholar, as well as the light touch of one accustomed to making difficult theology plain. These qualities are in ample evidence in this volume, which readers will find warms their hearts as it instructs their minds. I heartily recommend it.

—Professor Oliver Crisp, University of St. Andrews

Confessing and Believing

Confessing and Believing

The Apostles' Creed as Script for the Christian Life

Trevor Hart

Fortress Press
Minneapolis

CONFESSING AND BELIEVING
The Apostles' Creed as Script for the Christian Life

Copyright © 2022 Fortress Press, an imprint of 1517 Media. All rights reserved. Except for brief quotations in critical articles or reviews, no part of this book may be reproduced in any manner without prior written permission from the publisher. Email copyright@1517.media or write to Permissions, Fortress Press, PO Box 1209, Minneapolis, MN 55440-1209.

All biblical quotations, unless otherwise indicated, are either from or based upon the New Revised Standard Version Bible, copyright © 1989 National Council of the Churches of Christ in the United States of America. Used by permission. All rights reserved worldwide.

Scripture quotations marked (NASB) are from the (NASB®) New American Standard Bible®, Copyright © 1960, 1971, 1977, 1995 by The Lockman Foundation. Used by permission. All rights reserved. www.lockman.org.

Scripture quotations marked (ESV) are from the *ESV® Bible (The Holy Bible, English Standard Version®)*, Copyright © 2001 by Crossway, a publishing ministry of Good News Publishers. Used by permission. All rights reserved.

Scripture quotations marked (NET) are from the NET Bible® copyright ©1996, 2019 by Biblical Studies Press, L.L.C. http://netbible.com All rights reserved.

Scripture quotations marked (KJV) are from the King James Version.

Scripture quotations marked (NKJV) are from the New King James Version®. Copyright © 1982 by Thomas Nelson. Used by permission. All rights reserved.

Scripture quotations marked (NLT) are from the Holy Bible, New Living Translation, copyright ©1996, 2004, 2015 by Tyndale House Foundation. Used by permission of Tyndale House Publishers, Carol Stream, Illinois 60188. All rights reserved.

Scripture quotations marked (NRSVA) are from New Revised Standard Version Bible: Anglicized Edition, copyright © 1989, 1995 National Council of the Churches of Christ in the United States of America. Used by permission. All rights reserved worldwide.

Scripture quotations marked (TPT) are from The Passion Translation®. Copyright © 2017, 2018, 2020 by Passion and Fire Ministries, Inc. Used by permission. All rights reserved. ThePassionTranslation.com.

Scripture quotations marked (WEB) are from the World English Bible.

Scripture quotations marked (NABRE) are from the *New American Bible, revised edition* © 2010, 1991, 1986, 1970 Confraternity of Christian Doctrine, Washington, D.C. and are used by permission of the copyright owner. All Rights Reserved. No part of the New American Bible may be reproduced in any form without permission in writing from the copyright owner.

Cover image: The twelve Apostles receiving inspiration from the Holy Spirit and composing the Creed, from Sommele Roy, a moral compendium/Wikipedia
Cover design: Laurie Ingram Art + Design.com

Print ISBN: 978-1-5064-8547-8
eBook ISBN: 978-1-5064-8548-5

For our granddaughter Ailsa, born on 16th November 2021 just a few days after this book was completed. In the hope that some day you may read it, and discover in it questions worth asking and stories worth telling about the world into which you have been born.

Symbolum Apostolorum

Credo in Deum Patrem omnipotentem;
    Creatorem coeli et terrae.

Et in Jesum Christum, Filium ejus unicum, Dominum nostrum;
    qui conceptus est de Spiritu Sancto,
    natus ex Maria virgine;
    passus sub Pontio Pilato,
    crucifixus, mortuus, et sepultus;
    descendit ad inferna;
    tertia die resurrexit a mortuis;
    ascendit ad coelos;
    sedet ad dexteram Dei Patris omnipotentis;
    inde venturus judicare vivos et mortuos.

Credo in Spiritum Sanctum;
    sanctam ecclesiam catholicam;
    sanctorum communionem;
    remissionem peccatorum;
    carnis resurrectionem;
    vitam oeternam.

                                      Amen.

The Apostles' Creed

I believe in God the Father almighty,
  creator of heaven and earth.

I believe in Jesus Christ, his only Son, our Lord,
  who was conceived by the Holy Spirit,
  born of the Virgin Mary,
  suffered under Pontius Pilate,
  was crucified, died, and was buried;
  he descended to the dead.
  On the third day he rose again;
  he ascended into heaven, he is seated on the right hand of God
    the Father Almighty,
  and he will come to judge the living and the dead.

I believe in the Holy Spirit,
  the holy catholic Church,
  the communion of saints,
  the forgiveness of sins,
  the resurrection of the body,
  and the life everlasting.

Amen.

CONTENTS

Preface		xiii
Memorizing Mere Christianity		1

I

1.	"I believe . . ."	13
2.	"God the Father almighty, creator of heaven and earth . . ."	39

II

3.	"In Jesus Christ, his only Son, our Lord . . ."	67
4.	"Conceived by the Holy Spirit, born of the Virgin Mary . . ."	83
5.	"Suffered under Pontius Pilate, was crucified, died, and was buried; he descended to the dead . . ."	99
6.	"On the third day he rose again . . ."	117
7.	"He ascended into heaven, he is seated on the right hand of God the Father Almighty . . ."	141
8.	"He will come to judge the living and the dead . . ."	157

III

9.	"I believe in the Holy Spirit . . ."	179
10.	"The holy catholic Church . . ."	209
11.	"The forgiveness of sins . . ."	235
12.	"The resurrection of the body, and the life everlasting . . ."	275

Notes	297
Selected Bibliography	329
Index	335

PREFACE

"OF THE MAKING of many books there is no end."¹ Like any biblical text, this one lends itself to different inflections. Read perkily, it might gratefully be adopted, for instance, as the strap line for a hopeful new publishing venture. Or perhaps more in keeping with the Eeyoreish tone of the book of Ecclesiastes, it might be heard instead as a writer's weary reflection on the mismatch between authorial idea and aspiration on the one hand and the cruel conditions of human finitude on the other. So many great books to write; so little time. It behooves authors, therefore, to think carefully about which projects are worth the expenditure of their perpetually diminishing reserves of time and energy, lest they labor long and hard to produce books of which the best that can be said is that they fill much-needed gaps in the market.

By way of an apologia for this particular volume and the considerable time and effort expended in bringing it into the world, I offer two considerations variously to my prospective readers; my wife, Rachel; my congregation; and anyone else at risk of being or having been adversely affected either by the process or by the product itself.

First, as its subtitle reveals, this is first and foremost intended as an exposition of the Apostles' Creed, and despite reasonable expectation, there are not so many books already dedicated to this task as to make yet another self-evidently superfluous from the outset. The list is relatively slender, and the short list of those worth spending much time with is more slender still. Too many are insubstantial, tending at best merely to whet the appetite rather than granting it any lasting satisfaction. Others are "classics" which, for that very reason, must satisfy despite inevitably having a rather dated feel where their assumptions and cultural allusions are concerned. So a fresh treatment of this topic, adding yet one more to the many books of whose making there is no end, seemed warranted so long as any such book would wrestle deliberately with a number of challenges.

Such a book should, of course, grant careful attention to the actual substance of "the faith that was once for all entrusted to the saints," reckoning with this in relation to both its biblical roots and its faithful development and transmission in the life of the church across the centuries.[2] In other words, the book must meet the needs of the contemporary reader seeking a reliable and sufficiently meaty account of the so-called Vincentian canon of Christian convictions—"what has been believed everywhere, always, and by all."[3]

This alone, though, might end up encouraging Christian navel-gazing of a self-indulgent and unhealthy sort unless it also reckoned seriously with the wider human contexts within which these same convictions have arisen and in relation to which they always have been and must today be articulated and made sense of. To deploy a convenient shorthand that I have used elsewhere, the proposed book's concern must be not only with the "internal coherence" of the world of Christian beliefs and practices represented by the Apostles' Creed but with its "external coherence" too[4]—that is to say, with its integrity relative to the wider set of beliefs we and our fellow citizens of late modernity typically hold concerning all sorts of things, most of which fall identifiably beyond the range of concern of either Scripture or creeds and about which, therefore, they do not presume to tell us anything at all. And yet, of course, the implications of those things that they *do* tell us about are of such magnitude and scope that we are bound to ask and to answer questions about the reasonableness of believing them and allowing them the primacy of consideration not just in some secure silo of our lives marked "religion" but across the whole territory of our living to which, if true, they lay legitimate claim.

That the attempt to discover or establish an underlying coherence between our understanding of the gospel and our wider understanding of the world should be a challenging and sometimes uncomfortable one ought not to surprise us—the intellectual and cultural contexts of the twenty-first century themselves being far more tolerant of fragmentation than most others and typically resistant to being asked to bear too much truth except in certain randomly privileged areas. The responsible search for a coherent and meaningful outlook on reality (even though this reality, being unfathomably deep and rich rather than shallow, may forever frustrate our attempts to get our heads around it completely) is incumbent upon Christians, whatever others may be prepared to rest content with. For it belongs to the Christian's wider creed that God, in love, eternally purposed a creation marked by order rather than chaos and so fit for human habitation and flourishing together with God and with our fellow creatures.[5] Seeking to understand this cosmic order to the best of our ability is thus an imperative contained within the summons to worship this same God not just with all our heart, all our soul, and all our strength but with all our mind too.[6] And, of course, we can hardly expect to offer to others any compelling reason for the hope that is in us if we do not pay respectful attention to their own professed commitments, not only when these differ from or clash head-on with our own but even when they are widely shared and, for this precise reason, hardly ever taken out, dusted down, and subjected to careful examination.[7]

The second consideration is of a different sort, having to do with the book's provenance and the anticipated ease of producing it. Its genesis actually lay in a series of sermons delivered during the seasons of Lent and Easter 2018—having heard which, a number of people generously inquired whether I had considered the possibility of making them more widely available in print form. They would, I was encouraged to suppose, make a worthwhile book for use by other congregations or for the benefit of readers interested in an accessible introduction to "mere Christianity." Furthermore, such a book, I was told (and increasingly came to tell myself), would do little to consume the small proportion of my time available for writing, most of the work having already been done in preparing the sermons themselves. All that was needed was to print them out, go through them quickly with a red pen, do the relevant tidying up, and ship them off confidently to a publisher. It did not, of course, work out quite like that. Sermons are not book chapters, and the demands of the two genres are rather different. This fact, and my aforementioned desire to avoid offering anything merely equivalent to a selection of theological canapés in place of fare at once more nutritious and more satisfying to the appetite (if not always the taste) of the hungry reader, compelled a more thoroughgoing reworking of my original texts than was compatible with the phrase *lightly revised*. If the result of this reworking is thus some extra bulk and ballast (Episcopal congregations typically get twitchy after twenty minutes or so of preaching, and none of the original "chapters" exceeded two thousand words), I hope, nonetheless, that the treatment of themes will not be judged to be "heavy." The accessibility of the prose style, the ideas, and the illustrations is deliberately pitched quite widely, though I also hope that habitual readers of theology may find here sufficient to provoke their interest and hold their attention long enough for them to identify more than the mere reiteration of the already familiar. In short, this is a book offered to the whole church and, indeed, to any inquiring minds outside it. Whether it be used to prepare candidates for baptism, to stimulate and deepen the believing of the already baptized, to inform the merely curious, or as a cure for sufferers with chronic insomnia (whatever their fiduciary commitments), my hope is that it will indeed be useful to someone, and preferably by being read.

My thanks are due to Fortress Press and in particular to their visionary executive editor Carey Newman, who, despite having been present in St Andrews to hear one of the original sermons preached, agreed nonetheless to publish them.

Trevor Hart

ALL SAINTS' DAY, 2021

MEMORIZING MERE CHRISTIANITY

BEFORE WE GET to grips with the content of the Apostles' Creed, it might be useful to say something briefly about creeds in general and this one in particular. What sort of thing is it that we are looking at, and where did it come from?

Like many English words (not least those having to do in one way or another with the life of the church), the word *creed* owes its origin to another language altogether—Latin. For many centuries in the West, Latin was the language that educated people used for formal communication (whatever part of the known world they were living in), and it was the language of the church's public life and worship too. The Bible itself had been translated into Latin fairly early on, a version we are familiar with as the so-called Vulgate edition, produced in the late fourth century CE by the theologian Jerome. So Latin was de rigueur in Western Christianity, a language shared with officialdom and by the whole church so that it helped bind the church together across national and linguistic borders. It being the language of power and privilege, though, Latin also tended to exclude from understanding anyone who, through no fault of their own, spoke only the local lingo—this, of course, being the vast majority of people and the bulk of the poor and uneducated classes in particular. That's why at the European Reformation, there was a democratizing move to translate Scripture and key liturgical texts into more accessible versions—so that even those who couldn't read for themselves could nonetheless hear them being read and be able to make some sense of them. Otherwise, in a service where everything was said or sung in Latin, most people, then as now, would struggle to follow or make sense of what was going on and so be unable to share meaningfully in the dynamic of personal receiving and responding of which the heart of Christian worship consists.

In its original Latin form, though, the opening words of the Apostles' Creed are "Credo in Deum" (I believe in God), and it is from that very first word, "Credo," that our familiar English term *creed* comes. *Creeds*, then, we may properly say, are statements of things *believed* by Christians, though far from all being the same as we might expect, they actually come in quite different shapes and sizes. This is primarily because they were all written in different contexts and for a variety of different purposes, and that affected what people thought was helpful to include in them. Some creeds, for instance, were written in order to clarify and state the church's official understanding when some maverick or "heretical" view on an important matter of faith was being propagated unhelpfully within its ranks. Here too, therefore, there was both a binding together and an excluding involved. In this case, though, those excluded were not the illiterate poor but anyone whose views differed significantly from the catholic mainstream that was being clarified and encapsulated. Those who subscribed to the creedal version of things, on the other hand, were included identifiably in the acknowledged fold of an emergent theological "orthodoxy."[1]

A good example of this sort of creed is the one still used most widely in those churches that still recite creeds regularly at all—namely, the so-called Nicene Creed, traditionally included in the eucharistic liturgy. This creed was drafted by theologians and bishops and formally adopted by two so-called ecumenical church councils, first at Nicaea in 325 CE and second (in a slightly updated and expanded version) at Constantinople in 381 CE.[2] The main focus of this creed was and is the church's understanding of the "incarnation"—namely, what it means to say that Jesus is the Son of God and that in him, God himself has, "for us and for our salvation," as the creed puts it, "taken flesh" and dwelled among us humanly.[3] This very precise doctrinal concern rather skews the content of this creed. It makes it a bit lopsided in coverage at points, giving lots of space to some things while covering others in seeming haste and passing over others still in silence. In fact, the reason for updating the creed slightly at Constantinople was the desire to add something about the Holy Spirit, who had, with the benefit of hindsight, been granted insufficient consideration in the original version. The Nicene Creed is also frankly rather technical and "unbiblical" in some of its vocabulary for most Christians' purposes, and my suspicion is that many believers who recite this creed regularly nonetheless remain less than clear about what exactly they are professing, being bemused or perplexed by some of its more specialized and unfamiliar language ("of one substance with," "begotten, not made," etc.). Such terminology, though, was vital to the context of the creed's drafting, being borrowed from the precise, technical lexicon of the philosophers in order to pin down and clarify the meanings of biblical words and phrases which otherwise remained dangerously ambiguous, an ambiguity with which the substance of the good news itself was placed in jeopardy.

The debate lying behind the creed itself concerned the gist of Scripture's teaching about Jesus's identity. Was Jesus truly God himself, present here in person and in human form? Or was the one who forgave sinners, healed the sick, taught us to love our enemies, and willingly gave himself up to death "for us and for our salvation" not God at all but a third party sent by God to do all this in God's name and God's stead? A huge amount rests on the answer so far as our narrating of the good news and our characterization of God himself are concerned. Both parties in the debate were able to quote scriptural phrases left, right, and center, but this did not resolve anything because it was precisely the meaning to be ascribed to those same phrases that was in question, and simply repeating the phrases themselves again and again could not pin this down. So, ironically, in order to secure what they believed to be a biblical *meaning*, those who drafted the creed were driven to resort to words and turns of phrase of a decidedly "unbiblical" ilk. The Nicene Creed, we might say, dips its toes identifiably in the waters of Greek philosophy, even if (having some very un-Greek things to say) it avoids falling in and succumbing to baptism by total immersion in the process.[4] It retains a biblical core, and its task is the clarification of biblical teaching about Jesus. Yet despite its prominent place in the tradition and widespread liturgical use, this particular creed may not actually be the most obvious choice as a focus for seekers' groups or confirmation classes.[5] Intelligent exposition of its teaching is certainly to be commended for those seeking to deepen their understanding of a faith already grasped and indwelt but not, perhaps, for those exploring or seeking entry into it. Whether in that circumstance it should retain its prominent place as a formulary recited publicly by all present whenever Holy Communion is shared is probably a topic best reserved for another occasion.

The Apostles' Creed is a rather different sort of animal. Its purpose was *not* to respond to deviant ideas with intellectually rigorous reiterations and clarifications of particular beliefs but rather to provide a convenient overview of what C. S. Lewis helpfully dubs "mere Christianity"[6]—that is, the basic collection of things which being a Christian involves someone believing in and which have been and are held to be true by most Christians most of the time and by the church officially everywhere and all the time. There are, of course, lots of things about which Christians disagree and about which, while not exactly unimportant, they are content to agree to disagree, even though in practice, such disagreements have from time to time led to unfortunate divisions and to the forming of different Christian "denominations" within the church. But there are other things altogether more central to the stuff of what it means to be a Christian at all, and the Apostles' Creed is, in effect, a digest of what might reasonably be reckoned to be the bare minimum of these—of the gist, we might say, of the apostolic teaching.

So while it certainly isn't intended to be exhaustive, this creed is reasonably comprehensive and evenhanded in its coverage. It's a short, relatively easily memorized answer to the question, What is it, then, that Christians believe? This is a question any Christian believer might reasonably find themselves being asked and, as the apostle Peter suggests, to which they ought to be willing and able to give a clear answer.[7] This is true even if exploring and unpacking that answer at length—a task, we should note, needing to be done not just once in some definitive version but ever anew so that the answers will be fresh and speak directly into each new context, each new generation, each new location within which the church is called to dwell and to bear witness—remain the preserve of a cohort of curious individuals identified by the church as its "theologians." And for this purpose of effective witness, among others, the Apostles' Creed is far more accessible too than its Nicene counterpart. It is identifiably based on little more than the language, the teaching, and the overarching pattern of Scripture. Its language is clear (none of those complex, philosophical technicalities to worry about), and it follows a broadly narrative sequence, echoing the story that Scripture itself has to tell about God's dealings with the world in Jesus but crunching this story down into a concise format. Ironically, it is a format that, in a technological age which increasingly breeds dependency and gradually atrophies rather than enhances our natural skills (of imagination, among others), might well find itself subjected to that essentially nonnarrative, unpoetic, and generally unimaginative approach to visual communication known and bemoaned by mind-numbed audiences the world over as "death by PowerPoint."[8] But bullet pointed though it may be, the Apostles' Creed is nonetheless a power-packed summary designed precisely to capture our imagination and, far from shutting it down or rendering it otiose, to send it into paroxysms of visualization, curiosity, and exploration, and its brevity and clarity make this particular creed far more useful in practical terms than some others. It is a pity, therefore, that the otherwise welcome rediscovery in many contemporary churches of Eucharist as the norm for a congregation's regular diet of worship means that this particular creed is now rarely used and hardly known. (In many Anglican churches, for instance, it now occurs only as part of the relatively niche service of Choral Evensong, being included in the prayer book settings of Morning and Evening Prayer but not in more recent liturgical revisions of these services.)

So where did the Apostles' Creed come from? Well, despite its name, this creed didn't come from the apostles themselves. There are, to be sure, identifiably "creedal" bits and pieces in the New Testament itself, such as the fragments echoed by the apostle Paul in Philippians 2:5–11 ("Christ Jesus, who, though he was in the form of God, . . . emptied himself, . . . being born in human likeness," etc.) and 1 Timothy 3:16 ("He was revealed in flesh, vindicated in spirit, seen by angels, proclaimed among Gentiles, believed in throughout the world, taken up in glory").[9] These texts, too, seem likely to have served in the early church as easily memorable formulae summing up important aspects of what Christians believed about God and about Jesus and which could either be used in worship or else called readily to mind when summoned to bear witness to the gospel. But while there is a delightful legend about the Apostles' Creed which has each of Jesus's disciples on the day of Pentecost, under the direct guidance of and inspiration by the Holy Spirit, composing and contributing his own personal clause or "article" to this creed, it *is* only a legend that grew up in later centuries. It's easy enough to see why the legend grew up. After all, if this creed did indeed come directly from the apostles, then neither its importance nor its authority could seriously be challenged. But although it is very ancient, the creed was dubbed "apostolic" not because the apostles themselves composed it but because it was, as I have already suggested, an attempt to provide a faithful digest of the pattern of the apostles' own testimony to Christ in the writings of the New Testament, interpreted properly within the canon of Scripture as a whole. Its *apostolicity*, therefore, like that of the church itself, lies in that same relationship of faithfulness as it is laid hold of and used by the Holy Spirit to bear witness to the truth as it is in Christ.[10]

The particular version of this creed that we use today probably reaches back only as far as the ninth century CE, but there exist far earlier versions of it. Of particular importance is a Greek creed used in baptisms as early as the middle of the second century CE by the Christian congregation in Rome. This creed was in a question-and-answer form (as creedal affirmations are in many modern baptism liturgies too), but in other respects, it bears a striking resemblance to the more polished indicative version that has come down to us in Latin. The link with baptism ties in nicely, of course, with the supposition that this creed is, in effect, a convenient summary of the sort of things which becoming and being a Christian involve someone believing. Candidates for baptism would, in the early centuries, typically be prepared or "catechized" during the weeks of Lent and then baptized early on Easter Day itself. A large part of that preparation would no doubt have been invested in helping them grasp how the various articles of the creed they would soon profess publicly were rooted in the soil of the Old and New Testaments and where and how they fitted in with or else called into question the wider pattern of beliefs and practices of the contemporary cultural and intellectual milieux. And it is natural to suppose that some version of this creed itself (or one very like it) would have been used as the working outline for such an introduction to and elementary nurturing in the intellectual, practical, and other entailments of a newly born Christian faith.

In the days when the main diet of Anglican worship on a typical Sunday was not eucharistic, Morning and/or Evening Prayer being either said or sung instead (with Holy Communion celebrated only, perhaps, on a fortnightly or even monthly basis), it was sometimes suggested that any devout and self-respecting Anglican Christian ought to be able easily to recite from memory at least the Lord's Prayer and the Apostles' Creed. Whatever the presumed benefits of this eagerly anticipated party piece for either performer or audience, though, being able to *recite* something is in itself, of course, only ever of limited value. Those limits may perhaps be more expansive than we tend to suppose—a level of familiarity with the poetry or "music" of liturgical or scriptural texts itself having a rather more formative benefit in spiritual terms than first meets the eye (as those texts gradually soak into us, their sedimentation forming settled habits of heart, will, and body as well as mind, working under the radar to help shape and color our perception of the world around us). And as we shall see in the next chapter, in reality, all of us live in any case constantly, comfortably, and with impunity with at most a partial and provisional grasp of the majority of the things we take to be true, and none of us will ever arrive at an exhaustive understanding even of those things we claim to have fathomed most fully. Nonetheless, as we grow up in the Christian faith, we need and we should desire to go further still, seeking a deeper level of *understanding* of what it is that—when we utter the words of the creed, for example—we are actually *professing to believe*.

This matters a good deal because "saying the creed" is not just a recitation but what philosophers of language like to call a "performative utterance" or "speech act"—an act of saying, that is to say, that rather than reporting or describing some state of affairs actually *does* something as we say it, as when, for instance, we say in particular contexts "I do . . . ," or "I pronounce you . . . ," or "I baptize you . . . ," or "I sentence you . . . ," or "I'm Spartacus . . . ," or (after a suitable dramatic pause and with a Donald Trump– or Alan Sugar–esque pointing finger) "You're fired!" Saying the creed, with its threefold iteration "I believe . . . ," is without question a performative utterance in this sense. These are not empty words to be toyed with, therefore, or ones that we can sit loosely to as we say them. In the context of worship or witness, they are words charged with meaning and power, and in uttering them, we are *doing* something—taking a stand, declaring our allegiance, identifying ourselves as belonging to Christ, professing personal commitment and promising personal faithfulness, and rehearsing an outline of faith's imaginative and ideational content, all in front of anyone who cares to look or listen.[11] Public *profession* in both these senses (promising and rehearsing) is thus another important aspect of this creed's purpose and use, and in order to mean what we say rather than perjuring ourselves, we need as we say those words to fill them with whatever meaning we are capable of grasping.

Another Latin term that can be translated by the English word *creed* is *symbolum*, which, as we might guess, also means a symbol or a sign of something. In ancient times, a *symbolum* might be something material, a token or badge that could be worn on a costume or clothing, serving as an outward and visible indicator to others of someone's allegiance to a particular group or party or organization within society.[12] So too a creed (and this creed in particular, with its catechetical potential and its links with the event of Christian baptism[13]) was not to be thought of as or permitted to become an essentially private and individual "code for life" or a bit of esoteric spiritual knowledge shared by holy huddles largely in secret and away from the world's gaze. It was, and it is and should be, that version of the truth as it has been made known to us in Jesus which Christians are prepared to take a stand for and be known by, and that means again, of course, that to the best of our ability, we should be willing to give some account of not just what the creed says but also what it means when it says it and how that variously converges with, clashes with, or offers a critical response to all sorts of other things people in our society take as true (including, of course, the self-referentially corrosive insistence that the truth is that there *is* no truth deserving of the name).[14]

In answer to our initial question, then, this particular creed can be thought of and treated helpfully both as a tool for Christian nurture—encouraging a grasp and understanding of the basics of the faith—and as a mnemonic device to be deployed in presenting the gist of that faith conveniently to a wider public as it looks on and asks questions. It is, in other words, an articulation of "mere Christianity" in Lewis's sense, likely to be of invaluable use in both feeding the flock and fostering the fringe, the systole and diastole of the church's heartbeat that eschews equally the blinkered, "inward-looking" mentality of a private religious club and the untethered, indiscriminate absorption of the world's own alternative creed in a misguided bid to prioritize "relevance" above all things.[15]

I

1

"I BELIEVE..."

IF, NOW, WE turn to the creed's opening words, "I believe . . . ," what are we to make of them? Perhaps the first and most obvious thing is that, left like that, these two words make absolutely no sense at all in English. *Believe* is, as grammarians say, a transitive verb, which requires an object. In other words, we can't just "believe"; we have to believe *in* someone or something. And the Apostles' Creed supplies a helpful list of things that Christians "believe in."

It *is* a list, one I have chosen to distribute over twelve distinct chapters in this book. In a sense, though, most if not all of the "articles" that follow are simply an unpacking of the first and most important of all. It has been said that as Christians, it is not so much *what* we believe as *whom* we believe in that sets us apart, and that, of course, is God—not any old "god" but the particular God who makes himself, his name, his purposes, and his promises known to us through Scripture's witness to the history of Israel, focused in the person of Jesus. That's why the larger part of the creed itself is concentrated on Jesus and earthed in claims about particular things held to have happened at particular times and in particular places. Christianity is not a set of timeless "religious" truths about the cosmos but an awkward insistence that the world itself is a stage on which a divine drama has been played out in history. It is a drama traces of which should show up on any radar sensitive enough to register the "facts" of the matter and which embeds those facts within a story of God's action and human response and answers some of the perennial questions of human existence in the world: Who are we? Who are we called to be? Where are we headed?

Nonetheless, before engaging the drama and some of the particular claims that belief in this God involves us in grappling with, it is worth pausing to take stock of what such "belief" itself amounts to and demands of us. For ease of expression as much as anything else, though, I'm going mostly to stop talking at this point about belief (which perhaps connotes something a bit rarefied, intellectual, and abstract) and talk about "faith" instead. This word points to something more concrete and engaged, as will be apparent at once if we translate *Credo in Deum* differently as "I have faith in God" or even "I put my trust in God." As we shall see in due course, it's not possible to "have faith in" someone or something without a significant input of *ideas* and some responsible thinking about those ideas, but faith of the sort the creed is speaking about amounts to considerably more than that, a surplus without which it cannot properly count as "belief" in the Christian sense at all.[1]

Faith as Gift

PERHAPS THE FIRST thing to note is that having faith (or "believing") in God is not a human lifestyle choice (let alone any sort of meritorious performance or accomplishment) but something in which God himself is involved from first to last. In the Bible, Abraham is the great exemplar of faith in God, and like the many other "faithful" individuals who follow in his wake, when we first encounter him, we don't find him sitting around musing on life and its meaning or flicking distractedly through a catalog of available religious options to see whether any of them catch his eye. On the contrary, Abram (as he still is named at this point in the story) is a busy man with a lot on his mind. Responsible for the well-being of his family, worldly goods, and an entire retinue bequeathed to him by his father soon after migrating from Iraq to Syria, he is probably still weighing up the expense of relocation, the prospects for trade, and other available opportunities for self-betterment in the new neighborhood. But at this point, just as everyone is settling in and settling down, we are told God *calls* Abram—unsolicited and seemingly apropos of nothing—and summons him into a relationship. Despite its abruptness, this is precisely a call rather than a suggestion or an offer; it anticipates no resistance, taking the form of instruction as well as promise, and exactly who this God is will only become clear as the story which begins here slowly unfolds. Abram, though, in what is subsequently hailed in Scripture as an exemplary response, does exactly what God summons him to do.[2] He loads up the family goods and chattels and prepares (no doubt against his own better judgment and in the teeth of their grumbling) to launch everyone on yet another magical mystery tour in the desert. But exemplary or not, it's perfectly clear that the initiative and the motive force for the whole enterprise lies not with Abram at all but with God.

In fact, this is the pattern throughout Scripture's narration of various "faithful" individuals. Faith begins when God calls and makes himself known to them, and their faith consists not in a creed (though it may involve *believing* rather than *not* believing certain things or believing other things instead) but in a relationship into which God summons them and within which God holds and sustains and equips them. Faith is, we might say, a free and undeserved *gift*—the gift of knowing God and living our lives intentionally in the light of God's own presence and involvement with us.[3] Furthermore, it is a gift that is constantly given afresh, and like life itself, were God to withdraw it rather than holding us securely within it, we should have no resources of our own to replenish it, no magic lamp to rub which would summon it up again, genie-like, from the void of absence. The gift of a relationship, of being permitted to get to know someone, always begins and continues with an invitation freely offered and renewed, and if we accept that invitation, it changes who we are because our identities and our characters are shaped in significant measure by the relationships we indwell and own.

This is why the polarization sometimes posited between "faith" and "works" as the basis of our standing before God, whatever version it arises in, is always misleading and will not finally hold. Faith itself, as I have already noted, is not a triumph of the human heart, mind, or will that we have each satisfactorily to accomplish in order to win

God over but a relationship in which God lays hold of us, establishes us, and sustains us. But nor is faith ever a vacuous, passive, or morally and intellectually disengaged relationship. On the contrary, being drawn into and held in this relationship can and will, unless we resist and deny it (thereby putting it under strain and at risk), involve us in thinking, desiring, and doing all sorts of things which are more "godly" than "godless." As Jesus himself confirmed (citing the so-called Shema of Deut 6:4–5), a person drawn into such a relationship with the God he knew as his Father is expected to devote all their heart, soul, mind, and strength to loving God. That is what entering God's "kingdom" or devotion to God as King means.[4] That's why Jesus's brother James, in his epistle, insists that "faith without works is dead."[5] "Works" (for want of a better and less theologically loaded term) are the natural *fruits* of faith, of being embedded and rooted in God, held by God, nurtured by God. Works are not the prior condition of God's summoning us into a relationship but the natural condition of anyone who indwells and enjoys the sort of relationship with God that faith properly is, a condition that our continuing sin and faithlessness as believers contradict, chafing and causing us to suffer. So to ask whether works or faith is more important is, as C. S. Lewis notes, as meaningful as "asking which blade in a pair of scissors is more necessary."[6]

Faith as Assent

FAITH, THEN, IS much more than intellectual acquiescence (let alone the dubious accomplishment of believing "as many as six impossible things before breakfast"[7]). Faith is more than this, but it is not less. Faith does, in other words, involve "believing" certain things in the sense of granting appropriate intellectual assent to them and reflecting on the implications of doing so for our wider knowledge and understanding. It is not an alternative to intelligent reckoning with the reality we apprehend and indwell but a form of it, and it certainly provides no excuse for anyone to refuse to grapple with or think through some of the hard questions with which reality confronts us. Facing up responsibly to the command to love God "with all your mind," in other words, cannot permit retreat into a comfortable, unthinking ghetto where the things of faith themselves are concerned, and we should demand no less of ourselves as reasonable and reasoning beings here than we do otherwise.[8] But let's be clear: this demand for parity and intellectual respectability does not mean, as is sometimes suggested and supposed, that we should refuse to believe something until we have understood it fully or until its reality has been demonstrated by the sort of evidential demonstration or logical "proof" that we sometimes crave and which contemporary culture sometimes insists upon as the only respectable gauge of what may reasonably count as real or be accepted as true, not least where matters of religious belief are concerned.

Where the reality we speak of as God is concerned in particular, in fact, for Christians (and perhaps for others, though I will not presume to speak for them), there is something nonsensical about the suggestion that we must hold off, refusing to entertain or invest belief in whatever we cannot fully grasp or know to be true on grounds independent of God's own approach and self-opening to us. To suggest this, the believer may properly insist, is simply to have misunderstood what the word *God* itself actually means. After all, *God*, in biblical and Christian terms, refers us to a reality lying way beyond the natural range and reach of anything of which our bodies, minds, and languages together are properly adapted to know and speak. This is part of what it means to speak of God, as Christians do, as the uncreated source of "all things, visible and invisible." To say this of God is, as we shall see duly, to set God radically apart from everything else that exists rather than identifying God as just one more "thing" among others (albeit the biggest and most powerful "thing" imaginable), susceptible in principle to the same human initiatives of exploration, mapping, and intellectual colonization as anything else. If we cannot lay our hands on or get our heads around the reality of God, in other words, this is neither an indication that God is not "real" nor an index of our intellectual incapacity or the unsophisticated state of our tools. It is, in the first instance, simply because God is God.

In passing, though, we should note that this same claim about God's intrinsic otherness and unknowability (what theologians sometimes refer to as God's "transcendence") is one that arises, ironically, only with God's decision to "reveal" himself. It is not something we can know from experience or on the grounds of so-called pure reason but something that God tells or shows us in opening God's mind-blowing reality up to us, doing so necessarily in ways that leave our minds (and our words) nevertheless well and truly blown rather than handing God over for inspection, analysis, and convenient definition. That's why the continued use of words like *mystery, ineffable, infinite, poetic*, and others in relation to our knowing and speaking of God is not simply a cop-out in intellectual terms, a sort of excuse for not being forced to think hard or to say anything precise or meaningful. On the contrary, Christians have always thought hard and felt bound to say things (often very precise things) about God. When they have been most careful and responsible in their thinking and speaking, though, they have remembered this most fundamental thing of all and so avoided falling into the trap of supposing that in God's "revealing" or opening up of himself to us (doing so by turning a plethora of images, ideas, words, objects, events, places, relationships, and other creaturely realities into appropriate signs and symbols of his own), God's reality is put at the disposal of our knowing so that by flexing our intellectual muscles, we might now squeeze that reality satisfactorily into categories that will render it available to us and demonstrable to others as and when we choose, let alone to know or speak it exhaustively. Neither God's reality nor the reality of "revelation" is like that. Furthermore, therefore, if God really is the sort of God we know in God's self-giving initiative toward us, then both capitulation to external demands for independent "objective" verification, on the one hand, and claims by believers to possess "revealed truth" which automatically trumps every rival truth claim and grants a hard and sharp instrument with which to bludgeon them into intellectual submission, on the other, are not only misguided and highly "unscientific"[9] but forms of intellectual disobedience to boot which Christians should be extremely wary of committing.[10]

Faith as Knowledge

AT THIS POINT, though, we need to pause and allow the pendulum to swing back slightly in the other direction. Because while the case of our knowing and speaking of God is and must by definition be unique in all sorts of ways, closer inspection suggests nonetheless that some of the considerations just identified are not ones wholly without analogy on a much wider front when it comes to the manner in which reality, as we might perfectly well say, discloses itself in various ways to our attempts to know it. In particular, the exercise of faith, intellectual humility, and an underlying openness to the mysteriousness of things all play indispensable roles in the ways in which we typically know things and are thus always constituent parts even of our best and most thorough knowing and understanding of things rather than shoddy alternatives to them.

This is apparent from an analysis of the ways that science itself works, where in reality, a huge amount is and must be taken on trust; where tradition and voices of institutional authority function constantly to direct patterns of practice and privilege methodological and theoretical "orthodoxies"; where intuition, imagination, and creativity are vital foils to the disinterested gathering of evidence and recording of data; and where both personal commitment of a high order and the deliberate holding of certain unproven (and unprovable) beliefs are paramount.[11] But the same point can be made from a different angle with even the briefest consideration of the things we take ourselves satisfactorily to know as we go about our daily living. For we do so for the most part, I suggest, on the basis of all manner of things we hold to be real and claims we take for granted as true but of which we *personally* have relatively little understanding and for the verity of which, if the proverbial gun were to be put to our heads, we *ourselves* should certainly be in no position either to muster evidence relevant to satisfactory demonstration or watertight logical proof. Of course, we need to grasp a certain amount in order to be able to say that we believe or trust it at all, but that grasp may take many different forms and will in many instances be quite modest. So many things fall into this category on any day in any individual life lived that it is pointless even to begin to list them.

To acknowledge this is simply to observe that most of us nowadays have a high level of understanding, expertise, or practical skill related to only a very few things in life. It is one of the great ironies of the modern world that its strides forward in science, technology, and learning have if anything left us poorer rather than richer in terms of the quality of our personal engagements with things, less well adapted to "know" reality on its manifold fronts, in fact, than our premodern forebears were. This is not to deny, of course, that in all sorts of ways, humankind now knows and understands and is able to accomplish far more than ever before, whether for good or ill. But the increasingly specialized nature of knowledge at the cutting edge means, paradoxically, that even the most expert individuals in a field now tend to know immeasurably more about considerably less than their predecessors even a few generations ago, a concentration which raises the bar of competent understanding or "mastering" of disciplines and practices across the board ever further beyond the reach of the larger educated populace and threatens to drive the genuine polymath (always a rare species in any case) into extinction. Meanwhile, the remarkable technological achievements of the digital age, more thoroughly even than its industrial precursors, continue in the name of efficiency, convenience, and economy (profit) to enfeeble rather than enable us. No longer having to do all sorts of things for ourselves, we eventually forget (and are no longer taught) how to do them, and whole manual and mental skill sets perish, to be lost to us forever. At the level of our individual dealings, it must surely be admitted, all this leaves us less well adapted and proficient than we used to be on a wide range of reality's many fronts—the fact that one may be the world's leading expert on some infinitesimal sliver of it notwithstanding. It means, therefore, that where the bulk of what we generally accept as "reality" is concerned, we are bound to lack either the relevant skills or access to other specialized conditions under which, alone, the sort of "evidence" typically taken to be relevant to the authoritative demonstration of "truth" may be weighed, measured, and pronounced upon. And that's before we remind ourselves that there are all sorts of things (generally, in fact, the sorts of things that matter to us most, the most "human" realities of all) that do not lend themselves to the methods of evidential demonstration or logical proof in any case but which none of us seriously doubts the reality or the truth of as we get up and go about our business day by day.

I drive a car and use a laptop (not at the same time, I hasten to add). I believe implicitly and absolutely in the capacity of these and other similar devices to do all that I want and need them to do, even though I have absolutely no idea how they do it, and much of what they are actually capable of remains unutilized, lying beyond the scope of my practical "need to know." Where these things are concerned (and many, many others—things upon whose efficient traction on the surfaces of reality I rely daily and without which I would now find it impossible to function), I am quite content to rest in the knowledge that there are folk somewhere who *do* understand it all. And even were I capable of (and life's fleeting duration to permit) the relevant learning involved, the truth is that I feel no personal need whatsoever to get my head and hands around the theory or the technical know-how prior to turning the ignition key, booting up the hard drive, or whatever else is involved in the idiot-friendly process of harnessing the power of gadgets, gizmos, and mechanical conveyances. True, things can go wrong and the wheels can come off (metaphorically or otherwise). If they do, though, I can and do fall back gratefully on the twenty-four-hour help line, and as long as I have paid my roadside recovery or AppleCare premium (and as long as it's not my iPhone that has malfunctioned), my lack of knowledge and technical know-how is quickly made good by a friendly technician whose knowledge and judgment I trust implicitly, precisely because they are infinitely in excess of my own. That's what they get paid for, right? In the aforementioned specialized climate of modernity, of course, I wouldn't allow the same "expert" to perform a root canal on my teeth or approach them for personal financial advice—not, let's be clear, because I myself possess expertise in those fields but because they almost certainly don't either, and when it comes to dentistry or the Dow Jones, therefore, both of us would be better advised to seek out an appropriate third party in whose training and skill we are told we have reason to believe. In such circumstances, as in so many others that populate all our day-to-day lives, if we would engage with the reality of things at all, we are compelled to do so in ways that have nothing to do with our own competent hold on large chunks of it or even our capacity to assess the bona fides and expertise of those claiming to grasp it in our stead and on our behalf. Instead, we operate in large measure within an ecology of trust, unstinting acts of faith, and the contented holding of beliefs whose truthfulness we cannot (and really feel no need to) prove to the satisfaction of the determined skeptic.

Similarly, I mostly have no ready access (in terms of either equipment or training in the skills relevant to using it) to whatever it might take to "prove" to the skeptic's exacting standards that all sorts of things I take to be real and true are *actually* real and true. I believe, for instance, that there are microscopic things called bacteria, and I expend energy each day seeking carefully to avoid what I'm led to believe otherwise is the likelihood of their assault on my immune system. Of course, I've never knowingly seen any myself, and the provision of a convenient microscope beside the washbasin in my bathroom wouldn't really help much in this regard, since I wouldn't have a clue how to use it properly or be capable in the slightest of identifying what I was seeing if I did. Someone would have to show and tell me, and I should have to either trust them or not. Mostly (rightly or wrongly) I do, for which the purveyors of hand soap are no doubt grateful. In circumstances like that, we might note, even a seemingly straightforward appeal to "the facts" of the matter can carry little weight, since facts have to be recognized before they can be agreed upon, and recognition demands a level of interpretation (in this case, I imagine, of specks and squiggles wriggling or swirling in a blob or liquid, or something like that) of which I myself am not and, at my stage of life, am unlikely ever to be capable. There are more enticing and important skills to learn. Often, in other words, what counts as "the facts of the matter" is itself something to be taken on trust rather than something self-evident to everyone in the room. In all sorts of contexts, most of us, though we have eyes and ears, still lack "eyes to see" and "ears to hear" what is apparently there to be seen and heard by those equipped to do so. But again, the *reasonableness* of believing in the reality of such things (and behaving accordingly) is not contingent on our personal ability to marshal evidence or arguments that would pass muster with professionals whose job it is to understand and deal with them. Like most people, for myself, I'm content to trust the testimony of folk who know what they are talking about and what they are doing and, perhaps naively but in practical terms, *necessarily* to heed their advice.

Conviction of Things Unseen[12]

FINALLY, I HAVE no way (because there is no way) to prove "scientifically" that lots of things whose reality most of us take for granted daily are actually real at all or, as we say, "exist."[13] Of course, they exist in some sense in the hearts, minds, and imaginations of those who speak of them and appeal to them in the stuff of everyday living, but they cannot be seen, heard, touched, tasted, or smelled; they cannot be weighed or measured, not just in practice but in principle, because *materiality* is precisely what this category of things lacks. Goodness, for instance. Or beauty. Or thoughts. Or meaning. Or truth itself. Most of us structure our existence in one way or another around the belief or assumption that such things are real, even if we can't always identify, determine, or describe them very precisely. But their "reality" is, it is sometimes held in our materially focused and materially preoccupied world, not the *right sort* of reality, not leaving any identifiable trace on the sophisticated instruments we rely on in the laboratory to register and provide us with data about the "real world." So it's not uncommon to come across the suggestion that such nonmaterial entities *lack* reality or are in some self-evident way *less* real (or at least *differently* real, the implication being "not *really* real at all") by comparison with the hard stuff that physics, chemistry, biology, and their various subdisciplines and specializations get their hands dirty with. Since they are "there" and won't go away, though, these putative "realities" must be accounted for, and the most obvious way of doing that, it is widely supposed, is to locate their origin in the rich imaginings of human beings like ourselves. In other words, we invent or "make them up" as we go—not as individuals but as groups, communities, societies, and cultures.[14]

Those who suggest this, of course, do not typically suppose that whatever fragile hold such nonmaterial realities have on "existence" is of a sort either requiring or even permitting God to be brought meaningfully into the picture. Their appeal to the productive workings of the human imagination is meant precisely to exclude the need for any such wanton commandeering of the deity as an explanatory device and to erase God's name finally from the scripts of both "nature" and "culture," the twin spheres that human existence seems to straddle. But that's a sleight of hand or, at best, a non sequitur, and it's certainly a move we need not make. It is perfectly possible and proper to admit that some such things (codes of morality, value systems, aesthetic sensibilities, meaningfulness) would and could not exist at all apart from the languages—both literal and metaphorical ones—that humans have invented by way of response to the world, languages which we learn and upon which we rely in order to describe and make sense of it. It is possible, too, to recognize that the shapes and substances of these "languages" vary, sometimes quite significantly, from one time and place and human culture and community to another so that we encounter difference and are compelled to translate not just our utterance but the distinct outlooks lying behind and embodied in it. In doing so, though, we can perfectly properly refuse to relegate all this to the category of something "*merely* made up," as though it were simply epiphenomenal spume thrown up by the raging storm caused in the human breast variously confronted with an indifferent and finally meaningless material cosmos.

Instead, we might understand it as a diverse set of human responses—contingent on time, place, and culture—to a world vested already at its creation by God with the potential for certain moral, spiritual, semantic, and other nonmaterial realities to develop and be drawn out of it by the action and imagination of creatures like ourselves, furnishing a home to be indwelt fruitfully with our fellow creatures and with God. In this sense, we might insist, the reality of the cosmos as a whole (precisely as a "world" that, as the Nicene Creed reminds us, consists of things both "visible and invisible") is a creative project toward the realization and flowering of which God conscripts our active participation rather than handing us a finished product for passive consumption or, at best, careful preservation.[15] Creation is about not just what God has already made, in other words, but in a perfectly proper sense what God and human creatures "make of this" together within the give-and-take of a faithful covenant relationship.

It is not only in the realm of meanings, values, and other cultural "products" with our human fingerprints all over them, though, that significant nonmaterial realities must be and are identified and reckoned with. At a more basic level still, the realm of realities and relationships within which we and others exist identifiably as "persons" confronts us with realities of just such a sort and that, even if in our encountering of them they are tangled up inexorably with the sphere of cultural productivity just referred to, cannot simply be reduced to it any more than it and they together can be reduced to the pulsations of matter. Indeed, the reality of culture, we might suggest, is as much a response to the existence of persons as it is to the world of material nature, objects, and "facts." These are all mixed together in the texture of our experience, but that's no reason for us not to indulge briefly in some careful disentangling.

We can, for instance, demonstrate to our satisfaction the presence of other bodies occupying the material "space" of a room with us. We can, if they will allow us, measure the dimensions and establish other physical qualities of such bodies. We can register, by means of our senses and various technological enhancements of them, the movements and the sounds that such bodies make. We can do all of this and provide a factual report which is perhaps likely to satisfy most people present as regards its truth or falsity. At a different level again, we can identify and interpret certain such movements and sounds of these same material bodies as constituting meaningful communication, or as forms of intentional action possessed of a particular moral quality. Or we may ascribe to such material bodies and their movements aesthetic qualities, identifying in them varying degrees of grace, beauty, and loveliness or perhaps the opposites of these. At this level, though, the ways things are typically ascertained in the laboratory cease to be of much use to us, and we are compelled to resort instead to different sorts of instruments in order to recognize, classify, evaluate, and talk about their reality.

There is, though, a further level yet to be reckoned with. For meanings, intentions, values, ideas, and feelings of one sort or another do not, we tend to suppose, exist as self-explanatory and independent entities, free-floating in a nonmaterial ether. On the contrary, as we have already seen, in order to account for them (rather than simply denying their reality), thoroughgoing materialists are typically driven to appeal to the constructive meaning-making capacity of human beings, and I myself have suggested we might think of them in various ways as creative human *responses* to the world. While their theological implications may tug in rather different directions, what both of these viewpoints have in common is their tethering of the various "languages" in one way or another not just to the world of the body (investing particular material realities with significance so that they function for us as "signs") but to the reality of the world of "persons" too. For "persons," we tend naturally to suppose, are not themselves languages but those who invent and speak them; not feelings but those who experience them; not values but those who hold, cherish, and exalt them; not meanings but those who make and trace and indwell them; not even relationships but those who have their being in and are formed by them. In apprehending or interpreting a gesture, a cry, or a sound as "significant," a meaningful sign as distinct from merely a sensory datum, therefore, we grasp it as grounded in a complex, intelligent, imaginative, intentional existence analogous to our own—the existence of another person.

But the reality of persons and the relationships within which persons alone exist cannot be demonstrated, "proved," or charted by the scientific means that our culture generally exalts as the gold standard of genuine knowledge. The very things the existence of which makes our lives most worthwhile, most meaningful, most *human*, in other words, do not lend themselves naturally to such weighing and testing at all but resist those advances. So what do we do? Well, of course, none of us puts our lives on hold and refuses to behave as if such things were real simply because we cannot *prove* that it is so. We take the reality of other persons, of moral and aesthetic qualities and standards, and of all sorts of other things *for granted* as part of the complex and variegated "reality" with which we have to deal daily and don't worry at all about the fact that their very existence remains "unproven." Philosophers might worry about that (professionally), and some scientists may insist on telling us that we have no right to believe in the reality of such things just because their instruments and preferred methods are incapable of registering them. But most of us suppose that this is daft and even arrogant. And rightly so. Reality, we prefer to presume, is simply too big, too deep, too "mysterious" to fit into the laboratory or ever to be mapped adequately in scientific terms. And grateful for rather than resentful of that fact, we get on with living meaningful lives instead.

Knowing God Bodily

IN THE CASE of God, as in the case of other things, of course, it is reasonable to suppose that there are ways of knowing and interpreting that are appropriate to God's own peculiar reality and others that, try as we might, will grant us no purchase on it at all. And just as we cannot know another person's character or hopes and fears by weighing them, or putting them under a microscope, or sniffing the air to smell them (these being ways of "knowing" that are appropriate to other sorts of things but not to *persons* as such), so too there is little point to approaching the reality of God with instruments, methods, or assumptions dictated by our successful dealings with some other sort of reality only to complain that, as far as we can see, there is nothing there and conclude that we must have demonstrated that God does not "exist" or is not "real." The problem may be precisely that we are looking in the wrong place, or looking for the wrong sort of thing, or focusing on the wrong level while what we seek is all the time sitting in front of our noses. But we lack eyes to see, being blinded from the outset by a dogmatic refusal to put ourselves in a place or adopt an outlook or approach which, the widespread testimony of others suggests, is altogether more propitious for the quest than the empiricist box we are currently refusing to think outside, placing it instead over our heads so that it inevitably obscures our vision and occludes whatever lies beyond its edges.

None of this means that the world of material realities is irrelevant to our knowing of God, as if the latter were contained in some hermetically sealed, purely "spiritual" and mysterious sphere, accessible only to those prepared to adopt a flesh-denying regime of hair shirts and icy showers. But God's reality cannot and will not be *contained* within the categories of materiality any more than the realities and relationships that constitute our own personal existences can be. This seems particularly significant because, of course, it is precisely in terms of the analogy of *personal* existence and relationships that Scripture most often encourages us to imagine the reality of God. Again, there are no doubt ways in which God's "personhood" is quite unique, but the permission to think of God in this way suggests, perhaps, that our ways of dealing with and knowing other human persons will likely furnish the most appropriate sorts of expectations, assumptions, and approaches when it comes to knowing God.

So, for instance, there is nothing unreasonable or illogical about the claim that God, too, can make himself known by appropriating sounds and signs and through the material realities of the world, just as human persons do in sharing their lives with others.[16] These can become and be God's "language" just as surely as black squiggles on a page, or noises emitting from our vocal cords, or facial expressions and bodily gestures "speak" to us of an inner reality of "persons" that we cannot otherwise see or hear at all.[17] The case is parallel, and just as we take the reality of other people (i.e., their existence as more than hunks of flesh, blood, and bone) for granted, it is reasonable enough for believers to treat what they take to be the signs of God's activity in a similar way—identifying objects and events and actions they encounter in the world of embodied experience as "bodying forth" God's own communication with them—and not torment themselves endlessly about God's "reality" simply because that reality as such lies beyond the reach of material demonstration.

The conviction that this is precisely how God approaches and engages us lies, as we shall see duly, at the heart of the Christian insistence that in the life of the man we know as Jesus of Nazareth, God's "Word" himself has "become flesh" and dwelled among us. But the fact that God does not—outside this particular, unique, and world-transforming occurrence—have a larynx need not dissuade us from expecting God to lay hold of other material means to "speak" to us and solicit our responses. That might be through such familiar and divinely promised channels as reading and reflecting on Scripture together, involvement in other practices proper to the life of the believing community, or time spent in some palpably "holy" or sacred place (literal or metaphorical). Or it might come unsought and unexpected (and possibly undesired) from beyond the relatively controlled and comfortable environments of the church—in our dealings with people in "secular" contexts outside the congregation; through some sudden, destabilizing turn of events in our own lives, or the life of someone we love, or the life of the world; or as the result of a vertiginous encounter with nature in its enormity and terrible beauty. Like the flesh of Jesus itself, which lies properly at the center of this ecology of divine discourse and self-giving, any and all of these things may be laid hold of by God to become the material markers of divine meaning, the self-authenticating vehicles of God's "speaking" to us. After all, the Swiss theologian Karl Barth muses wryly, God in God's sovereign freedom can turn all creaturely reality to his own ends and, should God choose to do so, is perfectly capable of speaking to us through anything from the beauty of a Mozart flute concerto to the disgusting spectacle and smell of a dead dog—which is to say, anything from the sublime to the ridiculous.[18] This does not mean, though, Barth insists, that we should approach anything and everything in our experience as though, like Balaam's ass, it might suddenly prove to be the unexpected bearer of vital divine communication. On the contrary, God's speech has a distinctive "vocabulary" and a grammar, the rules of which we should certainly seek to learn, even if God, in God's freedom to improvise, is not bound by these and sometimes catches us out by his refusal to be. Of course, once we have experienced God approaching and speaking to us in any way at all, it would make little sense *not* to expect and to look out for further communication from God, to make a determined effort to "learn the language" God speaks, able not just to identify the signs in the future but to interpret them so that we may begin to understand what God may be saying to us and so become acquainted with God more closely and completely.

Faith as Personal Knowledge

A WELL-KNOWN DEFINITION of *theology* is that offered by the eleventh-century archbishop of Canterbury Saint Anselm in his book *Proslogion*. Anselm refers to theology as "faith seeking understanding"—the attempt to get our heads more fully around something the reality of which we believe ourselves already to know because we have had and continue to have personal dealings with it. Anselm is referring to the reality of God. But *faith seeking understanding* is actually a perfectly good description of the dynamics not just of theology but of much of our human knowing of the world. We encounter something, or are encountered by it, and it crops up identifiably on our radar from then on so that we might reasonably say that we "know" it or at least know something about it. We also know, though, that as yet, we are very far from understanding it or integrating our knowing of it into the wider pattern of things we hold ourselves to "know" or that others tell us we should believe about the world. Being creatures typically driven by curiosity and the desire for meaning, therefore, we commit ourselves, so far as opportunity permits, to learn more, to make sense of what we know, and to fit it meaningfully into the pattern of things we take to reflect "reality." We don't put our currently partial and provisional knowledge on hold, refusing to admit its value until we know everything (which, of course, we never will in any case). Instead, we use that knowledge as a springboard or a platform from which to advance ever further and more fully into the regions currently lying beyond our knowing. And it's like that, Anselm argues, with theology too (because *theology* is simply the name we give to what happens when faith *thinks* about things, something which anyone with faith is bound to do at some level and to some extent).[19]

Faith, I have been suggesting, is most helpfully thought of as a relationship into which God draws us and in which God holds and sustains and gradually becomes known to us. As such, faith is a dynamic starting point filled with promise rather than an end point. Faith is not a point of arrival after a journey of searching and struggling (though these may undoubtedly sometimes be involved) but a point of departure from which we are called to venture ever further in our grasp of God's promises, purposes, and ways of working and in understanding how these factor into the larger picture of "reality" that each of us gradually builds up from the sources of knowledge and experience available to us in our time and place. Of course, God only ever calls and expects us to venture as far as we are able, but God does call and expect us to do that, to take the risk and the leap of knowing God more fully.

In another classic discussion of the nature of believing, the nineteenth-century theologian John Henry Newman reminds his readers that there are two quite distinct ways in which we "know" things and grant assent to them.[20] The first he calls "notional assent," and this is what we grant to ideas, propositions, the conclusions of arguments, and the like, and it is the stuff of which critical reflection and intelligent reasoning are made. But it is precisely *thinking about* things, and that goes on and can only go on once we have withdrawn from our immediate engagement or encounter with the things themselves. The other sort of assent (what Newman calls simply "real assent") is a much more personal sort of response and is called forth from us in our face-to-face dealings with reality itself, the things that are presented to us in our concrete experiences of daily life. What we take to be "real" in this way, Newman observes, is precisely what gives us things to "think about" and duly come to understand. Both sorts of assent may be important in one way or another, but assent which is *merely* notional, while intellectually stimulating and impressive, lacks much purchase in or hold on reality and is in itself a purely academic form of "believing in." While, for its part, real assent lacks the clarifying and critical force of notional assent, it nonetheless furnishes the living substrate and impulse that earth our thought in the realities of human existence. Thought needs something to think about, to make sense of. And believing in something is much more than subscribing to a set of intellectual categories and relations, no matter how fully grasped and articulated.

Newman applies this distinction to the life of the English church of his day, where, he complains, there was rather too much "believing" which turned out to be of a mostly notional sort—creedal subscription, scriptural literacy, liturgical propriety of an impressive standard—but all rather remote from evidence of a direct, living engagement with the concrete realities of which such ideas were originally and properly intended to speak. Religious truth (though not religious truth alone), he suggests, is of a sort which "believing in" properly entails living participation and indwelling and not simply intellectual gymnastics or prowess. And in this sense, the uneducated or theologically unformed "simple believer" who grasps and assents to the basic claims called forth and engendered by a living engagement with God is more solidly grounded in his or her beliefs than the most learned student of the Bible, theology, and liturgy whose prayer life has atrophied or whose involvement in the life of the community of faith has grown cold and remote.

Our word *knowledge* itself, of course, can mean more than one thing depending on the context of its use. There is "knowledge" of an abstract and inert sort—the information *about* things that can be recorded in books or databases and the categories and schemes in terms of which we classify, organize, and reflect on it. And then there is the actual personal "knowledge" (or, as we might rather say, "knowing") *of* things as we are immersed in the complex, messy, multilayered, and multivalent stuff of our immediate experience of them. We can acquire lots of knowledge *about* all sorts of things by reading books, watching documentaries on TV, surfing the internet, attending lectures, or listening to podcasts, yet none of this necessarily arises from or feeds back into that sort of knowledge that can only come from having our noses rubbed in reality. In the best situations, though, these two sorts of knowledge belong and go together. We learn more about something or someone precisely through spending time with them—getting to "know" their character, their qualities, their capacities, their various quirks—and so becoming better able to provide a descriptive account of these. Or we may begin at the other end, with voracious devouring of knowledge of an abstractive sort, rapidly becoming a mine of information, but we shall only come genuinely to understand and grasp the truth of the things we read and the things we say when we are able to gauge their relationship to reality, ceasing to be a mere armchair specialist and allowing our learning to enable and enrich (and to be corrected and enhanced by) our actual up close and personal dealings with whatever it is. Where "whatever it is" happens to be another person or persons, of course, this knowing is also bound to be a two-way street. We can't really get to know someone properly, in other words, unless they are *willing* to be known, allowing us to get to know them and not withdrawing, withholding, or hiding themselves behind the ambiguous material realities (bodies, body language, facial expressions, gestures, words, texts, actions, and so on) upon which any first person encounter or meeting inevitably relies.

While, therefore, knowledge of the first sort (knowledge *about*) is an important part of Christian faith (which involves us knowing and believing all sorts of things *about* God), genuine faith will always be a compound of both sorts of knowing and cannot be less than "first personal." We need not presume upon the sort of cozy familiarity with God (as, in effect, a cosmic Buddy) that too easily verges on irreverence in its lack of a proper theological perspective, but we must certainly insist that faith involves us in a relationship in which we know and are known by the God of whom we speak. It involves us not just in believing that God is "there" but in meeting God, communing with God as with a father, a friend, a shepherd, a king, a judge, a lover. It involves us not just in believing that God forgives sins but in allowing God actually to forgive our sins. It involves us not just in believing that God is trustworthy but in actually trusting God with the realities of our own lives. And so on. There are plenty of folk in our churches who would profess "belief" in such realities as abstractions and who recite the creed with integrity and even vigor but who have never actually met God in person, or known what it means to have their sins forgiven, or stepped out in faith when God has called them.

Faith as Personal Response

A STORY IS told about the famous nineteenth-century acrobat Charles Blondin, who, in 1859, amazed crowds in North America by crossing Niagara Falls on a tightrope. As if this feat were not remarkable enough, Blondin added some theatrical twists and turns.

"Do you believe," he asked the crowds, "that I can walk across wearing a blindfold?"

"Yes!" they roared. And he did.

"Do you believe I can walk across, stop halfway, sit down, and cook and eat an omelet?" he asked.

"Yes!" they roared. And he did.

"Do you believe," he asked them again, "that I can walk across pushing a wheelbarrow?"

"Yes!" they roared. And he did.

"Do you believe," he asked, "that I can walk across pushing a wheelbarrow with a man in it?"

"Yes!" they roared.

So he turned to a particularly enthusiastic man in the front row. "Will *you* be that man?" he asked.

It's the difference between a certain sort of merely academic "belief" which is happy to assent to things from the safety of a detached observer's position and the belief which is also *faith*—an engaged, committed, trusting disposition of the whole person to the truth of things. Will *you* be that man?

Credo doesn't just mean "I believe" in the former sense. It means "I put my trust in" the truth, the reality, the reliability of the one in whom I believe and am willing to stake my life on it. It means joining the queue of those nervously willing to climb into the wheelbarrow, and that's something we clearly ought not to do lightly or without consideration of the possible consequences. Think of Abram again, having only just emptied his suitcase and buried his father after one long, dangerous, and costly journey, wanting nothing more now, no doubt, than to take stock, put down some roots, and build up some credit among the movers and shakers of Haran and make it feel a bit more like home—but faced at once with God's personal summons to join God on the unappealing tightrope of yet another risky trek into the wilderness, leaving behind security, a pension plan, and prospects in search of a place that God doesn't even bother to name and holding on to what must seem like a bunch of crazy promises about how it may all pan out eventually. And so when Abram "believed God," as Scripture says, it was no mere intellectual dalliance with questions of credulity;[21] Abram's belief was a wholesale response of heart, mind, imagination, will, and body, a venture of personal trust and commitment embarked upon in the context of a personal relationship in which, even more so than in any other, a high level of mystery and uncertainty was bound always to be in play. Yes, God "revealed" himself to Abram, but in God's self-unveiling, as in any other, much remains veiled, and we are compelled precisely to *trust* because the surety of absolute certainty is inconveniently unavailable. And yes, as I have been suggesting, Abraham's faith itself is a "gift" from God, a response of his whole being which he can only make at all because God has first approached him, and called him, and invited him to walk with him. A response that God constantly undergirds and underwrites, holding the relationship secure when Abraham repeatedly falters and breaks faith with it or seems bound to do so. But a response which nonetheless matters and which must be freely made even though it is tarnished by Abraham's doubt and fear and sin, falling back upon God again and again; because this same faith, this trust and commitment, is the very substance of the covenant God makes with Abraham and with humankind as a whole—a human response in which God's approach to us is met with reciprocal love and holiness fit to dwell in union with and to share in God's own. That, for humans, is the essence of our "salvation." Of course, it finds its fulfillment not in Abraham or, indeed, in us but in another: one of Abraham's many sons who, it turns out, is able to embody the reality of the covenant from both sides at once and to do so in a manner that includes us within and draws us into that reality. But let's not get ahead of ourselves.

Like Abraham's, our faith begins when God draws close to and calls us, challenging and promising and longing to begin the work of changing us.

And like Abraham, we can only respond, can only have "faith" because this call, this approach by God, has happened and continues to happen afresh each moment thereafter. But our response matters. No matter how weak and feeble it may be, God will grasp it and hold it and enable it to flourish. And God is patient with us. But God doesn't coerce or force us. And unless and until we grant our consent to God's laying hold of us, we shall remain on the periphery—drawn, tantalized perhaps, but largely untouched and unchanged by the reality of God's forgiving and transforming love, which is there, waiting for us, longing for us to respond. To resist is to deny the reality of who we are and the promise of God concerning who we shall be and become, a reality and a promise that we cannot elude forever. But God won't coerce or force, because deciding to put our trust in him means taking the first step on a wholly new and different and in many ways unattractive and scary way of living our lives. That's the point of the New Testament's language of "repentance," which, as many readers will already know, means simply "turning around." To turn to God in faith and to trust God are incompatible with continuing to invest ourselves and our energies in lots of other things, some of which are simply bad and others of which are perfectly good as long as they don't get elevated in our lives to the status of "false gods." Faith in God is exclusive of putting our "faith" in a whole host of other things at the same time. And turning to God in faith, therefore, means, in reality, "turning away" from these other things, turning our backs on them, perhaps permanently and at least until our sensibilities and priorities are reordered and until we can see them and judge them aright. That means that we shall stand out from the crowd, and it means that we shall be forced to resist many of the assumptions, values, and priorities that the world holds as its unquestioned orthodoxies, often making ourselves downright unpopular in the process. It's a life-changing decision (and, in truth, it's a decision we shall continue to have to make daily), and no one can or should be coerced into it. And no one ever is. That's not how God works. God is always ready to welcome us into the wheelbarrow and longs for us to be ready for him to do so, but God won't bundle us into it against our will. That would be pointless because it is not in the high-wire act itself but in our willingness to trust God in and through it that our salvation begins and consists.

Faith of the sort to which the creed gives expression changes the world, and not always obviously for the better (for the time being, at least)—because once one's life is orientated properly to the God who is its source and whose character it was always created to reflect, the accumulation of very different bits and pieces out of which the tapestry of any life is woven suddenly looks and feels and tastes very different. The bits and pieces (the "things" of various sorts) are largely the same ones, but viewed from the wheelbarrow rather than the security of the cliff edge, they take on a quite new hue, flavor, and significance. And the taste can be a bitter one. Believing in God is no bed of roses, and despite its reputation as some sort of intellectual crutch for the emotionally inadequate, it doesn't provide a set of easy answers to life's questions and problems either. More often, it stirs them up or complicates them. Yet those who know themselves to be on the receiving end of God's call and, having considered carefully the options of feigning deafness or jumping on the nearest bus out of town, find themselves taking the step of faith, which closes the circle and draws them in, mostly find that the view is worth it and that the costs are ones oddly worth bearing.

❦ 2 ❦

"GOD THE FATHER ALMIGHTY, CREATOR OF HEAVEN AND EARTH..."

God the Father

JESUS IS CONSTANTLY appealing to our imagination as he teaches his disciples and the crowds and challenges their religious understanding and their behavior. "To what shall we compare the kingdom of God?" he asks them playfully.[1] "What parable shall we use to describe it?" In other words, "What is it *like*?" That's a question we constantly ask as we seek to get some grasp on something new and unfamiliar or deep and mysterious. We want helpful comparisons to be drawn with other things, things more familiar to us, to help us begin to get our heads around it. And teachers of all sorts find themselves constantly resorting to the same strategy: "It's a bit like this . . . ," they say, or "Think of it like this . . ." Those sorts of imaginative appeals are fundamental to the way in which we learn about and come to understand anything. And they are at the heart of Jesus's life and teaching and the wider patterns of Scripture within which we learn about him.[2]

The kingdom of God, Jesus suggests, is like lots of things. It's like treasure hidden in a field. It's like a merchant seeking out the best pearls to buy. It's like a net cast into the sea. It's like a field planted with wheat and tares. It's like the party to end all parties. And so on. Of course, it's not any of those things, and it's different from all of them in all sorts of ways. But there's something in each—a shred of similarity that, when we grasp it, illuminates our appreciation of the kingdom. And Jesus does the same thing where God is concerned. To what should we liken God? How should we picture God in our mind's eye in helpful and healthy ways? How should we address God in worship and in prayer? The answer Jesus gives more consistently than any other is to encourage us to picture God and address God as our Father.

The image of God as a father has become so familiar within Western religious culture over the past two thousand years or so that we easily forget how distinctive it actually is. Again, of course, God is not *literally* a father any more than (as Scripture suggests elsewhere) God is a shepherd, or a judge, or a rock. And yet each of these biblical word pictures points us suggestively to something true about God's character—something about God that, despite the huge differences between God and ourselves as his creatures, draws close to things with which we are familiar in our human experiences of fatherhood, shepherding, and so on. These are central to the way in which God gives himself to be grasped by us, taking our imagination captive and helping us think and speak meaningfully about and to God. And for Christians, the image of God as "our Father" plays a particular and prominent role in all this.

Judaism certainly knows the image of God as a father and uses it. So, for example, it crops up in the traditions about God's choosing and calling of Israel and especially God's rescuing of Israel from slavery in Egypt. Moses is told by God to say this to Pharaoh: "Thus says the LORD, 'Israel is My son, My firstborn. So I said to you "Let My son go that he may serve Me."'"[3] Here notice it is *the nation of Israel as a whole* that is God's child (as we might properly say) and so, by implication, able to think and speak of God as her Father. And what grants her that peculiar privilege is God's choosing of her to be his people and God's entering into covenant with her. Fatherhood in God is linked to Israel's election and adoption, her calling and vocation as "my people," and to God's promise of salvation (release from captivity in Egypt). Later on, we find individuals spoken of in a similar vein. For example, in 2 Samuel 7:12–14, God says to David, "When your days are complete and you lie down with your fathers, I will raise up your descendant after you, who will come forth from you, and I will establish . . . the throne of his kingdom forever. I will be a father to him and he will be a son to Me" (NASB). Historically, the person concerned was Solomon, but the verses were soon interpreted as having a longer reach than this and read as a prophetic promise concerning the Messiah—the one who would come and establish God's kingdom of justice and peace and human flourishing. The Messiah would embody in himself the purposes and promises invested by God in Israel of old and so fulfill her calling to be the proper covenant partner of God ("You shall be my people, and I will be your God"[4]), a calling she had never yet managed to fulfill. And so the Messiah would be the true "son" of God, as Israel had been called to be and become. Thinking and speaking of God as Father, then, is not unknown in the Old Testament, but it generally comes highly charged and is linked to some of the most highly charged religious moments and ideas in Israel's history. It wasn't language to be bandied around lightly.

In fact, a simple glance at some statistics reveals quite a disparity between the two Testaments of our Bible in this regard. In the Old Testament (which was, more or less, the Bible of Judaism in Jesus's day and is still in our own), God is referred to as "father" just fifteen times (to which we should add the nine occasions where the term *father* itself is not used but where Israel or someone else is spoken of as the "son" or child of God, presupposing the same image). In the New Testament, on the other hand, the image of God as Father crops up hundreds of times, especially in the Gospels, where it appears on the lips of Jesus alone on more than 160 occasions. It is Jesus's favorite way of referring to and addressing God (interestingly, Jesus never addresses God as "Lord," the most common term used by Jews), and he teaches his disciples to think and speak of God as *their* Father too.

When Jesus teaches his disciples to think and speak of God in this way, of course, part of what he is doing is deliberately drawing on and evoking some of the stuff about God as Israel's Father in the Hebrew scriptures. In other words, he is expecting that when they hear him addressing and referring to God as "my Father," they will immediately think of Israel's ancient calling and mission and God's promises to bring in his kingdom and to save his people from oppression, both political oppression and that other sort of "enslavement" that blights human life and prevents God's kingdom (his reign in our lives) from triumphing—namely, our enslavement to sin. Jews in Jesus's day might well have occasionally referred to God as "our Father," meaning the father of the nation. But for someone to speak openly of God as "my Father" was, in effect, deliberately to set some theological bells ringing and to associate themselves directly with the agency of God's coming kingdom. It was to evoke the hope of a new exodus and to raise expectations of its being close at hand.[5]

But that doesn't really explain the frequency and single-mindedness with which Jesus speaks of God as his Father. It isn't just, as it were, a bit of religious shorthand, laying claim to a particular role in the pattern of God's ancient purposes. To do that, all Jesus would have needed to do would have been to use the term publicly on a number of well-minuted occasions. Instead, what we find is that the image of God as Father is everywhere upon his lips, in his private conversations, and in his public pronouncements—and, crucially, in his own prayer life. It is clear that for him, the full meaning of God's fatherhood goes well beyond formal associations, lies at the very heart of his personal understanding of who God is and who he himself is, and structures his own relationship and approach to God. There is an intimacy and a warmth about his account of God as "my Father," and this is captured especially in the fact that the word he is thought typically to have used (because the New Testament occasionally preserves it) was the Aramaic *Abba*, a word used by children (of all ages) within families and probably roughly equivalent to our own use of the term *Dad*. There is no known instance prior to Jesus of any Jew thinking of or addressing God in this familiar or colloquial way (the more formal Hebrew term *Ab* would have been used, if any). Jesus is flagging up the fact that God is his Father in a special and new sense which earlier uses of the term hadn't even begun to fathom, and part of this newness is an awareness of the love and intimacy that characterize Jesus's relationship to God.

In fact, the course of Jesus's teaching and his own prayer life as we see them in the Gospels shows us that this special relationship between Jesus and his heavenly Father is something quite unique and has something to do with who Jesus is not just humanly and historically but eternally. In other words, the language of *Father* and *Son* is how God chooses to express for our sake a distinction and relationship in God's own life, revealed to us when the "Father" sends his "Son" into the world to be "God with us" and God for us. This means that there is something in who God is eternally that is most appropriately likened to the relationship between a human father (or parent) and son (or child). And so when God becomes a human being, the one who is eternally "filial" expresses his own relationship to God in terms of the corresponding image of *Father*. This means, in the language of the New Testament, that there is no other "Son of God" in quite this sense because this sort of sonship rests on Jesus's divine identity. He is the "only-begotten Son of God."

And yet Jesus is quite clear that the disciples should, as a function of their following him and of their new commitment to the cause of the coming of God's kingdom, begin to think and speak about and to God as their own "Father" (their Abba) too. Paul reflects the centrality of this radical element in Jesus's message and mission in Galatians 4:4–7: "When the fullness of the time came, God sent forth his Son, born of a woman, born under the Law . . . that we might receive the adoption as sons. Because you are sons, God has sent forth the Spirit of His Son into our hearts, crying 'Abba! Father!' Therefore you are no longer a slave, but a son; and if a son, then an heir through God" (NASB).

What does this mean? Well, it means first that to be disciples of Jesus is to make our own and to "own" active roles in the carrying forward of the ancient calling and promises of Israel. It is to identify ourselves with the coming of the kingdom and with the cause of the coming King (who is, of course, in New Testament terms, none other than Jesus himself). It is to align ourselves with the dynamics of the new exodus, the promised liberation from sin into a life of freedom and living to serve and worship God in a new way in the midst of history. More than this, though, to speak of God and to speak to God as "my Father" (as Jesus teaches his disciples to) is to recognize that as a consequence of his incarnation, his ministry, his death on the cross, and his resurrection, all undertaken "for us," we are granted access to a wholly new sort of relationship with God, something much more intimate, much more personal, and much more transformative than anything any human being could ever expect or accomplish. In Paul's language, we are "adopted" into a relationship which by right belongs only to Jesus himself, the one who earths within history and our own flesh and blood a relationship existing within the very life of God himself. That eternal relationship—between the Father and the Son, enjoyed in the power of the Holy Spirit—is now opened up for God's creatures to share and to enjoy. We are, in other words, permitted by God's grace and goodness to share in the joy and the love that are at the very core of God's own character and being. That, finally, is the mind-boggling thought contained in the seemingly simple reference to God as "my" or "our" Father in the way Jesus teaches.

Notice that the popular idea that we are all "sons and daughters" by virtue of our having been *created* by God is thus actually unbiblical. According to Scripture, we are granted the privileged status of sons and daughters *only* by God's own coming to share with us in our fallen, broken, and sinful creaturehood so that we might in turn (and in exchange) share in the loving relationship between the Father and the Son that is part of God's own eternal life, full of joy and glory. And to know God as our Father has some radical implications for our lives, keying us into his kingdom's purposes and promises as active agents rather than passive observers or recipients. It is something, furthermore, that we have actively to own for ourselves and grasp and make our own by that response to the work of the Holy Spirit that the New Testament calls "faith." As the Prayer Book preface to the Lord's Prayer puts it, therefore, "our Father" is something "we are *bold* to say" (emphasis added) because in a vital sense, our status as children is one we are still very much growing into and as yet fall far short of. So it's an edgy and potentially risky claim to make.[6]

God the Father Almighty

THAT GOD IS powerful might seem to us to be too obvious to need saying, but that's only because we are already so familiar with a cluster of ideas about God from Scripture and other sources. And that God is "all-powerful" (which, straightforwardly, is what I take "almighty" here to mean) is actually quite a distinctive claim. In the Old Testament, where many of our most significant theological ideas were introduced, worked out, and shaped up, it's not uncommon to find the unguarded suggestion that Israel's God, Yahweh (translated in English versions of the Bible as "the LORD"), was one among any number of deities attached to the various nations in the way that sponsors attach themselves to sports teams today, identifying themselves with the nation's fortunes and touting their particular brand in doing so. So, for instance, Psalm 95:3 refers to Yahweh as "a great God, and a great King *above all gods*" (emphasis added). By the time the Old Testament as a whole was written up and edited into the book we know today, Israel had moved on to a new level of theological sophistication, coming increasingly to the view that Yahweh was, in reality, the "only Lord" and other supposed "gods" must, therefore, be classified as the products of peoples' misguided religious imaginings or falsely conceived hopes and expectations. Even when the existence of other "gods" was a possibility seriously entertained, though, what was vital to Israel's faith was the conviction that Yahweh was incomparable, capable of great deeds that set Yahweh apart decisively from any other putative deity—"all-powerful," in other words, in ways that elevated Israel's God into a category of his own. So in the Song of Moses, after the exodus from Egypt, we find this: "Who is like you, Yahweh, among the gods? Who is like you . . . awesome in splendour, doing wonders?"[7] And the answer is, of course, *no one*. Yahweh alone has sovereignty over all things, including any "gods" who may be sniffing around hoping to pick up some of the action. Yahweh alone is "almighty," a claim that, as the Old Testament took shape, came to be associated particularly with Israel's understanding that Yahweh, the particular God in whom she believed and trusted and who had revealed God's name to her, was the one who had *created* all things.[8] Yahweh alone is without beginning and without end.[9] Yahweh alone is able to work without hindrance or resistance.[10] Yahweh alone, that is to say, is all-powerful.

By the time of the New Testament, this association of Israel's God with power was so well established that *the Power* could function perfectly well as a convenient synonym for *God*, which was very useful because by this time, uttering God's proper name, Yahweh, itself was proscribed as sacrilegious—so holy was that name held to be. So synonyms were the order of the day. And when, for example, in Mark 14:62, Jesus tells the high priest "You will see the Son of Man seated at the right hand of the Power," the statement is denounced as blasphemous *not* because Jesus speaks the divine name (which he carefully avoids doing) but precisely because what he says, in effect, is that he, Jesus, will be seated at God's own right hand—will share, that is to say, in God's own unique identity and power. That's a claim that renders sacrilegious slips of the tongue trivial by comparison.

The image itself, of course, is one borrowed directly from the corridors of human power, where a king or potentate would be seated on the throne, and anyone sitting at his right hand would naturally be either his son or some other exalted figure given to share in the exercise of royal authority while others groveled obsequiously on their knees, taking care to reverse out of the throne room so as not to turn their backs on the power in the land (and risk losing their heads for doing so). It's an image familiar from a hundred or more Hollywood versions of ancient as well as more recent history. And it raises important theological questions: Is God's rule *really* like that? Does the appeal to that sort of imagery not appear to legitimate or provide "divine sanction" for models of human power that we have come nowadays to recognize as highly problematic? In the age of democracies and constitutional rather than absolute monarchies, in other words, are we not bound to experience an uncomfortable crunch of gears when seemingly inhumane notions of power are associated with or ascribed to God?

These are important questions not to be shirked. Perhaps the first thing to say is that any image works with an interplay of likeness and unlikeness. That's true, say, of the image of God as shepherd. God is *like* a shepherd in some ways (he cares for his "flock" and is willing to risk himself in order to rescue wayward and foolish "sheep") but *unlike* a shepherd in other ways (he doesn't spend days and nights sitting in a field or on a mountainside). So the fact that God is pictured as like a human potentate on a throne does not involve us in supposing that all characteristics of such power arrangements are relevant in God's case; there will be some ways in which God is wholly unlike any human sovereign, and we need to figure out what those are. Such discernment is one of the key tasks of theology. Furthermore, when it comes to the images that Scripture uses, they are bound to be ones that reflect its provenance in the specifics of Israel's particular history, which is why we don't find God pictured as a software engineer, a chess master, or a neurosurgeon (all of which have definite theological potential). And in biblical times, the image of human rulers of one sort or another wielding absolute power within their territories was still the model of power most familiar to most people and therefore the most obvious one to pick up and work with theologically. While, though, we often refer to those who seem still to aspire to this sort of power (in politics or elsewhere) as "playing God," that is, I think, a misleading and dangerous misuse of language, suggesting not that we are taking Scripture too seriously but precisely that we are failing to take it seriously enough. Because while Scripture, like the creed, insists that God is "almighty" and pictures God as Sovereign, King, and Lord, its wider characterization of God makes it impossible for these words, in Christian liturgy and theology, to mean any longer what, in human terms, they once did mean. In other words, Scripture itself, precisely by appropriating these terms and using them of God, deconstructs and reforges them, granting them quite new sets of connotations. The metaphor (like all good metaphors) modifies our understanding of both terms involved in it and leads us to suppose that human power and lordship modeled on God's own are bound to be very different indeed from any version of cosmic despotism. The poetry of the text, that is, offers a radical critique of both the understanding and practice of power as found in most human contexts and, far from endorsing it, points precisely to its drastic need of redemption—something that Jesus is at pains to point out to the disciples when, like many readers of the biblical text today, they show that they haven't yet gotten it.[11] Lording it over is, paradoxically, not true lordship at all.

God's power, we might note, is not in any case absolute. The biblical and creedal claim that God is "almighty," that is to say, does not and cannot mean that God can do *absolutely anything*. It may well be true in some sense that, as the archangel tells Mary, "*nothing* is impossible with God," but there are at least two categories of things that fall with impunity outside the scope of this generous inclusivity.[12] Skeptics have sometimes mocked the idea of an all-powerful God by asking, for instance, whether God is powerful enough to make a rock so heavy that even God cannot pick it up. Whichever way that question is answered, the suggestion seems to be that God is not almighty after all. Mental games of this sort (Can God make a triangle with four sides or a square circle?) are entertaining, but they are not serious objections to the creed's claim, even though we are compelled to answer them in the negative.[13] These, we may confidently say, are things that God cannot "do" not because God's power is limited or inadequate but because, as C. S. Lewis points out, "meaningless combinations of words do not suddenly acquire meaning simply because we prefix to them the two other words 'God can.'" Nonsense remains *nonsense*, he continues, "even when we talk it about God."[14] In other words, God may be able to do anything that, in the terms vested in the world by God's own creation of it, is intrinsically possible. That even God cannot do the intrinsically impossible, though, is not an admission of God's weakness or the limitation of his strength by some insurmountable obstacle; it is simply a tautology, an artificial contrivance born of our language and logic.

The other category of things that God "cannot do," though, is altogether more important. We might sum it up in the words of 2 Timothy 2:13: "[God]," Paul writes, "cannot deny himself." Put more positively, God is faithful—faithful to his own character and faithful to the promises and purposes issuing from that character in God's dealings with us as our creator and redeemer. Again, to say this is not to suggest that God's power runs up against some sort of arbitrary limit that, were God truly "almighty," he would be able to break through. It is simply to acknowledge that the reality of God, *ultimate* reality, is a *moral* reality, and God's freedom and power are constrained precisely and only by who God is. Now, we might say, that word *father* turns out to have further vital importance. Scriptural images of God do not only modify our understanding of the human realities from which they are borrowed; they also modify one another as they take their place within the wider pattern of biblically sanctioned imagining and speaking. And so the sort of "power" that God exercises without limit, the creed is telling us, is no random, capricious, or morally neutral force, let alone an immoral or cruel one. It is the sort of power proper to one whose character is even more fundamentally that of a father—and a father of the precise sort that God, in his dealings with us and through his Son, has revealed himself to be, for "Father," too, is a creaturely image, which, in our application of it to God, necessarily experiences critique, deconstruction, and redemption.[15] And despite all the political imagery that comes into play, what matters most for faith is that the one who alone is all-powerful is the one we know as our Father in heaven. To call God "almighty," therefore, is not, for Christians, a logical inference that any intelligent person might make ("In order to create the world, God must be all-powerful"). It has a very distinct moral and spiritual force. It is, in these very precise words of the creed, God "the Father almighty" of whom we speak and to whom we entrust ourselves. The world, it tells us, and we with it are in the hands of someone infinitely good, loving, merciful, and faithful, not just some cosmic office administrator or (worse still) a morally unstable dictator on steroids.

To confess God as the Father almighty, therefore, is, in effect, to insist and to trust that God is capable of accomplishing God's "fatherly" purposes and promises in creation and redemption and that nothing (other than the constraints of God's own character, which are in any case already expressed in those same purposes and promises) can stand in the way of that accomplishment. In accordance with the ways in which those purposes and promises are unfolded in the narrative of Scripture, it is clear that this involves God working constantly and patiently with some recalcitrant materials and some self-imposed challenges. God has created human beings with a real measure of freedom and a world with its own integrity, contingency, and order, both of which, being who he is, God must work with rather than simply riding roughshod over them. It's difficult for us to imagine how that might be possible. One suggestion (already alluded to en passant above) has been to picture God as a grand master who is so good at playing the game that there is never any question that he will eventually win it, no matter what moves his opponent makes and despite the fact that, along the way, the moves God must make to win remain far from clear (possibly even to God himself). But pictures like that, while suggestive and helpful, are only of limited use. Therefore, as one writer puts it, "we should not be surprised that the working out of [God's] gracious purposes is often painfully obscure to us, that our patience is often tried to the limit, and that belief in God as both good and almighty is often exceedingly difficult."[16] Again, such belief is no matter of natural or logical inference from the evidence of our lives in the world. It is a matter of faith in who God has revealed himself to be in God's Son Jesus Christ. And it involves a form of "power," we must not forget, that is *so* powerful as to be able, in the pursuit of its purposes, to transform itself into its seeming opposite, the manifest weakness of Jesus suffering and dying on the cross. There is no greater challenge to or critique of our typical human notions of what power is or looks like than that. And since all human power is derived ultimately from God's own and answerable to God and ought therefore to conform to its pattern and character, this should be a sobering thought for any who exercise it, no matter the context.[17]

Creator of Heaven and Earth

IT IS THIS same all-powerful God, the one known to us as the Father, who, the creed insists, is the creator, the one who called all things into existence "in the beginning" and who holds them in existence from moment to moment. "Heaven and earth" is Scripture's shorthand for everything that exists besides God. The Nicene Creed goes further, borrowing Paul's terminology in Colossians 1:16 and directing us to God's creating "all things, visible and invisible." While the two formulations have a certain cumulative force when yoked together like this, in reality, they mean more or less the same thing, the latter adding only a bit more precise definition or contour to what is being said. What it reminds us, helpfully, is that so-called spiritual (nonmaterial and so "invisible") realities, too, are part of the same creaturely cosmos as their bodily counterparts. Like flesh and blood and grit and granite and stardust, they are all part of a multilayered reality that exists only because God chose that it should exist alongside God and which depends utterly for its continuing existence on God's faithfulness in sustaining it—constantly infusing into it, as it were, fresh creative energy and intent. Were God ever to withdraw from this world or to withdraw God's creative will from it, it would simply cease to be, returning to "nothingness," that void of nonexistence and absolute lack of potential which preceded the world's genesis and out of which God's voice alone summoned it to be. Thus, of the animal kingdom, the psalmist says to Yahweh in grateful wonder, "When you hide your face, they are dismayed; when you take away their breath, they die and return to their dust. When you send forth your spirit, they are created; and you renew the face of the ground."[18] But the same is true whether it's animals, humans, angels, "spiritual" beings of other sorts, planets and stars, beauty, goodness, truth, love, mercy, justice, creativity, or anything else we might have in mind. Whatever different sorts of things there are, God holds them all in being—in the palm of God's hand—and without that holding fast, they would slip into nonbeing in an instant.

That things do not simply disappear, that *we* do not disappear in that way, is because God holds on to us, even when we behave in ways that are identifiably displeasing, disrespectful, or even hateful to God. And that, again, is due to the fact that God's creative will and power are not those of a morally indifferent or capricious deity but the creative potency of a Father who is and remains true to himself and to his purposes and promises. God is good, and having created the world, God will not let it go until everything has been done that can be done to see that God's good purposes for it are fulfilled. It's important to stress this because it might otherwise be supposed that God created out of some need or lack in himself, that God, as it were, gets an important trade-off from the world's existence and so *cannot* let it go without leaving himself unfulfilled or incomplete. In the Bible, it is always God's faithfulness, to himself and to us, that is given as the reason for God's continuing goodness to a world undeserving of it and incapable as yet of responding to it well, let alone properly. This is important because, to return to another facet of knowing God as Father, we can say that it is out of God's love that God creates. Were it out of need or a sense of a lack in God's own being or identity, creating would be a self-serving and ultimately selfish action, and of course it would make God in some sense dependent on our continued existence. Scripture will have none of that. We are utterly dependent on God, but God is dependent on no one. And yet it is perfectly proper to say that, God being who God is, it "comes naturally" to him to create a world to share in his joy and his love and to enjoy his glory. God (who is eternally not just the Father but the Son and the Spirit too) is fulfilled in himself, an eternal communion of goodness, love, and joy, and far from a deficit or lack, creation is, therefore, better thought of as issuing forth from an overflowing or fullness of God's joy, which longs to share itself and creates in order that it may bless others with such sharing. God's life as the Father, Son, and Spirit is, we might say, a party already in full swing but one which creation is now invited to join in and to enjoy.[19]

That God is the creator also reinforces, of course, what the creed has just told us—namely, that God is all-powerful and enjoys sovereign authority over all things that exist. It also sets God apart decisively from everything and anything else that exists ("heaven and earth," "all things visible, and invisible"). God is without beginning and without end, whereas the remainder of reality is determined by time (it has a beginning and will come to an end) and, in the case of physical things, space too. God is the sole originator of things. Theologians have sometimes expressed this by saying that God created "out of nothing" (ex nihilo), which is an awkward, counterintuitive, and in some ways, therefore, not altogether helpful phrase. But its point is simple enough and captures a fundamental biblical insight. If God is indeed the creator of heaven and earth, of all things that exist besides God himself, then prior to his creative act, there *was* nothing *besides* God. God was all there was. That's a very difficult circumstance for us to imagine because our minds are adapted to deal with things that exist in time and space. So if we close our eyes and try to imagine a situation in which God is all there is, we'll probably end up picturing God (however we do picture God) existing in some sort of dark, empty space. But dark spaces themselves are part of the world as God has created it and tied to the way it is ordered. In fact, strictly speaking, we can't even properly talk about a circumstance "prior" to God's creative act because time too as we know it, with its "before" and "after," is also part of the world God has made. It gets complicated, and our imagination naturally and properly runs up against the buffers at this point. But one simple and important lesson to glean from it is that God has not, like a human craftsman, builder, or artist, fashioned the cosmos out of preexisting materials—because before creation (there we go again, carelessly using the word *before* . . .), there was only God, which means that whatever existed alongside God was stuff of God's own choosing and making, no matter how resistant and recalcitrant it may have turned out to be. God made it. And if it presents God with limits and challenges, they are only ones that God himself has chosen to live and to work with. God is all-powerful in relation to whatever exists because God made it, and he made it in accordance with a purpose, a plan, a promise that sprang naturally from God's character as the Father. And we're told in the Genesis creation story that God got great pleasure from doing so because what he made was good and satisfying—so much so, in fact, that God took time off straight afterward just to enjoy it and drink it all in.

One way of refreshing our reading of Genesis 1, perhaps, might be to picture God as an artist in the studio rather than (as we usually do) a cosmic potentate at whose authoritative command a host of nervous minions scurry around to obey. If we do so, then we may hear the words "Let there be . . ." less as a brusque injunction and more as the excited suggestion springing from a divine imagination in which ever more wonderful, colorful, and beautiful possibilities are unfolding. No image of God's mode of creating and fashioning the world is perfect, of course, and no doubt this one (and the way it involves us in "hearing" the text differently) has its own limitations. But "God as Sultan" and "God as Site Manager" have their limitations too, and both are prescribed and authorized by our habits of reading rather than by the text itself. At the very least, "God as Poet" or "God as Artist" may offer a worthwhile imaginative supplement, capturing, perhaps, something of the sense of God's joy, satisfaction, and love that not only constitute the motive force and inspiration for the project of creation as a whole but also characterize God's response to its establishment and gradual evolution, enabling us to take more fully into account those other words by whose reiteration the chapter is punctuated: "And God saw that it was good."

This same God, whose character was already well known to Israel through the law and the prophets and is known more fully still to those who hold him to have been identifiable among us as the man Jesus, is the one, the doctrine of creation insists, in whose hands the past, present, and future of the cosmos lie and with whose character, purposes, and promises the secret of its meaning is bound up inexorably. For Christians, this is the wider "theological" backdrop against which, for instance, science's testimony to the regular workings of nature must be placed, together with whatever other knowledge and understanding we possess about our world, if we are ever going to make proper sense of it and learn to live in it appropriately. And it is the purpose of the stories of Genesis 1–2 to sketch a vital part of that backdrop for us, picturing the world's beginnings with God in ways designed to lay bare something of God's character, purposes, and promises for our imaginative grasp and exploration. One literary feature of these stories of creation in particular dangles in front of us a striking theological suggestion that is easily missed but that, once we have noticed it, we can subsequently identify woven through the canon of Scripture as a whole, being a central thread in the pattern of its depiction of God's purposes and promises from creation onward, the removal or severing of which would see the whole thing unraveling horribly before our eyes.

The major concern of the doctrine of creation, I have suggested, is not with the *how* but with the *why* of creation. Why, that is to say, did God create at all? This question is bound up closely with others about the world's meaning and value and the meaning and value, therefore, of our own human existence and history as part of that world. Few questions, surely, can be designed to capture our imagination or grab our undivided attention more securely than this one. And it might do so if we would only switch off our TVs, tablets, and smartphones long enough to interrupt the incessant stream of trivia and titillation, by immersing ourselves in which we are, in Neil Postman's telling verdict, gradually "amusing ourselves to death" instead.[20] Well, no doubt, as Charles Dickens insists, "people must be amuthed, . . . thomehow" at least some of the time.[21] But the *why* of creation is, it turns out, far more exciting and urgent anyway than funny kittens on YouTube or the latest upload to Netflix. That's why Scripture foregrounds it from the outset and gives us tantalizing glimpses of it again and again, building up gradually to the great "must-see episode" in which, with the appearance of Jesus, "things hidden from the foundation of the world" are divulged, the unity, integrity, and overarching meaning of the drama in which God and the world are involved together finally brought to light and its denouement anticipated.[22] And all this is meant not to leave us—fascinated, excited, even "amuthed"—in the role of mere observers or consumers, eager for the next episode to begin. Instead, in a way that outstrips even the accomplishments of the latest "interactive" media entertainments, its aim is to draw us (no game consoles or VR helmets required) into the drama itself—imaginatively, intellectually, morally, bodily—for part of what was once hidden and now lies revealed is the fact that this has been our story, our drama, and our game and its "world" our world all along. And we have significant roles to play in whatever remains of it.

What, then, is the *why* of creation? In biblical and theological terms, any answer to the question is bound to resist easy summary, there being lots of things one might say in unpacking such a huge theme. But if a gun is pointed at our heads and we are denied the theologian's luxury of endless deferral and qualification, one theme does suggest itself as a convenient way of summing it all up. It is a theme that, I suggested above, may not be obvious at first glance as the camera directs our gaze to Scripture's opening scene, but as things come gradually into focus and we attend to the details, those already familiar with key characters and with later scenes will discover that the director has, in reality, etched it cleverly all over the set and between the lines of the dialogue. What we need are eyes to see. What I am talking about is the suggestion that God created the world so that God's *glory* might fill the world and so that we, together with other creatures, might dwell in the midst of and enjoy and come to share in that same glory—which is to say, dwell in, enjoy, and share in a place filled to the brim and unmistakably by God himself.

In the Old Testament, the glory of God is the focus of God's presence and is pictured mostly in terms of fire, light, and other forms of effulgence that are so remarkable that they threaten to dazzle, stun, overcome, or even destroy mere mortals, who, we are told, cannot even bear the sight of God's glory directly. God's glory, we are told, is "like a devouring fire," beautiful and deadly at the same time for creatures like ourselves;[23] even Moses is advised to look away as it passes by, being permitted a glimpse of its less impressive nether regions alone,[24] and too much time spent in close proximity to God's glory has some unintended side effects—forty days and nights on Sinai's heights sufficing to give Moses a tan to die for.[25] The final moments of Steven Spielberg's *Raiders of the Lost Ark* deploy the full range of Hollywood's special effects to provide for us a visualization at once horrific and humorous of the imagined consequences for mortals (let alone sinful mortals) of undue exposure to the fullness of God's glory. It's not a pretty sight, and (once the movie has ended) it's no joke either but a serious theological point.

For God's glory is the material symbol of God's holy reality and presence in the world, a reality that, as things stand, cannot be borne by us, cannot be enjoyed by us, cannot be experienced directly by us. It is sacred and, as the manifestation of God's own character, burns in its unwavering opposition to the moral and spiritual condition in which the world currently exists, and it is concentrated, for Israel, in the tabernacle and the temple, its "throne" being the aforementioned (long since "lost") ark of the covenant. But God, Scripture insists from the get-go, longs for nothing more than to dwell in our midst, to share his life with our lives, to inhabit the world together with us—to put God's glory in its and our midst in such a way that it transforms our lives and the world together, filling it to the very brim, "as the waters cover the sea."[26] This is the *why* of creation. This is what it, and the world's history, and our own lives are all about. And it's there already on the opening pages of the script where, as various biblical scholars have noted, there is a clear literary parallelism between the way in which the story of creation is structured and those chapters in the book of Exodus where God, through Moses, gives Israel the blueprint not for the building of the world but for the construction of the tabernacle—the place where, symbolically, God's glory is to be housed in the people's midst.[27] The parallels would take too long to recount here, but the parallelism is deliberate and developed, and the suggestion is clear enough: God, the poet who crafted these stories is insisting, creates the world not as an afterthought, or to fill up time when there's little else to do, or as an experiment to see what might happen next, or because God is in need of company. No, God creates the world as a *temple*, a place in the midst of which God's own glory can and will be shared and dwell openly so that all will now enjoy and be blessed rather than consumed by it. *That's* God's purpose in creating—so that what God creates might share in God's glory and so bear the hallmark of God's presence shot through every fiber of its being, characterized by the love, joy, and peace which are the proper conditions of God's own holy life as Father, Son, and Spirit and offering this life back to God in creaturely response to the gift and opportunity that creation itself occasions and affords.

That's the *why* of creation. That's God's purpose in creation. And the "good news" already being flagged at the story's outset (long before we get anywhere near the New Testament) is that, despite the obstacles and the challenges involved in doing so, this God is one who seems fully capable of bringing it off and fully committed to doing so. It is a theme shot through the whole Old Testament story of the covenant—flickering as that story does between instances of faithfulness and disobedience, the joy of Zion and the pain of exile, the presence of Yahweh with his people and his seeming withdrawal and absence—and in the form of a promise, it leaps across the gap between the two Testaments in our Christian Bible, to be picked up by the apostles in a way that would blow everyone's circuits by insisting that even the prophets' wildest dreams had not been wild enough. In the life of the man Jesus, John tells us in the prologue to his Gospel (opening, as it does, with those clear echoes of Genesis 1), the creative Word of God himself "became flesh and *tabernacled in our midst* . . . and we have seen his glory."[28] Creation purposes and promises come to a head here, and a landmark moment is reached in the story of the good news; in some sense, with this "coming of the Lord to his temple," the fulfillment of creation itself has already begun.[29] It's an exciting time to be alive.

Putting Us Helpfully in Our Place

THE DOCTRINE OF creation has lots to tell us about God, therefore, but it also has all sorts of things to tell us about ourselves and about the world in which we find ourselves, and some of these are things we need to hear loud and clear in our own generation, not least in the "developed" Western world.

First, it reminds us that life itself is a gift from God and not a right. And we should *receive* it as a gift, therefore, and treat it with care and respect. That obviously goes for the lives of others too, especially those for which we have some particular responsibility—our children, our aging parents, or whomever it might be whose well-being depends on our behavior and decisions. Since we are each created within a given network of biological and other sorts of relationships, others' lives are a gift to us too, and ours to them. We should neither take these gifts for granted nor treat them lightly. Life (and human life in particular) used to be referred to as "sacred," which captures something of this idea of a gift that *matters to* God as well as *coming to us* from God's hand.

To know that we are God's creatures disabuses us, too, of any supposition that we (personally or humankind as a species) are at the center of the cosmos. We are not the be-all and end-all even in our own lives, let alone in the wider pattern and history of the cosmos. And we are not and cannot finally be the lords of our own lives, though we may spend much of our lives trying to be. God does not just "own" us (in some ways, an unfortunate pecuniary image, albeit one with plenty of bite in a consumer age) and did not just make us: God made us *for himself*, and our lives will never be properly adjusted to the world, and we will never really feel "at home" in the world until we realize that and reorientate ourselves accordingly. That's not just something that is true in modern, secular, godless societies. It was already true at the end of the fourth century CE, when Saint Augustine could write, "You have made us for yourself (Lord), and our heart is restless until it finds rest in you."[30] It has always been true. We are restless, unable to find fulfillment or satisfaction of any permanent or deep sort. A large part of modernity's answer to that is the ideology of consumerism. But it doesn't work. It is just one more way of denying our creatureliness and supposing that we are the center and the measure of all things, existing for ourselves, and that is to be seriously out of touch with reality. Instead, as one writer puts it, "God's gracious purpose for us is that we should sustain our true dignity as creatures meant to be conscious and intelligent witnesses of his work, created to know, glorify and enjoy him forever."[31]

What, then, of the world, our natural environment, and the sentient creatures with whom we share it? Again, we might begin by recognizing that, like life itself, the world and its fragile and beautiful and diverse ecosystems come to us as *gifts* from God's hand but are not handed over to us to do with whatever we like or choose. The world, in other words, is not *ours*. We do not own it or even have the leasehold. The world is given to us so that we may share it with God and with other creatures whose habitat it is alongside us. This is almost certainly the most important thing for us to hear and to take seriously in the current moment of history, with its impending ecological crisis and the shadow of irreversible climate change growing ever darker. But the rot goes back a long way and ironically received a significant shot in the arm at the dawn of modernity from the appropriation and misuse of *biblical texts* to provide theological warrant for an ideology of exploitation, consumption, and the gratification of every conceivable human desire. The world became a warehouse of raw materials to be processed and sold at a profit to the highest bidder. This consumerist attitude coincided with rapid growth in human understanding of nature and the ability to manipulate it courtesy of science and technology. How should such tools be used? Surely, a generation of philosophers and theologians argued, in whatever way seems to suit us best. After all, does not the Bible itself say that humans are made in God's image and are to exercise "dominion" over and "subdue" the world? Well, that *is* what the Bible says in Genesis 1:26

and 28. These are not the only relevant texts when it comes to reckoning with a biblical view of our place within nature, but they are the ones that tend to have been concentrated on. And the question is, of course, not What do they *say*? but What do they *mean*?

At the time of the European Renaissance, this idea of a "dominion mandate" given by God was fused together with ideas about human beings that drew their inspiration far more obviously from strands of classical Greek philosophy than from the Bible.[32] Human beings, it was held, were essentially spiritual, godlike creatures composed of material bodies and divine souls, and their essential "godlikeness" lay in their capacity for reason. This, it was assumed, was what the Bible meant when, in the very same passage, it spoke of God creating humankind in God's own "image" and "likeness."[33] It was an interpretation containing the sort of implicit disparagement of all purely "material" realities (anything lacking a "rational soul," in fact) from which Christian theology and Western culture have struggled to free themselves whenever philosophical idealism of one sort or another has been allowed to dictate the terms in which Scripture is interpreted. The Renaissance, of course, was all about the rebirth of classical ideas in European culture, including the idealism of Plato and his followers, and armed with these decidedly unbiblical tools, theologians now set about unpacking what it might mean for godlike, rational beings to "exercise dominion" over material nature. God, it was widely contended, had put humans in the world in order to make it their own, to use it as raw material for their experiments and industry, to expand their minds by pulling it apart to see how it worked—all in the interest of sustaining and enhancing human knowledge and improving human quality of life and without any necessary regard for the well-being (short or long term) of nature as such. After all, it was simply a material playground, a warehouse of material bits and pieces, devoid of any "spiritual" qualities of its own, and of no lasting significance in the bigger scheme of things. Humans, on the other hand, were essentially spiritual beings who, while shackled for now to the clumsy processes of nature by their bodies, were clearly "above" nature and free to use and abuse it as they saw fit. This ideology of hubris and liberal consumption may only have lasted for a few generations, but it put in place attitudes and patterns of practice which are still very much with us and that possess terrifying potential.

So if the granting of dominion to human beings in Genesis 1 is not theological grist to that particular ideological mill, how, then, *should* we read it?[34] First, we should notice that there is no suggestion in this passage or anywhere else in Scripture that human beings are in any way elevated "above" nature. We are creatures, one species among many, and sharing with others a physical environment fitted for our and their survival and enjoyment. There is nothing, either, in the biblical idea of being "created in God's image and likeness" to suggest that we are "essentially spiritual." We have spirits, or souls (or call them what you will), but the idea that we *are* "spirits" with a troubled but fortunately only temporary link to bodies has no basis whatsoever in the Bible. It is another import from Greek philosophy, one that has generally been unhelpful when it has reared its head in Christian theology. The only sense in which humans are "set apart" in Genesis 1 is that God grants them a share in his "dominion" over the world. And *God's* dominion, as we have already noted (God's exercise of power), is that of loving care and concern for the well-being of his creatures. To be granted a share in it is thus, first and most importantly, to be given a huge responsibility for doing all that we can to ensure the good of both the animate and inanimate creations and, second, to be directly accountable to God himself, who does not disappear off the scene and leave us to "get on with it on his behalf" but remains fully involved and wants, through our cooperative activity, to extend his loving "rule" over all that God has made. And humans, we might say, share in that "rule" precisely *from within*, embedded within the networks of relationships that structure the world and so having their own well-being bound up inextricably with its own. As well as a divine command to exercise the sort of dominion in the world that *God himself would exercise if he were a human being*, therefore, our own self-interest ought also to counsel against behavior that plunders resources greedily and inflicts terrible and needless damage on our created home, something that all but the most obdurate or foolish are gradually coming to terms with as the evidence stacks up and the likely consequences of doing so grow both more terrifying and more immediate.

In any case, this isolated text[35] needs to be set within a wider biblical context where other perspectives, too, are offered on our place as human creatures within God's world. Richard Bauckham, in his book *The Bible and Ecology*, does a first-rate job of showing how, for example, Job 38–39 offers a sustained vision of the animate and inanimate creations from God's point of view and in which human beings are only fleetingly alluded to.[36] The point of these speeches by God to Job is to put him (and, with him, us) firmly in his place and to induce a form of "cosmic humility" about just how little we humans are able to understand and to do where the patterns and processes of created lives other than our own are concerned and compared with God himself. Today, of course, it must be admitted that natural science has improved our understanding of things that to Job would have been wholly mysterious. But that improvement is comparatively superficial when considered under the barrage of God's questioning in his chastening of Job. If anything, scientists at the top of their game today are more conscious than ever of the amount that remains still to be discovered, let alone understood, and to the likelihood that "the big surprises will be the answers to questions that we are not yet smart enough to ask."[37] And despite popular presumption, there is certainly no basis for supposing that human minds will ever be able to understand *everything*. It is perfectly possible—highly probable, in fact (Why, other than from an inflated sense of our own importance, should we reckon otherwise?)—that we shall eventually run up against limits that our minds are inherently incapable of crossing, just as our senses are calibrated to deliver data only across a certain spectrum of what is there in the world to be seen, heard, smelled, and so on. It may be galling for us to have to admit that in certain respects, dogs, cats, bats, birds, and even bees have a clear edge over us in their capacities to navigate certain tiers of material reality, but it is true nonetheless. Our bodies simply aren't designed to register things in the same way as theirs. So it's reasonable enough to suppose that our minds, too, may forever run up against limits, leaving much of creation shrouded in humbling mystery. The point is not in any way to belittle human understanding but simply to set it in an even larger and humbling perspective and, of course, to insist that, despite being made in the image and likeness of our creator, we are certainly not God and have no right to lay claim to God's prerogatives. It would undoubtedly help, though, if our efforts both to understand and to live in God's world were more directly to reflect God's own "lordship." For finally, we are called not to exercise God's power so much as to share God's delight and joy in what God has made, and the exercise of whatever human power we have must be consistent with that delight and joy.

3

"IN JESUS CHRIST, HIS ONLY SON, OUR LORD..."

IN 1993, THE musician Prince suddenly disappeared from the music charts. At least, he appeared to disappear. In reality, he was still there, still writing and performing and recording music that excited and entertained millions of fans. But Prince had unexpectedly changed his stage name, adopting an unpronounceable (and untypeable) symbol instead of a word and causing all manner of headaches for Warner Bros., with whom he was in dispute over the release of his back catalog. It wasn't long before fans, radio stations, and others coined the sobriquet "the Artist Formerly Known as Prince," which was a bit of a mouthful, to be sure, but easier to say than ☥. In the meanwhile, the wider music industry and its consumers wondered where Prince had gone and, when they discovered he was still there, how to reckon with the significance of this peculiar rebranding.[1]

Sometimes rebranding can serve a useful purpose precisely by causing us to question the familiar, making something strange and so compelling us to stop and look again and more carefully. Notice that this article of the creed reiterates the opening "I believe." It does so because the creed follows a trinitarian structure, and the threefold repetition of the verb draws attention to this. Christians don't just believe in "God." In fact, I sometimes think that it would be better if we abandoned this word altogether, finding or inventing some other identifying marker to take its place and so causing folk to stop and look again. The word *God* itself is in serious danger of being worn out by overuse and careless use and comes so loaded with misunderstanding and a variety of definitions that people suppose they know more or less what it means when, in fact, what *they* mean by it may turn out to have little at all in common with what Christians mean by it (or *should* mean by it). And no doubt something similar is true for adherents of other religions too. *God* needs some careful attention in our religiously plural and avowedly secular society if believers are going to say what they mean and be heard rather than misheard and misunderstood.

Bishop Tom Wright recalls his conversations as a chaplain with undergraduates arriving at an Oxford college who, during a statutory cup of tea and interview, would nervously admit that they didn't really "believe in God" and so probably wouldn't be putting in many appearances at the college chapel. Tom's stock response was "Oh, that's interesting; which god is it you don't believe in?" Surprised answers to this line of questioning generally trotted out some version of an all-powerful, prudish old man with a white beard and clad in a white nightgown, spying on the world from some place high up and far, far away, gathering evidence sufficient to convict large numbers of people of moral and religious crimes warranting their eventual imprisonment in a hell of his own devising (think Guantánamo Bay but with fewer creature comforts) and, grudgingly perhaps, allowing those remaining to share eternity in his exalted company instead. A classic pastiche of bits and pieces drawn from all over the place but un–thought through and singularly badly informed by exposure to Scripture's testimony to the character of God. "That's good," Tom would continue. "I don't believe in *that* god either."[2]

Unfortunately, the truth is probably that many folk who are regular members of Christian congregations also harbor some inadequate and distorted views of God—so powerful are the popular cultural memes and stereotypes and so reluctant are people in our day and age to *think* about their faith. But this won't do. Christians don't believe in "god." Or, we might better say, the God Christians do believe in has little in common with popular caricatures or vague religious impressions. In chapter 2, we saw that the Jews of the Old Testament knew their god by a particular name (Yahweh, which lies behind the old English rendition of the name Jehovah) and insisted that he was quite unlike the gods of other nations. Christians, too, know this same God by a particular name—in fact, because they meet and know this God in three different ways at once, it is a composite name: Father, Son, and Holy Spirit. And what is known of this God is strikingly different from popular accounts of the "god" in whom people sometimes insist that they don't, can't, and won't believe. That's why, when we embarked on our consideration of the creed in chapter 2, I decided for the time being to pass over the word *God* ("I believe in God . . .") largely without comment. That might seem odd to many readers given the centrality and importance of the word for Christian faith, liturgy, and theology. I did it, though, precisely *because* it is so central and so important, and its meanings and associations, therefore, are important to get right rather than wrong—because there is a proper sense in which we are only able to fill this word with its proper Christian content once we begin to unpack what we believe about Jesus, in whom, Christians believe, God has shown himself most fully and finally. Prior to and apart from that, we are working, at best, with something less than what God has given us to work with in our knowing and speaking of God and, at worst, with vague, shadowy, and often quite misleading (and un-Christian) notions.

I suppose reasonable questions for a thinking Christian to ask at this point are, Well, what about those people in Old Testament times? Did they or didn't they *know* God or have a clear idea of who God was and what God was like? Those are good questions and put their finger on something very important—because it's vital to affirm that Christians do indeed know and worship the *same* God as was known and worshipped by ancient Israel. The God of the New Testament is not a new variety of God, nor is this God the *real* or *true* God who, having left things until now inexplicably in the hands of an apprentice or warm-up act (of dubious character and credentials), finally steps up to center stage and into the spotlight to take control and please the crowd. That was the sort of view associated with Marcion in the early church, and although it was officially rejected, it raises its head whenever and wherever, for instance, people contrast in an unthinking manner an Old Testament "God of holiness, wrath and law" with a New Testament "God of love." Both inevitably turn out to be caricatures, and neither has anything much to do with God. Where God is concerned, the wider canon of Scripture tells us, holiness and love are mutually defining rather than mutually exclusive qualities, and any attempt to separate them, therefore, necessarily results in a dangerous corruption and misunderstanding of both. God's love is, as the Scots Congregational theologian P. T. Forsyth used constantly to remind his readers, precisely "holy love"[3]—the love of the God who is above all things holy, a holiness that is itself love's own burning opposition to evil and all that threatens to damage or distort what God has, in God's love, created. Furthermore, of course, Jesus was a devout Jew who worshipped the God of his Jewish forebears, treated the Hebrew scriptures as the authoritative Word of God, and made sense of his own mission and ministry in terms of Yahweh's purposes and promises.

So yes, the people of the Old Testament certainly *did* know God, and the God they knew (and knew *about*) was the same God as the one we encounter in the pages of the New Testament.[4] And what they knew was important and remains important for Christians precisely *because* it was important for Jesus and because most of it is taken for granted in the New Testament as theological "stuff" we need to have to hand if we're going to make any sense of Jesus at all and know how to respond to him. (If the New Testament has much less to say about God's *holiness*, for instance, that's not because holiness is now passé or theologically embarrassing but precisely because it is so basic, so important, so unquestionable as an attribute of God that no one felt any need to say anything further in order to reinforce it. If there are "Old Testament" things that have changed, the New Testament doesn't keep quiet about them—it tells us so.) For this reason, some theologians prefer to speak of the *First* Testament rather than the Old Testament, avoiding any suggestion that this larger part of the Christian Bible is somehow past its use-by date, yesterday's news, rather than an essential and abiding part of the apostles' own news about Jesus.[5] While, though, Jesus worshipped the same God as Abraham, Moses, and the prophets had, his coming was certainly not just the same old, same old. On the contrary, in Jesus's appearance in Israel's midst, God was doing a new thing, and it was a new thing bound either to occasion religious and theological scandal or, more constructively, to provoke a revolution or paradigm shift in Israel's knowing and believing.

An illustration may help us grasp the tension of continuity and discontinuity involved here. On a visit to the theater, we are all familiar with the way in which, in any drama, things known about a key character in acts 1 and 2 can be transfigured by things that only come to light in act 3. The change in our perception may be and often is radical, and once we have experienced it, we can never go back and see acts 1 and 2 in the same way again. The same is true with the early and later chapters of a novel or of episodes in a Netflix "box set." But what we knew of the protagonist in our first encounter with the drama was certainly not "nothing," nor was the larger part of it false (though what we did not yet know may, in retrospect, have been misleading). It was simply what the playwright intended us to know at that stage and for the sake of his or her purposes in constructing and unfolding the plot and characterizations meaningfully for our enjoyment. And, of course, its "truth" and its vital importance are obvious if we ask what sense we could have made of things had we stumbled into the theater at the beginning of act 3, after the drinks interval, with no prior knowledge of the play whatsoever. We should almost certainly become one of those annoying people who whisper their questions (loudly) to the person sitting next to them through the remainder of the performance. So Christian faith in the Father, Son, and Holy Spirit is in an important sense *faith in the same God* known to Israel, and it can only be uninformed and malformed if we do not know our Old Testament well, because the New Testament writers often remain silent whenever they can simply take the Old Testament plot and characterizations for granted. And yet what is known of this God and his purposes is now (in the light of later events) so much more and in certain respects radically new and different. It transforms our ways of relating to God, and in some ways, it is bound to create a crunch of gears or a problem for anyone working with an Old Testament understanding alone.

Jesus Christ . . .

THE POSITIVE RELATIONSHIP between the Old and New Testaments in terms of the God about whom they speak is already clearly flagged for us in the words *Jesus Christ* alone. The name Jesus is a Greek version of the Hebrew/Aramaic name Yeshua, or Joshua, and like many Hebrew names, it is a contracted statement about God. It means something like "Yahweh saves" or "salvation of Yahweh." So when the angel instructs Mary about how to name her son, he isn't just expressing a personal preference; the name comes already theologically highly charged. In most English-speaking contexts today, hardly anyone would choose to call their son Jesus, presumably nervous of such designation being deemed inappropriate, if not sacrilegious, in a "secular" culture still so clearly haunted by the associations of its long-standing Christian heritage (although, oddly, the popularity of "Joshua" remains entirely unperturbed by such considerations). Theologically charged or not (and we should remember that *lots* of biblical names are theologically charged), Jesus/Yeshua/Joshua was a very common name for Jewish boys in the first century CE, not yet having been rendered awkward by the fact of its bestowal upon the Word made flesh. That's no doubt why, in due course (and in a society that functioned without surnames), Jesus came to be known commonly as Jesus of/from Nazareth—pinpointing his hometown in order to clarify *which* Jesus was being spoken about among all those other Jesuses in the telephone directory.

The name Christ, too, is packed full of theology. In fact, it's not really a name at all; it's a title, one to which there is a very full role description attached. So we should really say not "Jesus Christ" but "Jesus *the* Christ," the one who, within the purposes and promises of the God of Israel, has a very specific role to fulfill. The word *Christ* comes from the Greek *Christos*, which is itself the translation of the Hebrew *Mashiach*.⁶ *Mashiach* (the transliteration of which into Greek as *Messias* lies behind our English "Messiah") meant "the anointed one" and referred generally to the anointing with oil of special figures (most notably kings and priests) in the life of the nation of Israel. The oil was symbolic of God's Spirit, who was held to empower and enable these figures for their ministry. So a *mashiach* was someone special whom God had set apart to perform a special role in Israel's life and in the accomplishment of God's purposes. And *the Mashiach* (the Messiah) was a figure in Israel's religious hopes and expectations who, it was widely believed, would be raised up and sent by God to restore the nation's fortunes, fulfilling the roles of a king and priest and so setting Israel's life on a firm footing in both political and religious terms—as the people called and set apart by God.

When we read about Jesus in the Gospels, he often seems reluctant to apply the term *Christ* to himself and is cautious about others speaking of him using that term. It is unlikely that this was the result of undue modesty. Much more likely is that Jesus was only too aware of the limitations and problematic features of what messianic expectations had become and of the gap between such expectations and the ways in which he would actually fulfill them in due course. There was no point in stirring up misunderstanding and exciting ill-adjusted hopes. It was better for people to discover gradually, by what he did and said and suffered, that God had sent a rather different sort of messiah than they had been expecting and hoping for, one who would accomplish something much more profound and world changing than their limited hopes had anticipated. His power would be exercised through suffering, and his victory through death.

In calling Jesus "the Christ," though, Christians are insisting that Jesus is nonetheless the true Messiah of Israel; "the one who is to come" has indeed here come and, in coming, has fulfilled the meaning of Israel's institutions of monarchy and priesthood and the promises embodied in and associated with them.[7] Again, even though these expectations are, in their fulfillment in Jesus, blown wide open and shown to have fallen far short of the full reality of what God had always intended, they are nonetheless the background to and preparation for his coming, and we cannot begin to understand the significance of his coming properly unless we attend to them. That's why the Old Testament remains a vital part of the church's sacred text in which the story of God's dealings with Israel and, through Israel, the world is told. Acts 1 and 2, we might say, are just as important as act 3, which *makes absolutely no sense* without them. That's why the proclamation "This is the Word of the Lord" is an appropriate thing to say after the Old Testament as well as the New Testament reading in church on a Sunday morning. It is the whole book, the whole story told here, which the church acknowledges as the God-breathed testimony to God's character, purposes, and promises. Of course, we have to read particular parts of it in relation to the whole book. But *all of it* matters and has its proper part to play in making God known.

Jesus is Israel's Messiah. That claim, with all its entailments and whatever difficulties it throws up, is fundamental to the church's faith. It's what it means to be *Christ*ian at all. And that has implications beyond our attitude toward the Jewish scriptures. As one theologian notes, it involves us in acknowledging also "the special place of the Jews in God's plan of salvation, recognizing and accepting them as the kinsfolk of the one Jew, the universal Saviour, in whom and for whose sake they were and, in spite of unbelief, disobedience, and rejection, still are—now in mysterious partnership with the church—God's special people."[8] The Messiah looked for and longed for by Israel was to be a man who, like his ancestor David, would be raised up and anointed by God, a key agent in the fulfillment of God's purposes and promises for the people. Jesus, in his fulfillment of this messianic hope, transformed it beyond recognition, but the hope's shortfall, when compared to reality, had to do not only with what the actual *Mashiach* did and did not *do*. There was something else: something that even in Israel's wildest dreams she had never imagined possible and that she would have the hardest time getting her head around and coming to terms with.

God's Only Son . . .

"WHEN THE FULLNESS of time had come," Paul writes to the church in Galatia, "God sent his Son, born of a woman, born under law, in order to redeem those who were under the law, so that we might receive adoption as children."[9] He's talking about Jesus, of course, but setting Jesus's life and ministry now in a rather different perspective. What from one angle can and should be understood as the fulfillment of a trajectory within history—the raising up of a man who would fulfill the role of Israel's anointed King, albeit in a way no one quite expected—from another angle must now be recognized as God's sending of *his own Son* into the world, becoming a man in order to redeem his own human creatures. There was, we might say, a movement from above and one from below that met in the person of Jesus, but both were movements originating in God's own life as God on the one hand and human on the other. Because God had not simply raised up a human king for Israel; he *had himself become human* in order to fulfill that role—God and humanity united in a single human life.

The phrase *son of God* was, to be sure, used from time to time in the Old Testament of other figures, including the King, the promised Messiah (who would also be the "son of David"), and Israel herself as God's chosen and anointed people.[10] So this biblical phrase already had political and religious form. In the New Testament, though, Jesus is singled out as *the* Son of God (deserving of a capital *S*) or even, in John's further underlining of the point, God's "only begotten" Son,[11] which is what lies behind the Apostles' Creed's own "God's only Son" here. This New Testament insistence was clearly grounded in Jesus's own awareness of having a relationship with God as his Father not just of an unparalleled intimacy or special symbolic significance but in some way unique to himself, and while it certainly evoked a host of Old Testament political and religious resonances, the realization to which the first Christians gradually came was that this close relationship between Jesus the Son and his Father was not something to be made sense of in human and historical terms only. Jesus wasn't just a man "raised up" by God to fulfill Israel's own long history of expectation and promise (though he was certainly that) but someone whose relationship to God as "son" was of another order altogether, one that could be made sense of only by saying that Jesus the Son had "come from" and been "sent by" the Father into the world, earthing within the flesh and blood of our humanity and our history a filial relationship that *already existed in God*. It's quite clear that this is what Paul understands by the term—so that to call Jesus the "Son" or "Son of God" is for him to identify Jesus without further ado as God, whether eternally (in what is sometimes clumsily called the Son's "preexistence") or present among us in human form. So, for example, Paul tells us that it is God's "beloved Son" who is "the image of the invisible God" in whom and through whom *all things were created*.[12] John, too, in the prologue to his Gospel, makes the same link explicit: the one who was the Word of God, active in creation, is also the Son, who has become a human creature and revealed God's glory in the flesh, "the glory as of a father's only son," and in doing so, John observes, "God the only Son, who is close to the Father's heart," has made the Father known.[13] We are dealing with the same "person," that is to say, whether in the primordial darkness with which Genesis 1 opens, or teaching and healing and antagonizing the religious authorities in Jerusalem, or suffering and dying on the cross of Golgotha, or at the Father's right hand receiving and mediating our worship and our prayers; and his "personhood" is filial from first to last because, it seems, there is something analogous to the relationship between a father and a son in God's own way of being God. That's why the Christian naming of God as Father is something peculiar and special. God has shown us that God is eternally the Father by coming to us humanly in the person of his eternal Son.

Discussion of this momentous claim has always lain at the heart of Christian theology, and the attempt to pin it down and unpack it was one that dominated the first few centuries of theological debate—so great were the consequences of taking it seriously or of failing to do so. The terms in which this debate was mostly conducted were, as we noticed in chapter 2, often ones borrowed from the intellectual tool kit of the philosophers, insisting, for instance, as the Nicene Creed does, that to call Jesus the "Son of God" is to acknowledge that he is of one nature (or consubstantial) with the Father.[14] To share God's "nature" in this sense means to be God himself. But the language of natures and substances is, for most of us, more redolent of biology and chemistry lessons than talking about or to God and isn't language that Jesus himself or the apostles would have been at home with either. Despite the absence of this philosophical vocabulary from its pages, though, the New Testament isn't woolly minded or vague about the issue, deploying its own precision tools very effectively to hit the relevant theological nail on the head. Biblical scholar Richard Bauckham has made this point quite emphatically in some of his recent work.[15] The New Testament authors may not know or have much to say about "natures," he points out, but as good Jews in the so-called Second Temple period, they will know perfectly well that there are things about the God of Israel that are unique and that to breach this uniqueness—to think or speak or behave as though these things were true of anyone else—is not merely to make a misleading category error but utterly inappropriate in religious terms too.[16] At the heart of this unique "identity" of God, as Bauckham refers to it, are two features in particular:[17] God alone is the creator of all things (there is a sharp distinction that must not be blurred between God and all other reality), and God alone, therefore, exercises a unique sovereign rule over all things. On the basis of these two aspects of the divine identity, furthermore, God alone is deserving of creation's worship, an attitude the intentional misdirection of which is both unthinkable and religiously disastrous when it occurs. For the Judaism of Jesus's day, Bauckham writes, "God must be worshipped; no other being may be worshipped."[18] What is immediately obvious in the core apostolic testimony to Jesus, though, Bauckham points out, is its repeated unashamed willingness, apparently, to flirt with danger on all three counts: speaking quite deliberately and explicitly of Jesus as the creator of all things,[19] as sharing in God's unique sovereign rule over all things by sitting down on God's heavenly throne,[20] and as the fitting object, together with his Father, of creaturely worship.[21] What's going on here, though, is not flirtation with sacrilege but the deliberate (and, to be sure, scandalous and outrageous, if untrue) inclusion of Jesus within the unique identity of God himself, insisting, in other words, that Jesus himself is part of the answer we must give to the question "Who is God?" and that in him it is God (the one who creates, rules, and commands our worship and devotion) who acts and suffers. And in turn, that changes our understanding of who God is and what, in Christian terms, the word *God* itself means.

Our Lord . . .

LORD IS YET another term laden with significance in its New Testament application to Jesus. In everyday Greek, the word *kyrios* could be a simple term of polite respect, not far removed, for instance, from someone saying "Excuse me, sir" in English. Some of the uses in the Gospels reflect this perfectly ordinary usage. In John 20, for instance, when Mary Magdalene goes to the tomb and finds it empty, she tells the angels in great distress, "They have taken away my *Kyrion*!" Moments later, when Jesus (whom Mary mistakes for the gardener) asks her who she is looking for, she replies, "Sir [*Kyrie*], if you have carried him away, tell me where you have laid him." She's not expecting to see Jesus, so she can't and doesn't see him. And while she uses the same word here twice in quick succession, she uses it in two quite distinct senses. John, of course, is playing word games with his readers, indulging in a nice bit of linguistic as well as dramatic irony—because despite Mary's own suppositions and intentions, the one she addresses politely as *kyrie* (sir) *is* in fact her "Lord," as rapidly becomes clear. So it's a more than felicitous way to speak to this shadowy figure lurking in the dawn light, and for the knowing reader, it drips with secret meaning.

So what does *Lord* mean in this more highly charged sense? We've noted before that the Old Testament treats God's proper name, Yahweh, with a huge amount of respect, and in the Judaism that provides the backdrop to the New Testament, that name was widely held to be far too holy for day-to-day use. In synagogue worship, the practice of avoiding using it altogether grew, substituting for it when reading aloud another Hebrew word, *Adonai* (Lord). In due course, editions of the Old Testament texts appeared in which the name YHWH was ornamented with some vowels in order to aid those reading in public worship, reminding them that they should say "Adonai" instead of "Yahweh." English versions, therefore, typically translate this complicated Hebrew word as "the Lord," marking it out as a special use of the term. The Greek translation of the Old Testament, widely used and known in New Testament times, translated "Adonai" as Kyrios. So this otherwise mundane Greek word *kyrios* found itself conscripted and used in Jewish religious contexts to mean the same thing as "Yahweh" or "Adonai"—that is, it served as the name for Israel's God just as "the Lord" does in our English translations. When, therefore, Paul tells us, in the familiar passage in Philippians 2, that God highly exalted Jesus "and gave him the name that is above every name" and that at that name every knee in heaven and on earth and under the earth should bend, we should almost certainly understand this "name" to be this same sacred, unutterable name[22]—God's own name, Yahweh. Only God's name is above *every* other in this way, and only at God's name must *all things* (all creatures) bow their knees.[23] For Paul to insist this is simply another way, therefore, of including Jesus within God's own identity, "identifying" him as God.[24] It is generally supposed, though, that in Philippians 2:6–11, Paul is quoting a fragment of a song or hymn with which he expected his readers already to be familiar, which would mean that this same idea (Jesus sharing in God's holy name) would have enjoyed much wider circulation than its appearance in the New Testament suggests. And that fits, of course, with the knowing, deliberate, and widespread use of the title "Lord," or "Kyrios," or "Adonai"—the name Jews were allowed to use to identify Israel's God, whether speaking about or to God, without actually uttering the sacred name itself. So one of the earliest Christian creedal snippets or professions of faith—"Jesus is Lord!"[25]—was not merely a way of indicating that Jesus is special or extremely important. It was another concise and precise way of saying that the name, majesty, and authority of Adonai himself belong properly to Jesus, that he is none other than Israel's God, now present personally and humanly among us.

Everything in Christianity hinges on the integrity of this claim. If it is true, then we can trust that in knowing Jesus, we truly know God. Theologian Thomas F. Torrance recounts an experience when he was a chaplain on the battlefields of World War II: a young soldier, fatally injured, in terrible pain, and with less than an hour to live, clutched his arm and asked in an anguished whisper, "Is God really like Jesus?"[26] That's the key question for many people when push comes to shove, a question that, Torrance observes, gnaws "at the back of people's minds but which they suppress and which come[s] to the surface only in moments of sharp crisis and hurt."[27] "Fearful anxiety arises in the human heart," he continues, "when people cannot connect Jesus up in their faith or understanding with the ultimate Being of God, for then the ultimate Being of God can be to them only a dark, inscrutable, arbitrary Deity whom they inevitably think of with terror, for their guilty conscience makes them paint harsh angry streaks upon his face. It is quite different when the face of Jesus is identical with the face of God."[28] Can we trust that God is really like Jesus? It's a question in which the gospel itself, the "good news" about God and God's purposes and promises for us, is at stake. If Jesus is none other than "God with us"—God among us in human form, the human Son of God who faithfully reveals to us the character of a heavenly Father—then the answer is, of course, that we can and should. We can know that the one in whose hands the provenance and course and destiny of the world and its history and of our own lives are held is here shown to us in flesh-and-blood form—good, loving, merciful, and faithful; healing diseased bodies and tormented spirits; and offering forgiveness of sins. There are and can be no nasty surprises where God is concerned, no secret God hidden behind the back of Jesus, because Jesus himself *is* God, and in dealing with him, we are dealing with God himself. We see God's human face. And, of course, if Jesus is God, then our understanding of the word *God* must finally accommodate and include all that we know of Jesus. The sort of God we believe in is not one who remains aloof and remote in the comfort and safety of "heaven," sending other, lesser beings to get their hands dirty in dealing with the world. On the contrary, God is committed to the hilt to the well-being of his world and comes in person to bear the cost of its redemption and renewal.

This, then, is what, when we utter these few words in the creed ("Jesus Christ, God's only Son, our Lord"), we are affirming. That in the man Jesus from Nazareth, not only have all God's promises to Israel (and through Israel to humankind as a whole) found their fulfillment in the "Christ," the one specially anointed by God's Holy Spirit, but (far beyond Israel's and our wildest imaginings) God has done something far more drastic and wonderful still. And to grasp what is so wonderful about it lies simply in recognizing just *who* the Christ himself is. God's ancient purpose and plan for *creation as a whole*, hidden since the foundation of the world, has now finally come to fruition as God himself, in the person of the Son, has come down from heaven to experience being human for himself, to share our humanity and make it his own, to share our world by indwelling it together with us and as one of us, and in sharing it all to transform it, redeem it, and draw it into the web of relationships that is God's own life. And all this God has done not for God's sake but, as Paul says, "that we might receive adoption as children. And because [we] are children, God has sent the Spirit of his Son into our hearts, crying, 'Abba! Father!'"[29] Here, in Jesus, God and our humanity are reconciled to each other, united to each other in a human life lived in the power of God's Spirit by the one who is eternally and properly God's Son. And so those whose humanity God has made his own are set up now to experience a potentially vertiginous change of standpoint of their own, no longer beholden to sin as its slaves but adopted as God's own sons and daughters and set free to know and to love God as their own Father. What that means, as Paul's language reveals, is that we too are now drawn in, by virtue of Christ's solidarity with us, to share in the very love with which, in the Spirit, the Son eternally loves the Father and in that love that the Father, in the same Spirit, pours out reciprocally upon the Son. Salvation, therefore, is not merely about being sanitized so that we no longer create a foul stench in God's nostrils or forgiven and handed a "clean sheet" (something that experience suggests is simply crying out to be blotted all over again) but about being *made new* and drawn into the inner sanctum of God's own eternal life of love and glory and joy, which is where we were always intended to dwell. That's the thing we could never have imagined for ourselves, the amazing realization that follows on from the confession of Jesus as Lord, Adonai, the Son who is himself part of the divine identity, part of who God eternally is.

The creed, though, like Mary Magdalene, the apostle Thomas, and others, says not "*the* Lord" but "*my*" or "*our* Lord."[30] This reminds us again that we are dealing here with not a merely academic point of theological concern but a theological point that demands a personal and existential response and expression of commitment. By becoming one of us, God's own Son has made us his own and laid claim to us. To use Paul's pecuniary image, he has "bought [us] with a price," and we are owned by him.[31] Acknowledging this, and meaning it when we do so, means that we now in our turn can only hand over the "lordship" of our lives to him rather than continuing to claim it for ourselves or lease it out to sin. In doing so, though, we recall that the one who is our Lord is also our friend and our brother and has given everything for us. To say "our Lord" or "my Lord," therefore, is not only an act of willing submission but one of devotion and love too. As we shall continue to see, the things we say we "believe" when we join in reciting the creed together mostly have some fairly immediate knock-on implications for our wider patterns of living, and if those are things we're not entirely happy to commit to, then we might be better to keep quiet, lest God hear us and take us at our word.

4

"CONCEIVED BY THE HOLY SPIRIT, BORN OF THE VIRGIN MARY..."

MY GUESS IS that if there's any part of the creed that has people secretly crossing their fingers behind their backs as they recite it, it's this part. Its semisexual overtones already make it ripe as a target for mockery, innuendo, and ribald jesting. If, though, it has Christians velcroing rather than nailing their colors to the mast, I suspect there are two different sorts of problems needing to be addressed. First, there are questions of one sort or another about credulity (Could such a thing really have happened, and can we really take the claim seriously these days?), and second, there are questions about its *meaning*. After all, if we can't see something as significant, as full of meaning, then we are unlikely to invest much energy in grappling with questions about its historicity. So the two are linked together.

Those who drafted the creed factored it in prominently as something to be insisted upon rather than indifferent about, suggesting that the circumstances of Jesus's birth were for them part and parcel of grasping the full force of what God had done in taking flesh and coming among us as one of us in order to effect our salvation. Indeed, they chose to focus here—rather than, for instance, on Jesus's baptism—in narrating the series of redemptive events in Christ's life. So we can't trip lightly over it and move quickly on.

Scriptural Roots for the Doctrine

THE BASIS FOR this creedal claim, of course, lies in two particular passages in the New Testament section of our Bible. Those passages are Matthew 1:18–25 and Luke 1:26–38, each of which deals quite explicitly with the pregnancy of Mary and insists that it did *not* arise in the ordinary manner. Mary, Luke tells us, was still a virgin at the time of conception, which was due to the "overshadowing" of her womb by the Holy Spirit.[1] Matthew's formulation tells us less, but it indicates the same thing (i.e., Mary's virginity) by implication at least.[2] It may help at this point if we try to purge our mind's eye of the images of a thousand Christmas cards and the sentimentality and tinsel associated with the story and clarify what is at stake in the claim. A young Palestinian girl in the northern town of Galilee is, we are told, already betrothed to be married to a local tradesman, Joseph, but before they are married, and while she is still a virgin, she is discovered to be pregnant. Joseph presumes the obvious and considers a quiet termination of the agreement he has reached with her family, not wanting to "expose her to public disgrace."[3] When asked about the situation, Mary insists that she has had a vision or visitation some months previously where an angel told her that she would conceive and that this would be the result of the work of God's Spirit. Before Joseph can terminate the wedding contract, he too has an angelic encounter in a dream in which the peculiar circumstances of Mary's pregnancy are confirmed to his satisfaction. So he, at least, believes Mary, and until the baby duly arrives, together they ride the storm of sneering, stigma, and shame that inevitably arises from the neighbors who are sure of one thing: whoever the father *is*, it's not Joseph.

That's the testimony of the two Gospel passages. It seems most likely that their source lies in the memory and testimony of Mary herself, who, after the events surrounding Jesus's birth, as Luke tells us, stored up what had happened and pondered it all in her heart. Again, we should probably strip our imagining of the birth itself of some of the familiar Christmas card imagery, with its suggestion of a Hollywood-style son et lumière extravaganza that no one in the vicinity of Bethlehem could possibly miss. It almost certainly happened much more quietly, unnoticed except by those whose noticing of it was important to God. And yet even in its marginal occurrence (in a shed behind a motel), it was a happening in which a whole series of events in Mary's life came to a head, and she was indeed bound to ponder its significance. Such pondering, perhaps, is usual for young women whose first pregnancy comes to term and who suddenly find themselves for the very first time with the miracle of a fragile, newly born human life held vulnerably in their arms, utterly dependent on a mother's care, and already crying for the milk which will keep them alive. It's a ponderous responsibility and a watershed in any parent's life. And far from being any less so, it was almost certainly more so for Mary, whose level of responsibility was, if the angel was to be believed, of another magnitude altogether. Pondering there was bound to be.

That Mary pondered it all doesn't mean, of course, that she grasped its significance any more than any mother does where the birth of a child and its implications are concerned. But she and Joseph would certainly have had plenty to wonder about together over the coming years as they watched Jesus grow to manhood and maturity, and by the time Mary came to tell her story, a lot more water still had passed under the bridge, and no doubt some of it was finally beginning to make better sense. The fact that only two of our four gospels contain any account of this story is sometimes cited as a reason for doubting its authenticity. But Matthew and Luke themselves clearly know slightly different versions of the tradition, and their distinct versions of things corroborate rather than contradict each other, indicating that this was a story circulating in more than one form and probably enjoying quite widespread rather than limited familiarity within the early church. Furthermore, while neither John nor Mark tells the story, their gospels contain hints of their awareness of it and so testify again to its wider currency in the apostolic church.

So, for instance, during Jesus's Galilean ministry, the most reliable translation of Mark 6:3 has members of the synagogue in Nazareth asking one another, "Is not this the carpenter, the son of Mary and brother of James and Joses and Judas and Simon, and are not his sisters here with us?" The whole family is evidently known to those concerned, and each member is mentioned—with the exception of Joseph. That Jesus here is "the carpenter" rather than "the carpenter's son" indicates, perhaps, that Joseph (who was quite probably significantly older than Mary) is by now already dead and Jesus has inherited the family business. But the exclusion of all reference to Joseph (let alone to him as Jesus's father) seems likely to be deliberate rather than inadvertent one way or another and so to have an edge or an unspoken point to make—what historians refer to as a "pregnant silence" (an unfortunate metaphor, we might think, in this circumstance!). In his account of some similar mutterings, John, meanwhile, records the crowd's making mention of Joseph, a mention that, in the context of John's telling of the story, comes freighted with dramatic irony. Jesus speaks of himself as "the Bread of Life who has come down from heaven," to which the bystanders respond, "Is not this Jesus, the son of Joseph, whose father and mother we know?"[4] Given what Jesus has just been saying and what he goes on to say, the question cries out for the answer "No!" You do not know my Father, Jesus insists. Your actions and words and lack of faith make it clear that you don't know my Father at all. Of course, he has another Father in mind than Joseph, but the play on words allows him to make a powerful theological point and lifts the lid again, indirectly, on the whole question of who Jesus's father really is and how Joseph's place in Jesus's life should be classified. He's not the Father whom Jesus himself has come from, by whose direction alone others may come to Jesus, and about whom Jesus is constantly telling them.[5] Theology here trumps biology, but it does so in a way that nonetheless invites rather than sidelines altogether the question of whether a paternity suit might be warranted.

In John 8:39–47, too, questions of paternity (this time that of the crowd as well as Jesus) are at issue, and again, John records some words from the crowd that positively drip with irony. The whole thing kicks off with another bit of playful riffing on the word *father*. "You should do what you have heard from the Father," Jesus tells them. "*Abraham* is our father" (emphasis added), they respond with more than a hint of self-importance and a dash of religious self-righteousness to boot. You may be Abraham's descendants, says Jesus, but you're not really his *children*;

to begin with, there's no family likeness. In fact, he continues, now that I look more carefully, I *can* actually see a family likeness—but it's not Abraham's DNA that it points to at all. I suspect your real "father" is someone quite different, someone altogether less savory, someone you might want to keep rather quiet about in fact. . . . Unsurprisingly, this is sufficient to rankle the crowd, and as well as denying that they are the spawn of Satan (which, as v. 44 confirms, is the gist of Jesus's insulting suggestion), they add some abusive spin to their return of serve. "*We* are not illegitimate children," they say.[6] "We have one father, God himself." In other words, we have just the one father, and what's more, we *know* who *our* father is, Jesus. How about you? It's not we who should be worried about the integrity of our lineage or owning up to who our real father is.[7] And those who live in glass houses. . . . By the way, how's your mother doing these days?

We know that in due course, there were indeed attempts to turn the circumstances of Jesus's birth into a scandal, rumors growing up quickly in Jewish circles that he was illegitimate—a *mamzer*, as the Palestinian slang had it—and possibly even the product of Mary's passionate clinch with a Roman soldier.[8] Variations on the theme like this one were no doubt designed to discredit Jesus to the maximal degree—not just a bastard but the bastard of a foreigner, perhaps, worse yet, of an occupying stormtrooper. Hardly fit, one way or another, for decent Jewish society, let alone to be taken seriously as a claimant to the role of the Messiah. John seems already to be aware of some rumblings along just such lines and of the factual background to them—Joseph was by now widely known to have been not Jesus's biological parent at all but only his legal guardian.

Finally, there is the witness of a tantalizing allusion made by John in the so-called prologue to his Gospel. The verses refer to those who believed in the incarnate Word, to whom "he gave power to become children of God, who were born, not of blood or of the will of the flesh or of the will of man, but of God."[9] Translated in this way, the reference seems fairly clearly to be to that second "birth" that, Jesus will tell Nicodemus, is "from above," reinforcing the point that becoming a child of God is not the result of any natural, let alone biological, process.[10] And yet the ostentatiously drawn-out description that John provides resonates suggestively with the idea of that *other* birth which was "from above" and without the involvement of blood, or the flesh, or the will of a man[11]—that is, Jesus's own. That the resonances were audible to some readers in the early church at least is clear from the existence of a fairly well-attested variant reading of this verse in the Greek text, substituting a third-person singular pronoun for the third-person plural and so making Jesus rather than regenerate believers the subject of the second part of the sentence as well as the first: "He gave power to become the children of God, *who was* born not of blood or of the will of the flesh or of the will of man, but of God" (emphasis added). It is possible that this might even be the original version of the text, in which case it constitutes an explicit reference by John to the tradition concerning the virginal conception. But even if it is a secondary misrendering, it points to the striking parallelism between John's description here and the circumstances of the virginal conception, a parallelism more likely to be deliberate than accidental, and so again suggests the evangelist's awareness of that tradition and its central importance in early Christian circles.

One final bit of New Testament evidence comes from Paul, whose writings are generally acknowledged to be among the earliest written sources contained in the New Testament. Again, it is a matter of vocabulary: in Romans 1:3, Galatians 4:4, and Philippians 2:7, Paul refers explicitly to Jesus's lineage and birth. In each case, Paul uses the same Greek verb, *ginesthai*. Oddly, in each case, another similar Greek verb (*gennasthai*) would be the obvious choice for anyone reasonably fluent in Greek. So is Paul simply bad at languages and careless in his choice of words, choosing wrongly on all three occasions? It's possible, and Paul's Greek is certainly not the equivalent of Shakespeare's English. But here's the interesting thing: *gennasthai* (the word Paul avoids using, despite the fact that it is the most natural one to use and would score a higher grade on any translation exercise) has a distinct whiff of testosterone about it, its connotations tending to foreground masculine virility as the primary consideration in those familiar processes involved in a bit of successful "begetting." *Ginesthai*, though, is more politically correct and lacks these locker-room overtones. So rather than revealing his linguistic limitations, perhaps Paul is deliberately, and somewhat awkwardly, avoiding the more obvious expression here and deliberately using the "wrong" word instead—a word that does the job but, in doing so, avoids the unhelpful implication (unhelpful because in this case and this case alone it was untrue) that there was a man involved at some point. It is certainly very important to Paul that Jesus was indeed *born* (i.e., did not come down on the clouds or appear in a puff of divine smoke) and his humanity genuine, therefore, rather than a chimera; but that his birth was "of a *woman*" and "under the law" suffices for him to secure the fact of Jesus's solidarity with us.[12] None of this demonstrates for sure that Paul *was* aware, at this very early stage in the church's life, of traditions about Jesus's birth and parentage, but such awareness would account very well for what is otherwise an odd and seemingly inept choice of words on three separate occasions and may be the most satisfactory explanation.

It should be said at once, of course, that none of this demonstrates or "proves" that the virginal conception happened. It's difficult to know precisely what might be held to have constituted such "proof" in any case at that time, let alone now. But what we have seen does indicate that questions and claims regarding Jesus's parentage were almost certainly familiar to the mainstream of the New Testament writers and so likely to have been circulating in the wider church, whose beliefs the New Testament reflects as well as shapes. We are not dealing simply with a maverick idea limited to a couple of isolated passages and, should we prefer, ripe for pushing to the theological sidelines.

While we are still dealing with passages of Scripture, though, we should perhaps reckon with a couple of textual "problems" sometimes cited as casting doubt already on the historical veracity of the story of the virginal conception. First, there are the genealogies of Matthew 1 and Luke 3, both clearly concerned to establish Jesus's importance by tracing his lineage back to theologically significant ancestors. Matthew traces the line back only as far as Abraham (which is already quite a long way), while Luke presses on further all the way to Adam. In doing so, of course, both pass most significantly of all through the figure of King David, thereby establishing that Jesus was not just of royal descent but "of David's line," this requirement, as we have already seen, being built into the "person specification" drawn up for the position of Messiah. To do this, though, both Matthew and Luke trace Jesus's family tree back through the male line—which is to say, precisely through Joseph. The perceived problem is posed in the form of a Catch-22: either Joseph *was* Jesus's actual biological father, and hence the story of the virginal conception is inauthentic, or he wasn't, in which case Jesus wasn't truly a "son of David" at all, in which case the integrity (and theological point) of the genealogies is compromised. But Joseph was certainly Jesus's legal father, and in reality, this was a sufficient bond between them to count as far as the religious force of the genealogy is concerned.[13] Furthermore, of course, Joseph performed the *role* of Jesus's father in day-to-day family relationships, which is a sufficient explanation for Luke being able to refer to him as such without any sense of concern that, in doing so, he is contradicting or undermining the drama and theological force of his first two chapters.[14] Similarly, it is interesting to note that Matthew 13:55 affords a variant of Mark 6:3, alluding indirectly now to Joseph as Jesus's father ("Is not this the carpenter's *son*?" [emphasis added]). Again, having told the story of Jesus's birth in Matthew 1, it is highly unlikely that the evangelist feels bound or intends now to contradict it; the reference is better understood here, too, as a perfectly normal one to Joseph's "paternal" role in the family or, more likely still, to his legal status as Jesus's father, thereby underscoring that messianic pedigree to which Matthew, as the "Jewish" gospel par excellence, is even more keen to draw attention than other New Testament texts, with the possible exception of the Epistle to the Hebrews.[15]

The other "problematic" text sometimes cited is originally from the Old Testament, though it is enthusiastically cited in the New. In older English translations, Isaiah 7:14 reads, "The Lord himself shall give you a sign; Behold, a virgin shall conceive, and bear a son, and shall call his name Immanuel" (KJV). Aptly, it is precisely Matthew who picks up on this bit of prophecy and traces a link to the remarkable circumstances surrounding Jesus's birth, finding in these the fulfillment of the divine promise.[16] "Aha!" some have suggested. "*Here* we have the most likely source of the whole thing!" This is an ancient prophecy which enthusiastic Christians have seized upon, *inventing* the tradition of Jesus's miraculous birth in order to bolster their conviction that he was indeed the fulfillment of the Old Testament expectation, the son of David, the Messiah, and Immanuel. But it doesn't work. Modern translations of the Hebrew text have long since corrected the older English versions of Isaiah to reflect the fact that the relevant Hebrew word simply means "young girl," and while many young girls might also be virgins, Hebrew has its own perfectly good word for that biological condition, and it is one that doesn't make any appearance here. Nor, indeed, is there any evidence in pre-Christian Judaism of this text being interpreted to foretell a virginal conception. Nor, in fact, is there any evidence of this text being read to refer to the Messiah. It's easy to be misled at this point by the seemingly momentous name Immanuel ("God is with us"). But we should remember that *lots* of Hebrew children were given names that were "significant" in the sense that they made statements about Israel's God or God's dealings with his people. Earlier in the same chapter, for instance, we learn that Isaiah's own son is called Shear-Jashub, which means "A remnant shall return."[17] So what we are dealing with in the KJV and elsewhere is actually a case of enthusiastic Christian interpreters reading back into this Old Testament text significances that are absent from its original sense but doing so precisely because they believed (on quite other grounds) that the one who was Immanuel *had in fact* been born of a virgin and *was* the longed-for Messiah. The fulfillment, we might say, far outstripped the terms of the promise and transformed its meaning. The rich convergence of several distinct strands of expectation took place in the reality which was Jesus himself and meant that Isaiah's words were read in a quite new way by those who believed in Jesus.

Questions of Credulity

LET'S TURN, THEN, to wider questions about the credulity of the story of the virginal conception. I suppose the case for the prosecution goes something like this: We are modern, sophisticated human beings with an understanding of the world and its ways of working that is deeply informed by science. Surely to goodness we cannot and need not be expected to take seriously the claim that a woman was impregnated with and delivered of a child without the involvement at any point of a man. We know that such things don't happen, *cannot* happen, because we know all the biological processes that are required for the needful combination of chromosomes and what have you to arise in order for human life to be generated. Of course, we can forgive those in the ancient world who *didn't* have this scientific account available to them, who thought that such an event *was* possible, and who told this story about Jesus's birth because they wanted to stress how important and special he was to them. Furthermore (it might be added), this story about Jesus isn't unique; it's quite similar to stories you can find easily enough elsewhere in the ancient world about special men (and they were typically men) whose births were alleged to have been out of the ordinary and involved the special intervention of some spiritual being. Surely, in the light of all this, we can breathe a sigh of relief, uncross our fingers, and score out the offending words—or at least read them as "merely poetic," not making any claim that would scandalize our sense of intellectual integrity. Well (setting aside for now the implied slur on poetry and its dealings with truth), with the best will in the world, I think we can and should dismiss this sort of objection, which, far from the enlightened and "reasonable" attitude to the world to which it lays claim, is in reality both dogmatic and patronizing and reaches its conclusion far too cheaply.

It is *dogmatic* because it trades on the assumption (widespread in our culture) that science has, at this point in the human project, somehow got the whole world and its processes mapped in a determinative manner, having identified "laws" of nature that cannot be breached and thus, by definition, excluding the possibility of anything occurring that would constitute such a breach, which virginal conception certainly does. But that seems to me to be a thin and inadequate understanding of how science works and what it is competent to pronounce upon with authority. Science has been and is remarkably successful in helping us understand the regular processes and patterns of the cosmos and, in doing so, understand all sorts of things, the workings of which were once mysterious to us. But science (good science) is based on experience and is concerned precisely with those regularities in our experience of the world that can be mapped and described. It can thus tell us with a high degree of certainty what *probably* happened in some situation and what is *likely* to happen in the future. And in doing that, it helps us handle the world and live in and respond to it constructively as a place with order and meaning and predictability that we can come to rely on. But two things are worth observing. First, the best scientists know that, despite the huge accomplishments of science in helping us understand the world and its workings, the amount remaining yet to be discovered and understood massively outstrips what we currently know. The world remains laden with mystery, realities and depths of reality for which we do not yet even have language (which means, incidentally, that pioneering science is inevitably driven to poetic strategies—the use of simile, metaphor, and the like—in its efforts to describe the world). And second, scientists (qua scientists) are only able to pronounce authoritatively on the *regularities* in the world's workings—that is, on the ways things *ordinarily* happen (and so what we might reasonably *expect* to have happened or to happen in the future, all other things being equal). Science cannot, qua science, pronounce on what is *possible*, whether past or future. It can only work with the maps of the world and the tools for measuring and registering it that are at its disposal. Of anything that will not fit or show up on those maps or register on its instruments, it can say nothing more authoritative than that it is improbable or highly unlikely. To pronounce it "impossible" would be a form of dogmatism to which science as such is meant to be allergic—open-mindedness being of the essence of the scientific quest itself.

The objection is *patronizing* in its suggestion that the people of biblical times were credulous, primitive in their outlook on the world, and so capable of believing in such things as babies born to virgins. In reality, of course, they no more believed in such things than we do. As C. S. Lewis points out, they may not have been equipped with the technical vocabulary of spermatozoa, ovum, zygote, and all the rest, but they knew full well from a wealth of experience that a woman does not conceive unless she has taken a tumble with a man.[18] Mary's question to the angel is precisely the question we find ourselves asking: told that she is to conceive and bear a son, she asks, "How can this possibly be, since I'm still a virgin?" She doesn't need a biology textbook. Furthermore, she knows exactly how her neighbors, family, and friends are likely to respond when, as her belly swells in size and she is asked the inevitable question, she tells them, "The Holy Spirit overshadowed me." There can be little doubt that her answer will have elicited some bemused and incredulous responses and mutterings: *Are you having a laugh? You're kidding me, right? Apparently she was "overshadowed." . . . Never heard it called that before.* And in due course, as I mentioned earlier, there were indeed attempts to turn the circumstances of Jesus's birth into the stuff of scandal.

Whatever we make of all this, two things in particular are fairly clear. First, it seems certain that Jesus was known *not* to be the biological son of Joseph, and the question of his paternity was therefore a live one. And second, first-century Palestinians were no more credulous about the possibilities of conception occurring apart from the involvement at some stage of a man than we are. The claim that this was what had happened to Mary was precisely *not* an expression of a primitive view of things, therefore, but just as likely to be met with bemusement and disbelief then as it is now. The insistence that such things do not happen was the response of common sense *then* just as it is now. And, of course, whether then or now, it is part of the point of those events that we identify as "miracles" in the Gospels that they "do not happen"—namely, that they are striking, scandalous departures from the patterns which common sense and science alike tend to concern themselves with. That they are things that, ordinarily speaking, cannot and do not happen is of their essence and definition. It is precisely the point.

What, then, about the supposed parallels in Greek and Roman religion that are sometimes cited? I think the best thing to say here is that, on close inspection, they turn out not to be proper parallels at all but to contain, at best, pale and inadequate resonances.[19] If, for instance, we take the claims made about Augustus Caesar, that his mother was impregnated by the god Apollo, they are a million miles away both in tone and in substance from what Christians believe about Jesus's nativity. Here we have a demigod (the son of Zeus and Leto) who comes to earth to have a brief fling with a human girl, leaving her with the consequences to deal with on her own. The processes of procreation are all intact; it's just that the male role is, as it were, supercharged, being performed by a male demigod whose potency is hardly in doubt, even if he seems divinely unaware of the possibility of contraception. Nothing could be further from all this than the depiction by Luke's Gospel of what happens to Mary. Your womb, the angel tells her, will be overshadowed by the power of God, the same Spirit who hovered over the waters in the beginning, and out of its emptiness, God will call forth a life.[20] This is not impregnation by proxy; it's an act of creation directly parallel to the creation of the world, summoned forth out of emptiness, nothingness—Mary's virginal state, her empty womb, is (in and of itself) unable to bring forth life. But God creates life, turns Mary's emptiness into the site of a new creative act, fashioning for himself in her womb a human life which he will appropriate as his own, his own humanity, in which he will do all that needs to be done for the world's redemption. If there are indeed any pale echoes of this to be found in the mythologies of other cultures and religions, we might best reckon them, perhaps, as pointers and hints divinely intended to prepare and to point the way, outstripped and left looking wraithlike by the unthinkable reality itself when it arrives.[21] But they will be bound to mislead if we grant them any more significance than that and are perhaps best set aside altogether.

For those who believe in the God who created the heavens and the earth out of nothing, the claim that this same God called forth life in the womb of a young Palestinian girl who had not yet had sexual intercourse with a man will hardly be a stretch of either the imagination or the intellect. After all, calling forth life in the wombs of young girls is something this God does every day, the provision of a "microscopic particle of matter" from a man's body being simply the means by which God ordinarily does so, inserting a particular life into the reproductive biological line "that stretches far back beyond his ancestors into pre-human and pre-organic deserts of time, back to the creation of matter itself."[22] Those who believe, though, that this same God, having created the world and populated it in this way with human creatures, in the fullness of time purposed to enter the world himself as one of those creatures, may well, after all, be disposed to take seriously the suggestion that the circumstances of his doing so were marked by something odd, exceptional, unique. That God's appearance in the world should involve a theologically significant interruption of the patterns and potentialities of the ordinary is no less remarkable than the alleged circumstances of his eventual departure from it, the virginal conception and resurrection from death standing, as it were, like two theologically charged bookends, marking out the story of Jesus's life, ministry, and passion as a turning point, qualitatively distinct in all sorts of ways from what precedes and surrounds and follows it—a human life, to be sure, but not as we know it.

From Empty Womb to Empty Tomb

OUR DISPOSITION TO take it seriously will be aided further too, of course, if we can see this peculiar, messy, scandal-inducing event as more than a mere freak happening, more than an ostentatious, random show of divine power. It helps if we can see how this odd beginning to Jesus's life, to God's own life among us as a man, is charged with meaning, an appropriate sign pointing to what is actually happening here.

It may help first to dispense briefly first with what I take to be two misunderstandings. It has sometimes been held that the virginal conception was necessary in order to interrupt the transmission of "original sin" via the sexual act and thereby secure Jesus's sinlessness. In a church which seems always to have been preoccupied with sex and its relationship to sin, it's easy to see how such an idea might have grown up. But there are absolutely no grounds for it in Scripture. Furthermore, the idea fosters a very unhelpful notion of what Jesus's "sinlessness" (an intrinsically difficult idea to unpack) consisted in. Whatever is meant by it, if we allow Scripture to be our guide, sinlessness is something won through the struggle, sweat, and tears of temptation, testing, and obedience and not courtesy of immunity established in advance by divine genetic engineering.

Secondly, the virginal conception is not the necessary condition for the incarnation. That is to say, Jesus did not have to have a human mother and God as his "father" in order to be both human and divine. That's an odd idea that tends, in any case, to a peculiar account of the incarnation, as if Jesus were *half* man and *half* God ("he's got his mother's eyes but his Father's way with sinners and tax collectors") rather than God present among us *as a human being*. God, we may reasonably suppose, could have "taken flesh" and become a man through perfectly straightforward and ordinary biological circumstances, with a human father as well as a human mother involved. So the questions are why God chose *not* to do this and what God might have been saying to or showing us by choosing to do otherwise. If, in other words, the virginal conception and birth of Jesus are indeed "theologically significant"—that is, a *sign*—then what do they signify? What are they pointing to and expecting us to notice?

The secret, I suggest, lies precisely in the parallel with creation that I mentioned earlier. What this event tells us, if we ponder it in the light of the larger pattern of Scripture, is that here, in this particular birth as in no other before or since, God is making a fresh start, initiating a new impulse within humankind, regenerating our nature by taking it upon himself in order to become, as Paul has it, the first fruits of a *new creation*. The belief that the world's salvation will come and can only come courtesy of a radical new action by God the creator, that it cannot develop or grow out of the potentialities, possibilities, or potencies embedded in the way the world currently is, lies at the heart of Christian hope. That is the point of Jesus's resurrection from the dead: it testifies not so much to the possibility as to the *necessity* that if our world, marked as it is by corruption and decay, is to have a future with God, God himself must act to turn it around, bringing life—as only God can bring life—where otherwise there is only death, emptiness, and nothingness. Jesus on the cross and in the tomb is the sign under which our world currently exists, the symbol of its potency and potential when left to its own devices. The empty tomb is the mark of God's promise not to allow it to end there, the pledge of God to make good on his promise, to create and sustain new life where otherwise there would be none, life which is no mere replication of the life we know but qualitatively new, life woven together with God's own life, life to be enjoyed with God forever. That the moment at which this decisive new stage in the fulfillment of God's promises begins should involve a unique and striking act of new creation (filling emptiness, creating possibility where, biologically speaking, it is lacking), far from being a freak aberration likely only to cause incredulity and embarrassment, might, surely, be precisely the sort of thing we ought to expect? "Behold," it says in no uncertain terms, "I am doing a new thing."[23]

5

"SUFFERED UNDER PONTIUS PILATE, WAS CRUCIFIED, DIED, AND WAS BURIED; HE DESCENDED TO THE DEAD..."

Suffered under Pontius Pilate...

IT'S BEEN SAID that this clause of the creed contains every civil servant's nightmare.[1] *Suffered under Pontius Pilate*—one man's public misdemeanor or mistake recorded for posterity and so, no matter what his other accomplishments, becoming the thing that will be associated with his name and term of office forever. Pontius Pilate, the man who represented the authority of the Roman Empire, into whose hands Jesus's fate was fleetingly placed, who had the power to choose life or death. Pontius Pilate, the man who swithered back and forth, unsure of what he should do, finally giving way to the political manipulation of the Jewish authorities in order to preserve his own already fragile career, his hands therefore identifiably soiled with responsibility for Jesus's execution, but who sought (in a very public and notorious gesture) quite literally to wash his hands of the whole situation. Perhaps if his involvement in Jesus's story had been confined to the Gospel texts alone, he might eventually have enjoyed less notoriety and retired quietly with his reputation intact and his dreams untroubled, his part in the story having been swallowed up by the behavior of other actors on the stage. It is this inclusion of his name so prominently in a formulary intended to summarize the very essentials of Christian believing (the only male name to be included other than Jesus's own) that has, over the centuries, kept it alive and kicking in the public consciousness, keeping the spotlight on Pilate and guaranteeing him his place in Christian history as *persona maxima non grata*.

So why include it? Why does the creed pick on Pilate, as it were? Well, unpleasant though we may judge his actions to have been, it's not because his vacillation and hypocrisy are to be judged any worse than Judas's betrayal, Peter's denial, or the fickleness and bloodlust of the Passover crowds who, having sung hymns to celebrate Jesus's arrival in the Holy City earlier in the week, were baying like animals for his crucifixion by Friday morning. No, Pilate wasn't anyone special even in the contest for the most despicable character in the room. The simple fact is that his political career provided the church with a straightforward and convenient way to anchor the event of Jesus's death in history, Pilate's term of office being logged in the archives of the Roman government.[2] It reminds us that the story of Jesus is not one that we can treat as having happened "once upon a time" or "a long time ago in a galaxy far, far away," let alone ending with everyone living "happily ever after." Those are the literary devices beloved of fairy tales and fables and other imaginative constructs, stories which are powerful and deal with truth but which eschew any claim to document anything which actually happened anywhere to anyone in particular. They are typically about the sorts of things which might happen, or the clothing with imaginative flesh of general human hopes, aspirations, fears, and truths. And the "once upon a time" openings are there as a literary disclaimer, to remind us of that fact and shape our expectations accordingly.

What this clause of the creed reminds us, though, is that the gospel story is *not* like that. It's not the distillation of some ancient human wisdom that transcends time and place; it is earthed, anchored, grounded in *things that actually happened* at a particular time and place and offers an interpretation of the *meaning* of those events.[3] "Under Pontius Pilate" is precisely the sort of information that a historian expects to work with, enabling us to date Jesus's execution to somewhere between 26 and 36 CE, the years of Pilate's term as procurator of Judea. It tells us that the gospel is not a set of religious ideas or moral imperatives that

Jesus taught but that might equally well have been communicated by someone else; instead, it concerns claims about God coming among us and sharing in our history, acting and being acted upon in our history, doing and suffering things that can be pinned down to specifics of a time and place. That Jesus of Nazareth "suffered under Pontius Pilate" can be documented reliably from various sources, including the creed. Of course, the *significance* of the events is a different sort of thing, lying beyond the proper scope of what historians can tell us. But as a historical happening, the story of Jesus's passion and death is well attested. This, it has been pointed out, is the one clause of the creed that even a devout atheist should be able to say with integrity.

But the creed makes an odd leap here, we might notice. It takes us straight from the birth of Jesus to his last hours and his death, which is, I take it, what the phrase "suffered" here primarily refers to. In its eagerness to pin Jesus clearly on the map of history, it passes over in silence the whole of Jesus's ministry, as though that were simply an interesting preamble to the main event. Now, it's true enough that the Gospels give a seemingly disproportionate amount of space to coverage of the events of what we typically refer to as the "passion" story. In Mark, for instance, six out of sixteen chapters in total are given over to an account of Jesus's last few days, and in John, eleven out of twenty-one. It's not exactly a balanced bit of reporting, and it clearly suggests that this part of Jesus's story is of momentous importance, being in some sense where the center of gravity lies in any adequate answer to the question, What did Jesus come to do? But the three years or so of ministry that begin with Jesus's baptism by John can hardly be dismissed as insignificant, even in relative terms. In fact, I'd want to go further and say that we won't really be able to make much constructive sense of Jesus's passion if we isolate it from what preceded it, treating the ministry and the events of Holy Week as two hermetically sealed units rather than understanding them as organically connected. In this sense, I think it's important to say that Jesus's "suffering for our sins" begins not in the Garden of Gethsemane (or wherever, for convenience, we take the passion story to begin) but at the very outset of his public ministry and perhaps even earlier than that. As Karl Barth suggests, the Heidelberg Catechism of 1563 is more nuanced in this respect than the Apostles' Creed, the usefulness of Pilate as a historical marker notwithstanding: "What do you understand by the word 'Suffered'? That all the time of his life on earth, but especially at the end of it, he bore, in body and soul, the wrath of God against the sin of the whole human race."[4]

It behooves us at this point to stop and acknowledge our use of bad language, even if we refuse to apologize for it. So let's pause and unpack something of that "light-the-blue-touchpaper-and-retire-immediately-to-a-safe-distance" term *wrath*, an English word which jars modern "enlightened" sensibilities, seeming as it does to us to connote all sorts of dark things we would prefer not to have to associate with God at all. No doubt some of the problematic connotations may and should be stripped away. A quick online search offers us the following range of meanings: anger, rage, fury, annoyance, indignation, outrage, pique, spleen, chagrin, vexation, exasperation, high dudgeon, bad temper, displeasure, disgruntlement, cantankerousness, querulousness, and snappishness. None of those, though, seems really to capture the sense that *wrath* bears in Scripture. On the one hand, that is because some of these are indeed dispositions we hold typically to be problematic even in human terms, let alone when predicated of God. On the other hand, though, the problem is rather that they hardly seem to gauge the seriousness or force of what scriptural reference to God's "wrath" intends. *Anger* is perhaps the most sanitized rendering in modern translations, but even it falls short of catching the almost visceral force of *wrath*. *Rage* and *outrage* come closer, but as applied to humans (even the most well adjusted), these still evoke the sorts of responses that we might suppose are inappropriate for God.

The answer, I think, is not to dilute or tone down the force of the word *wrath* but instead to disentangle it a bit from the predominantly emotional meanings of some of its supposed synonyms. God's wrath is, no doubt, analogous in some ways to the forceful emotional responses we experience in the face of certain things, but it's also quite distinct from those responses and, if anything, *more* rather than less forceful than any of them. We might usefully think of it like this: God's "wrath" is God's being *utterly opposed* to evil, even the slightest trace of evil—evil itself being not so much something that angers God as it is a force or entity that is radically incompatible with all that God is. This is "antimatter" to God's "matter" and, as the Scots theologian P. T. Forsyth suggests, presents a genuine *threat* to God's existence, were God not determined and finally able to eradicate it.[5] Evil is not a mere irritant or even an outrage: it is that which contradicts and threatens God's being, and God cannot and will not finally coexist with it but has committed himself to purging it from God's world—not just for our sake but for God's own sake. And in the meanwhile, while God does and must coexist with its presence in the world, God *suffers* its presence.

Now, if we think of God's "wrath," or his relationship to sin and evil, in this way, we can begin to see what it might mean for this same God to commit himself to enter into his world humanly, to take our "flesh" and dwell among us as a participant in the relationships, the institutions, the experiences that make up life in a sinful world affected from top to bottom by the taint and the influences of sin and evil. We can begin to understand how simply *being in* the world in this fallen state would—for one whose character and moral and spiritual sensibilities are perfectly attuned to God's own (because they *are* in fact God's own human moral and spiritual sensibilities, the direct creaturely correlates of who God is as God)—already be an experience of "suffering" the sins of the world quite unique in human terms. Human analogies for divine realities can only ever take us so far, of course, and always risk collapsing into flippancy, but perhaps one or two are worth venturing. Think of the way in which, for instance, someone with that sort of finely tuned musical ear we refer to as possessing (or being possessed and haunted by) "perfect pitch" responds almost viscerally to the dire screeching of an amateur string ensemble having a more than usually bad day. Or think of the way someone exceptionally squeamish (perhaps by nature or perhaps due to some post-traumatic disorder) reacts when confronted with CGI-enhanced representations of gore and guts on the cinema screen. These are things, we might properly say in each case, that they *cannot bear* or tolerate under any circumstances, eliciting from them a degree of genuine distress and discomfort that others do not experience and cannot even begin to understand.

How much more distress and discomfort, we might ask ourselves, would be bound to be experienced by one who views, hears, and feels things in the world not with our dulled moral and spiritual sensibilities but with God's own—God for whom even the slightest shred of evil is unbearable, a threat to all that God is and all that God has promised the world will finally be? Simply to *be* "God incarnate," in other words, is, we might suppose, to be bound to suffer dreadfully. And in Jesus, of course, God does not simply *observe* this world of sin as a bystander. He is plunged into it and entangled in its webs, forced to wrestle and to struggle with it, to be victorious over it only one painful and difficult moment at a time. That's the point of Jesus's baptism being followed immediately by his departure into the wilderness to be tempted by Satan—a wrestling with the forces of evil which begins here and continues all the way to the crucifixion, where, as he dies, Jesus is able to utter those highly charged words "It is finished."[6] Not "*I* am finished" but "*It* is finished." Job done. The struggle with sin and evil, Jesus's "bearing" on his shoulders of the heavy load of human sin through his life and on to the cross, is here at last complete, and he can and does hand his life over to the Father, knowing that he has done what needed to be done to turn our way of being human around and to change the course of humankind's relationship with God forever.

So the suffering of Jesus during Holy Week and his death on Calvary are the climax, the culmination of what he came to do. But they must not be treated as a largely unrelated bolt-on to the package of his ministry, for they are the organic extension and the natural conclusion of a life and ministry in and through which sin was already being borne and suffered for, and victory over the forces of evil and death already being worked out in his struggle and obedience. Ministry and passion belong together, for they are a single reality. And the heart of Jesus's suffering even on "Good Friday," we should note, was not merely physical but ultimately spiritual. It had to do with the impact upon him—as God incarnate, in this darkest moment of all—when the forces of evil were most fully at work and most clearly ranged against him, threatening to swallow him up in death (sin's final weapon) and so to triumph over him. That he fathomed this terrible prospect is clear from those other words recorded by Matthew and Mark: "My God, my God, why have you forsaken me?"[7] But at the cross, as readers, we are invited to overhear the Father's words still echoing from Jesus's baptism: "This is my beloved Son, in whom I am well pleased."[8]

From a different angle, the insistence that Christ—and in him, God—suffered is important because it tells us that God is not remote from or unacquainted with the sorts of suffering, often dreadful suffering, that his sentient creatures typically experience in life. The scale of suffering in God's world is one of the biggest problems for believers and unbelievers alike when it comes to making sense of the world and of the claim that God is its creator and sustainer. This is a topic for fuller consideration elsewhere, but we need here at least to recognize again that the God people often say they "cannot believe in" is generally not the God of the Bible, who is known most fully and completely not for leaving us to get on with it, let alone inflicting it upon us willfully, but here, on the cross, in his determination to share with us up to the hilt in the very worst of our suffering (precisely the sort of suffering, ironically, that evokes the epithet "godforsaken") in order to sustain us through it and to break its hold over us. This is a God who is never closer to us, that is to say, than he is in the midst of our seeming "godforsakenness," and such suffering has no power to isolate or to distance us from God. He has been there before us, and he goes there with us.

Was Crucified, Died, and Was Buried . . .

THAT JESUS WAS crucified on Pilate's watch is a fact familiar to everyone. It is a fact reflected in the symbol of the cross, the instrument of Rome's most extreme legal measure, which has adorned over the centuries Christian architecture, clerical garments, the ceremonial utensils used in worship, and nowadays, arguably in defiance of good taste, a host of consumer items sold online and in Christian bookshops, including mugs, Bible covers, tote bags, and almost anything anyone could care to buy.

To some extent, the form of Jesus's dying is simply a function of the context in which he was arrested and tried and the charges of which he was found guilty. Crucifixion was not invented by the Romans, but the Roman Empire used it as a way of disposing of those it had reason to fear most—not just day-to-day criminals but insurgents, political thugs, and anyone who might be perceived as a threat to its rule, especially in the occupied territories.[9] Just a century before Jesus was executed, the revolt against Rome led by the escaped slave and gladiator Spartacus was put down by the legions of Cassius, and it is reported that six thousand of those rebels who survived the battle were crucified in a line stretching along the Appian Way, some 190 kilometers between Capua and Rome. It was a radical and cruel exercise in deterrence. The victims of crucifixion died horribly and slowly, usually from suffocation, as the weight of their own bodies gradually squeezed life out of them until, as John records of Jesus, they "breathed their last." In the meanwhile, though, the whole portfolio of human barbarism was played out in inventive and sickening variations of torture, and the heat and the flies and the crows and the dogs also worked their own peculiar brand of unpleasantness. As one writer observes, crucifixion was, in effect, "the attempt to manufacture a temporary hell for its intended victim," and no one who actually saw it would ever have dreamed of turning it into a piece of architecture or jewelry, let alone a logo for a tote bag.[10] And Jesus, of course, was charged with sedition. He was presented to Pilate as a pretender to the throne of

Israel and so a direct challenge to the authority of Caesar. And so once it became clear that Jesus wasn't going to deny the charges and that neither the crowds nor the Jewish authorities would rest content with him simply being beaten to a pulp in the cells by the pride of the Roman Empire and then released, Pilate assented to what was the normal punishment for his alleged crimes—a punishment that denied the humanity not just of its victims but of those who inflicted it too, as participation in degrading violence and evil generally does.[11]

At the human level, then, Jesus suffered this peculiarly degrading and dehumanizing form of death because it was the one his alleged crimes deserved. But in terms of God's purposes, we can perhaps read rather more into it than that. That God should become a man and dwell among us so as not just to identify with and redeem us from suffering and subjection to death but to bear the price of sin, which makes suffering and death so terrible, transforming them from mere consequences of mortal existence into the enemies which threaten to leave us "godforsaken," cut off from the God who holds us in life—all this makes it appropriate, perhaps, that Jesus should not die peacefully in his sleep or even suffer the quick, relatively "clean" death granted by other forms of execution available to Roman justice (such as beheading) but instead become the unfortunate victim of the most brutal form of execution known in his day or any other, one inseparable from the stigma of curse and godforsakenness. No doubt there are other, more painful ways to die (in fact, Jesus seems to have died surprisingly quickly, which means that those crucified on either side of him probably suffered longer and more—in physical terms, at least[12]), and we should not get hung up in any case, as theology sometimes has, on misguided questions about the precise "amount" of suffering Jesus had to endure, as though such a sickening calculus were even possible. But that he both died in solidarity with all the victims of man's worst inhumanity to man and died the death reserved for those guilty of the most inhumane offenses nonetheless has a powerful theological charge that should not be overlooked. That God was willing to allow himself to become such a victim, and to do so for our sake, tells us all that we need to know about the character of God's love.

Jesus's death was the climactic point of a divine action that, Christians believe, took place "for us" and "for our sins." His death wasn't just the inevitable outcome of his behavior and its provocation of the Jewish authorities. It was something that Jesus knew lay before him as the final step of his "obedience" to his heavenly Father, something that *had* to happen if the power of human sin was to be broken and human beings reconciled and restored to their proper relationship with God—justified to or "put right" with God and given a fresh start. Again, don't forget that this isn't a "take it or leave it" circumstance, as though God could simply decide to restore us willy-nilly by divine fiat. Sin and evil are far more serious matters than that. And if they are to be dealt with, and dealt with in such a way that opens up and creates the opportunity for the new or "eternal" life which God promises and Jesus is said to bring, then it would seem that the whole history of Jesus's suffering and struggling with sin that is implicit in the very fact of his being God in, as C. S. Lewis has it, "enemy territory"—which reaches a pitch in his public ministry and its climax as he hands himself over to be abused, tortured, and executed—is *necessary*.[13] It had to happen like this, or else sin and evil would remain and retain their grip on and their hold over God's human creatures.

The *death* of Jesus in particular is said in Scripture to be necessary for this process. Perhaps this is to some extent because, as we have seen, his death is the climactic point and seals and completes a dynamic that is present in the whole trajectory of his incarnate existence. So his "death" and sometimes his "blood" can and do serve usefully as symbols of what is a wider pattern of Jesus's action and experience. *How* his suffering and death accomplish and establish this divinely purposed redemption of humankind is a further question, and as Lewis again notes, it is a question to which a variety of different answers have been given over the centuries, none of which is essential to Christian faith. *That* they did so, he insists, is *the central Christian belief*, enshrined in our liturgies, our hymnody, and much else besides.[14] That is why the cross is the central Christian symbol, referring us again and again to this suffering and death as the place where the trajectory of human history was turned around, something done by God that left nothing the same as it had been previously. Without it and the resurrection from the dead that followed and placed God's seal of approval and promise upon it, the world would be left in a perilous state.

The theological shorthand for this "happening," or this divine action that put us right with God and created a new beginning for human life with God, is *the atonement*. To ask how the atonement works is to ask a good question, one in response to which Scripture itself offers us a number of different images to think about or turn over in our mind's eye. Again, these are answers to the all-important question, What is it like? As we saw in chapter 2, we can only ever understand anything by being able to grasp what it is like and how it differs from other things we are familiar with. That's why Jesus begins so much of his teaching with a direct appeal to imaginative comparisons and analogies—"To what, then, shall we liken the kingdom of God?" Well, he tells his hearers, it's a bit like a woman who, when emptying the Hoover bag, discovers an expensive earring she has lost. Or it's a bit like a mustard seed that grows so quickly and so large that it has the gardener reaching for the systemic weed killer. Of course, in all sorts of ways, it's *not* like those things at all. But each picture gives us a glimpse, and perhaps more than a glimpse, of something true to the reality of God's kingdom, something in our experience that it can be likened to. And Scripture does something similar here, too, when it comes to the atonement. It works with metaphors and similes.

So, for instance, Jesus's suffering and death are likened to some of the religious sacrifices that took place in the Jerusalem temple. There's something extremely important that his death has in common with these, we are led to suppose, though we can and should accept that it is also very different from them in other ways. To begin with, Jesus died not on an altar in the temple but on a gibbet in a Roman execution ground. So too, fittingly, the atonement is sometimes pictured in forensic or legal terms, as a matter of justice in which a penalty prescribed by law is meted out and borne. Elsewhere, the imagery is of a cosmic battle between good and evil, with Jesus winning decisive victories in occupied territory and striking a blow to the enemy that will finally set free those held captive. I have alluded already to the pecuniary image of "paying a debt" or "paying the price" for human sin, the latter image in particular being linked to another. The "redemption price" in ancient Israel was the sum of cash someone might pay in order to release a relative or friend from the social institution of slavery. And being liberated from bondage to sin is a further picture to which the New Testament writers appeal in drawing close to the meaning of Jesus's suffering and death. Elsewhere again, the picture is of our being "reborn" into a life which is "eternal" in quality or of orphans being adopted so that they now share a Father with the one who is the only natural Son of God. In each of these cases, we are to suppose that what occurs between Jesus and his Father and Jesus and humankind has some deep likeness to these various complicated human realities while recognizing that, in all sorts of ways, it will differ from any and all of them quite significantly.[15]

The key here, therefore, is to acknowledge that *none* of these images offers us an *explanation* or a literal description of what the atonement actually is and how it works. Each of them offers, at best, a partial imaginative grasp on its reality. But each, we may suppose, points us appropriately to some aspect of what goes on here, and taken together as a package, they grant us as good and rounded an approach to it as we can properly expect. After all, when it comes to asking how God relates to evil and how God has determined to deal with it and to fulfill his purpose in creation, we are in pretty deep water and might reasonably expect there to be a high quotient of mystery attached to it. Various more systematic "theories" of the atonement, claiming to explain its mechanics, begin with these biblical images but end up neglecting some in order to privilege others and pressing the ones they prefer way beyond the scope of their biblical roots. In "literal" terms, these things don't map onto one another properly at all, a sacrifice in the temple being *in reality* something quite different in both substance and spirit from a victorious skirmish on the battlefield, the payment of a massive debt by a wealthy benefactor, a legal penalty borne in another's stead, the restoration from disease or disability by a skilled healer, the birth of a child, the legal adoption of a child, and so on. None of these things is the same at all, and if we insist on treating them "literally" rather than acknowledging their nature as suggestive images, we are bound to choose among them, their differences being understood as mutually contradictory rather than taken up constructively into a rich poetic complementarity from which ever more meaning threatens to break forth. We may, of course, find one or more of the images particularly helpful for one reason or another and at one point or another in our lives, and Scripture itself grants more space to some than to others, suggesting, perhaps, degrees of significance and priority to be reckoned with in our attempts to hold them together and respect them. Talk of satisfactory "theorizing" seems to me, though, to be misplaced, tending to encourage unhelpful expectations about the force of what we come up with. And Christian faith, we should note, doesn't entail endorsing any of them in particular; on the contrary, it must be committed to treating them *all* seriously as part of God's redemptive harnessing of our imaginative capacity, calling it into play so that we might grasp ever more fully the meaning of what Christ has done for our sake. Where "mere Christianity" is concerned, it is enough to believe that Jesus's suffering and death were necessary, that they were embraced for our sake and for God's sake, that sins might be forgiven and we sinners drawn into the promised salvation of God.

    Although as a theologian I have often been compelled to reckon at length with confident-sounding explanations and theories of one sort or another having to do with the atonement, I have come increasingly to appreciate the implicit intellectual humility of Lewis's imaginative treatment of the matter in *The Lion, the Witch and the Wardrobe*, where Aslan meets with the White Witch and agrees to allow himself to be put to death on the Stone Table in place of Edmund, a grisly trade-off that will appease the Deep Magic. Aslan's resurrection to life and his victory over the forces of the White Witch are contingent on all this happening, we later realize, but there is no attempt whatsoever to theorize how that "worked." Nor is there any need for such theorizing in order to rejoice in the outcome and its implications. When it comes to the meaning of the atonement, we may sometimes wish to go further in our reckoning with it than its imaginative representations in Scripture, but if we do, we should tread very carefully indeed and make sure we continue to return again and again to those imaginative likenesses (all of them together, and not just some of them) and ask what they caution us against thinking and saying as well as what they encourage and permit us to think and say. This is holy ground, and human hubris would be an ironic thing to erect upon it.

The cruciform nature of Jesus's death is not only related to the wider shape and pattern of his own life and ministry in the New Testament, of course; it is also related directly to the nature of faith and discipleship and what it is reasonable for Christians to expect, aspire to, and pursue in their "following" of Jesus. Lots of different passages could be cited here, but we'll look briefly at just one. First Peter 2:20–25 reads as follows:

> *If you endure when you do right and suffer for it, you have God's approval. For to this you have been called, because Christ also suffered for you, leaving you an example, so that you should follow in his steps. "He committed no sin, and no deceit was found in his mouth." When he was abused, he did not return abuse; when he suffered, he did not threaten; but he entrusted himself to the one who judges justly. He himself bore our sins in his body on the cross, so that, free from sins, we might live for righteousness; by his wounds you have been healed. For you were going astray like sheep, but now you have returned to the shepherd and guardian of your souls.*

There is far too much here to get to grips with in full. But certain things are fairly apparent. Some ways of talking about the atonement suggest that at the heart of it—and in his suffering and death in particular—Jesus does something "instead of us" and something that we cannot do. Now, there is a sense in which that's both true and important. Some of the biblical images certainly encourage us to suppose something like this, and at the very least, the quality of Jesus's death as the devoted "only Son" of God the Father was unique and, in its uniqueness, redemptive.

In this passage from 1 Peter, though, we see a different part of the bigger truth of things, one that must not be downplayed or overlooked in enthusiastic talk about "substitution." For the insistence here is that—far from Jesus suffering and dying so that we might *not have to* suffer and die—in a vital sense, his suffering and death were precisely *to enable us* to suffer and die as we follow in his footsteps. Indeed, we might say that part of what sets him apart from us and makes his suffering and death unique is their capacity, as the suffering and death of God, to be *generative* of ours as we are united ever more fully to him by the Holy Spirit. As we grow more like him, so we too begin to "suffer" sin in the world and in ourselves (though unlike him, we continue, for now, to commit it), coming to see things as God sees them, to feel things as God feels them, our moral and spiritual lives being reorientated until our familiar bearings no longer grant us any stability or guidance. As the Spirit infuses us with the life and the "power" of Christ's obedience, we too will increasingly find ourselves at odds with the world and its values, and participation in its shared institutions and practices will begin to chafe at points like an ill-fitting shoe until we are raw. And as we find ourselves compelled from within by the work of Christ's Spirit to eschew the world's ways of thinking and behaving, we too will find ourselves increasingly discomforted and tormented by the responses of others and should expect not acclaim, popularity, and success but scorn, rejection, and failure as the probable outcomes of our faithfulness. But as Peter says, to this we were called, and for this—that we too might live cruciform lives, dying to sin daily that we might live to God—Christ bore our sins in his body on the cross, not so that *we might not have to bear the cross*, but precisely so that we might bear it day in and day out. Indeed, the apostle Paul puts it more strongly, insisting that because Jesus was none other than God himself, who had united us to himself in "taking flesh," in a very real and important sense, we have already been crucified in Christ's own death, and all that remains now is for this suffering and death to be worked out in the circumstances of our particular lives through his power at work in us so that we shall also share in the glory of his resurrection.[16]

So whatever it is that Jesus does or suffers instead of us, it's certainly not the whole story. As strap lines for marketing strategies or recruitment drives go, "Take up your cross and follow me" is one of the more unlikely ones. But it's the only one Jesus offers us. And the extent and nature of our suffering (as individuals, as congregations, as a community of witnesses in the world), not health, wealth, and success, are what are offered to us as the most authentic gauges of our faithfulness in doing so.

He Descended to the Dead . . .

IN THE JEWISH understanding of Jesus's day, the place of the dead was Hades (in Greek) or Sheol (in Hebrew), a shadowy underworld, an insubstantial place where the dead were thought to go while they awaited the coming Day of the Lord with its final judgment. We get glimpses of it in the Old Testament. So, for example, Psalm 6 tells us that those in Sheol were in some sense cut off from a proper relationship with God. "For in death," the psalmist writes, "there is no remembrance of you; in Sheol who can give you praise?" On the other hand, Psalm 139 points out that Sheol is certainly within God's reach, and no one should presume that by fleeing there they can escape from God: "Where can I go from your spirit? Or where can I flee from your presence? . . . If I make my bed in Sheol, you are there."[17] Jesus's parable of the rich man and Lazarus in Luke 16:19–31 gives us a more vivid depiction, though we should remember that it is precisely a parable, an imaginative tale told to make a spiritual and moral point, and not seek to build too much on its details in theological terms. Nonetheless, while the Jewish notion of Sheol/Hades cannot simply be identified with the later Christian idea of "hell" (which is a place of separation from God where only the impenitent wicked are dispatched, to remain there for eternity receiving the punishments due for their sins), it seems to be imagined as a place where the good and the wicked might at least be billeted separately rather than mixed up together, and the lot of the wicked is already one that, were any self-respecting sinner permitted to glimpse or be forewarned of it, should suffice to scare the hell out of them.

The addition of this clause, "he descended to the dead," to the creed may simply have been a way of underlining the fact that Jesus had actually shared to the full in human death rather than being snatched back from it at the last minute or (as some Jewish propagandists had been known to suggest) having never really died at all but merely fainted and therefore was not "raised from the dead." It really means "he descended to the place of the dead"—that is, went to Sheol/Hades as all humans were believed to do when they died. Pictured in this way, the circumstance naturally invites the question, What exactly was Jesus doing in between his "descent" to this "place" and his victorious resurrection on Sunday morning? It was this question and a resort to various bits and pieces of New Testament texts in seeking to answer it that led duly to the medieval doctrine of a Harrowing of Hell, the idea that Jesus had descended to the place where the dead were imprisoned not simply because he was himself dead but because he had a further stage of his mission still to complete—breaking into "hell" in person in order to bring "release to the captives," demonstrating his lordship over death and laying claim to its territory by sharing the gospel with those who, being dead, would otherwise never have the opportunity to hear it. Here, in other words, the imaginative logic of Jesus's own parable is reversed, the boundary between the living and the dead being transgressed not by one bearing a dire warning but by the one who is himself the embodiment of the good news. The relevant biblical bits and pieces are texts such as Matthew 16:18; 1 Peter 3:19–20; Ephesians 4:8–10; and Revelation 1:17–18.

While all sorts of questions are posed by this doctrine (which some Christians balk at), at the very least, it affords an imaginative way of extrapolating from the biblical insistence that in his suffering and death, Christ has broken the power and the hold of sin and death *for all* (and not just for those who, by accident of birth, are so situated in their time and place as to be able meaningfully to "hear" the gospel) and that the "place of death" need no longer hold any fear for those who put their trust in him. If we prefer, though, we can say this clause of the creed with impunity, intending by it no more than its original drafters probably did: that Jesus was crucified, died, was buried, and went wherever it is that the dead go—because he really was dead and not faking it.

6

"ON THE THIRD DAY HE ROSE AGAIN . . ."

I'M NOT A huge soccer fan. But just occasionally something happens in the world of the beautiful game to make even me sit up and notice. And one such occasion was in March 2012, when the Bolton Wanderers midfield player Fabrice Muamba suffered a heart attack in the middle of a game against Tottenham Hotspur and collapsed and died on the pitch at White Hart Lane. There was a cardiologist in the crowd, and he rushed onto the pitch but could only confirm that the player's heart had indeed stopped, all attempts by paramedics on the pitch to get it to start again having come to nothing. The ambulance into which Muamba's body was hurriedly stretchered took it to the London Chest Hospital, where they lowered its temperature to slow the rate of cell death, which begins as soon as the heart stops pumping blood to the vital organs. And then, remarkably, a whole hour and twenty minutes after he had died, they managed to restart his heart and—there's no other way of putting it—brought him back to life. Unsurprisingly, the press reached immediately for the theological dictionary to describe what had happened. It was, the headlines universally pronounced, a miracle. And for Muamba, and his family, friends, and Bolton Wanderers supporters the world over, no doubt that's exactly what it was.

Apparently, according to an item on a BBC radio news channel shortly afterward, the state-of-the-art technique used to reverse the dying process before it became irreversible (Muamba was technically "dead" for eighty minutes, and any doctor could have signed a certificate to that effect with impunity) was being developed and made more widely available. That's surely a good thing, and most of us might hope that were we to suffer an unexpected cardiac arrest, someone trained in the relevant procedures and a conveniently large refrigerator might happen to be close at hand. But of course, for all the obvious benefits these sorts of medical breakthroughs might be acknowledged to have in the case of someone otherwise dying far too young and leaving behind a young family as Muamba would have, the reality is that they can only ever defer the inevitable. The deferral may well be a very welcome one, but it is only a deferral nonetheless. No one gets to cheat the tomb. Death gets us all in the end, no matter who we are, what we have achieved in life, or how unready we may feel.

We might run from death's approach, stocking up on antiaging creams, hair colorings, rejuvenating tonics, and libido-restoring tablets, which suddenly seem less ridiculous as certain landmark birthdays come and go and our bodies threaten to become uncooperative partners in life, determined to play irritating and sometimes embarrassing tricks on us. But we can't hide. We might seek refuge in our society's effective banishment of death to life's margins, hiding the dying away embarrassedly first in "care homes" and then in hospital wards, from which they will never emerge until they do so feetfirst, rather than accommodating the fact and processes of their dying visibly in the midst of family, friends, and neighbors.[1] But where our own dying is concerned, we shall not finally be able to turn our backs on it or pretend it's not there. We may collude with the myth of immortality, which the self-image born of youth tends naturally to enjoy but which our own culture panders to and keeps alive long after we should have grown out of it, encouraging us to live as though death is something that only happens to other people and providing a thousand disavowals and distractions designed to shield us from the acknowledgment of our own mortality. But we will all die anyway—because death, to repeat, gets us all in the end. Universal human experience and scientific explanation of natural processes alike bear eloquent witness to the fact: human existence is part of a wider natural cycle of life and death, and while technological advances may tinker temporarily with the way that cycle plays out in particular cases, where there is life, death is bound to follow and to have the final say as surely as night follows day.

What, then, are we to make of this emphatic creedal insistence that having been "crucified, dead, and buried" on a Friday afternoon, on that following Sunday morning, Jesus, bold as brass, "rose from the dead"? What does it mean? And are we obliged not just to grit our teeth and affirm it but, in an apparent *sacrificium intellectus*, to believe what it says and even to put it up front and center in our confident presentation of Christian faith to others rather than sweeping it discreetly under the theological rug as the unfortunate intellectual legacy of a less sophisticated outlook on the world? Is such a claim not bound to provoke needless incredulity among those blessed by the insights of more scientific and "modern" ways of thinking and so to present a stumbling block to effective evangelism and intelligent catechesis? Because if the inevitability of death itself is a truth demanding universal acknowledgment, so too, the modern reader will wish to insist, is the fact that the dead, once properly dead, don't "rise" but stay dead, their gradually decomposing remains testifying to the fact that they are not just dead but dead and gone. I say "properly" dead because it is of course possible for a person to return from a "near-death" experience or for one who has technically died to be resuscitated—occasionally, as in the case of Muamba, some considerable time after their heart has stopped beating. But resuscitation and "resurrection" are not the same thing at all. Even Lazarus—whom, in John 11, Jesus "raises" from the tomb after several days—despite a temporary and no doubt welcome reprieve remains subject to the eventual claim of death upon his life, and we may safely presume the same to be true of Muamba. So we need to be clear on what we're talking about.

No Conjuring Trick with Bones

EVEN A CASUAL glance at the resurrection stories of the Gospels makes it clear that what the disciples were repeatedly encountered by was no resurrected corpse. The resurrection, as the erstwhile (and widely misquoted) bishop of Durham David Jenkins points out, was not just "a conjuring trick with bones" but something far more profound (and probably less creepy).² It was Jesus himself present among them again, they insisted, "in the flesh," and yet this was a flesh now wholly transformed rather than merely resuscitated, manifesting qualities which divulged its belonging to a wholly new sort of physicality. Its presence in their midst ruptured the familiar categories of manifestation, description, and explanation: not subject to the usual limitations of time and space—appearing and disappearing unpredictably, passing inexplicably and unhindered through solid walls and locked doors—it resisted easy recognition even by those who knew Jesus well. Yet what they had been dealing with, they insisted stubbornly, was no mere "apparition," ghost, or disembodied spirit either, let alone a corporate hallucination born of communal grief (phenomena perfectly familiar in the stories, beliefs, superstitions, and experiences of the first century just as they are in the twenty-first). And it was definitely Jesus. They were in no doubt about that.

No, Jesus himself was back among them, reassuringly the same in all the ways that mattered but spookily different in others, "enfleshed" now in what the apostle Paul bends language to describe as a *sōma pneumatikon*, usually translated as "spiritual body."³ Here, though, we should remind ourselves, as more generally in Paul's writings, "spiritual" doesn't mean "lacking in material substance." Instead, it refers to a reality belonging properly not to history or the world as we know and understand it but to a new era of God's dealings with the world, one heralded by a decisive, fresh outpouring, action, and indwelling of God's Holy Spirit (*to pneuma to hagion*) and thus in one way or another bound to be at odds with the characteristics and qualities of the same old, same old.⁴ As such, the body of the risen Jesus is definitely odd; it doesn't really "fit" the reality of here and now, and yet it is no mere surd anomaly or sensational aberration tearing the allegedly seamless robe of a "closed system" of natural cause and effect. It is a tantalizing sign that has its meaning, its center of gravity, and its explanation only in a reality lying as yet beyond history in the promised future of God with the world.

And what the crucified and risen body of Jesus points us to, therefore, is precisely a relationship of both deep identity and radical discontinuity between these two realities, which are, in truth, not *two* realities at all but *one* reality glimpsed at two very different points on God's time line. Jesus's body is not left to rot in the tomb, to be replaced by a new, turbocharged version, but "resurrected," redeemed, and renewed, made fit now to share in the glory of God, which was always the intended inheritance of our humanity, bodies, and souls. Likewise, the new creation, we are to suppose, will be not a creation de novo as the first creation was but precisely the recreation, renewal, and redemption by God of the same world that we currently indwell, rendering it at last fit to share in the glory of God, which was always its intended destiny. And life in the new creation, resurrection life, "eternal" life will be not *less* substantial than the life we know now but *more* so, laden with the ballast or (in C. S. Lewis's felicitous phrase) the "weight" of glory and to be enjoyed only now and at last "in all its fulness."[5]

The creedal claim we are concerned with, therefore, simply rehearses the gist of an event about which the New Testament makes no bones. The various stories of the empty tomb and Jesus's appearances to his disciples are the climax of the drama with which the Gospels more widely are concerned and are the very core of that "gospel," or good news itself on the truth of which the New Testament as a whole is premised. To set it aside, therefore, or even to push it, embarrassedly, to the margins of concern in the interest of fashioning a message more plausible (and so more likely to commend itself) to "intelligent people nowadays" is not an available option for a church grounded securely on the self-witness of God in Scripture. To "spiritualize" it (as though it would make no difference to what it signifies "religiously" if Jesus's bones were still lying in some Palestinian grave or ossuary), on the other hand, is to do serious violence to the natural sense of the biblical text, imposing our own modern, Western discomfort with the material and the bodily (and the idealist intellectual prejudices arising from that) onto a culture that does not share it. If we take seriously the claim that God's purpose in coming among us was to show us something of God's purposes and promises for the world and for ourselves, then such self-imposed blinkers are bound to blind us to the truth about our own humanity (that we are not imprisoned souls or minds cruelly hindered by the particularities of our situation in the body); about the horizons, contours, and qualities of the world's future in God's hands; and (vitally) about the value that God places on material existence as such. A world, let alone a church, that is unable to take seriously the resurrection of the body as part of its future hope is always likely to struggle to take the material creation itself seriously and will find it hard to resist the rapacious stripping and consumption of the world's resources or prioritize the well-being of the wider environment on anything other than grounds that are pragmatic and, finally, just as selfish as those that fuel such abuse. Never has belief in bodily resurrection, in other words, had more political, economic, and social urgency than in our own generation. And a church which does not hold fast to it and proclaim it to the world as the very heart of its theology is guilty not of mere intellectual squeamishness concerning an alleged freak occurrence a long time ago, but of a fatal doctrinal meltdown that threatens to leave it unable, if pressed, to provide serious theological warrant for protesting governmental, industrial, agricultural, economic, and other policies and practices fueling a major global crisis with which the world's immediate (not just its mid- or long-term) future is bound up. Bodily resurrection, then, is both central and essential to what Christians believe God has told us about God's purposes and promises for the world God has made; it is the event on which everything hinges rather than a peripheral accretion, and any attempt to strip mention of or allusion to it out of the New Testament would, if done thoroughly, leave little behind finally other than a tattered collection of isolated moral sayings bereft of any narrative underpinning or framework of understanding in terms of which they ought to be taken seriously. We shall see more fully in a subsequent chapter how belief in the resurrection and the mandated shape of Christian living are in all sorts of ways intimately related rather than distinct.[6]

Enough Wishful Thinking Already?

LET'S RETURN, THOUGH, to questions that might legitimately be raised about the stories of Jesus's resurrection. At this point, someone might legitimately ask, What, though, about the Old Testament? After all, Jesus's disciples were Jews raised in an atmosphere saturated by the teachings of the Jewish Bible, and the apostle Paul himself insists that Jesus's resurrection took place "according to the scriptures," a reference to the teachings of this same Bible.[7] Must we not reckon seriously, therefore, with the possibility, perhaps even the probability, that what we are dealing with in the disciples' insistence that Jesus was not dead and gone but had been raised by his Father from the dead is a sort of religious wish fulfillment—a conviction that if Jesus really was the Messiah and the fulfillment of all God's promises in the Old Testament (as the apostles believed he was), then he *must* have been raised from the dead, because that's exactly what the Old Testament led Jews to expect would happen? Naturally predisposed by their existing religious convictions to believe that the Messiah *would* rise from the dead, in other words, were they not bound to be suggestible as regards the claim that Jesus had indeed done so, even if there was scant evidence on which to base such a belief? In those circumstances, we can understand, surely, how even the slightest hint or a whiff of secondhand testimony or indication would be seized and picked up on gladly, exaggerated and elaborated (as tends to happen when people begin to tell stories) until suddenly everyone was saying that Jesus had been seen (by someone else), and everyone finally came to believe this. Of course, they would all be perfectly content to be several steps removed from the alleged historical reality itself and still believe in it, because it enabled them to tie up the messy loose ends and patch the unsightly fissure that Jesus's arrest, crucifixion, and burial had torn in their hope that he had indeed been the Christ (of whose story, "according to the scriptures," such things could not possibly be the final chapter). They *wanted* to believe it, so (without any disingenuous intent) they did.

This is a fair question and worthy of a considered response. It is, of course, another appeal to the credulity of the disciples and those who reckoned with their version of events, couched now in terms specific to their Jewish heritage rather than a putative premodern willingness to believe that things that "these days we know to be impossible" could and did actually happen. It's worth pausing again to challenge this latter suggestion, at least by observing that the people of biblical times were almost certainly no more (or less) credulous on this particular front than we are, the substance of universal human experience not having changed much in two millennia. Many of them (certainly not all) may have entertained ideas or beliefs about what we clumsily refer to as "life after death," and as I have already suggested, accounts of ghosts, "spirits," and apparitions of various sorts populated the hinterland of their experience as, despite the prominence of scientistic materialism, they actually continue to for plenty of people in our culture today. But when it came to death, no one seriously believed that there were any exceptions to its claims or its finality as far as the life of the body was concerned. Personal survival of death is one thing. Restoration of bodily existence after the body has died—let alone in a renewed and transfigured form, healed of its natural mortality—is something else altogether. And no one believed that anything like that *had* happened or, inasmuch as common sense and the overwhelming evidence of experience was interrogated as a guide in such matters, that it *could* happen. In fact, most popular religious beliefs about "life beyond the grave" would have reckoned such an idea ludicrous and substandard because it was the soul or spirit of a person that was naturally immortal, its incarceration in the body being a bit of a bind from which bodily death was looked forward to as a happy release. Wider intellectual prejudices about bodily resurrection in premodern times, in other words, were not a million miles away from our own supposedly "modern" ones.

Bodily resurrection, therefore, was a very odd and even unattractive image and not the sort of thing people believed in or looked forward to at all—except, that is, the Jews, whose vision of reality was always more "earthy" than that of other peoples and cultures in the ancient world, more liable to celebrate the life of the flesh, to embrace the material world as a good gift of God in creation, something to be enjoyed rather than endured, relished rather than resisted or rejected, and for whom, therefore, mere survival of death was a bit of a miserable affair in which the soul, stripped of its body (and so of any experience of sight, sound, taste, smell, or touch), was relegated, as we have already seen, to the shadowy, wraithlike existence of Hades.[8] So in one sense, it is unsurprising that the promise of God as it takes shape in the Old Testament and in postbiblical Judaism also "takes flesh," having little at all to do with the survival of death by "immortal souls" (except in versions of Judaism shaped thoroughly by Greek philosophy, for which such ideas were, one might say ironically, meat and drink).[9] And while there were strands of Judaism in Jesus's day which did *not* believe in it (the Gospels themselves mention the Sadducees in this respect), the notion that salvation would entail a "resurrection" of the dead—their restoration to a new sort of embodied existence in a "renewed creation"—had by now entered the religious and theological mainstream, even those who didn't believe in it having a reasonable idea of just what it was they were not supposed to believe. So the image of resurrected bodies would certainly have been familiar to those who followed Jesus and who began, falteringly at first, to claim him as Israel's Messiah and the Son of God. All of which brings us back to this question and its skeptical premise: even if the disciples might not have been credulous simply as citizens of the "unscientific" intellectual world of the first century, would this background belief in resurrection not have rendered them *religiously* credulous and so entirely likely to want to believe and even to fabricate stories about Jesus having been raised from the dead in order to minister to their own cognitive dissonance and to justify (to themselves as much as to others) their public association with those who owned Jesus as the Christ?

On Expecting, Seeing, and Believing

WHATEVER ATTRACTIONS SUCH a hypothesis may hold for anyone seeking grist for a skeptical mill, it doesn't hold water when applied to the evidence we have. To begin with, one of the first things to strike any reader of the resurrection stories is that, despite what we have just seen to be true about the wider hopes of Judaism, the disciples of Jesus themselves certainly weren't expecting what happened and had the hardest time recognizing it and taking it on board when it did. If, for instance, we take John's account of what happened on the Sunday morning after the crucifixion and burial of Jesus, when Mary Magdalene arrives at the burial site to find the stone removed and the tomb itself empty, she runs excitedly to find Peter and the disciple whom Jesus loved and tells them . . . what?[10] That Jesus has risen, just as he said he would? That they should go and tell the others and prepare for a celebration? No. She tells them exactly what she concludes must have happened: "They have taken the Lord out of the tomb, and we do not know where they have laid him." Mary's natural supposition when confronted with the empty tomb, in other words, is hardly that of an overactive, credulous religious imagination so heavenly minded as to be unable to see some fairly obvious down-to-earth realities. On the contrary, we might even be inclined to accuse her of demonstrating a lack of biblically informed faith and judgment; but then again, we've read the rest of the story and she hadn't. So she supposes what anyone might naturally suppose in the circumstance. Someone, probably the authorities, has been here at an hour even earlier than Mary herself, adding insult to the injury of Jesus's execution by indulging in a macabre bit of Burke and Hare by exhuming Jesus's corpse, stealing it, and presumably dumping it in an unmarked grave where it could rot with discreet anonymity (perhaps to prevent his tomb from becoming a focus for unhealthy sentimental attachment and even religious pilgrimage among his followers). It is still shock and grief that Mary pours out to her friends, not yet the excited good news of verse 18. So much, then, for Mary. But here, next, come the men—Jesus's closest friends and associates. Surely we can expect better from them. They'll get it sorted out and into a proper theological perspective, won't they?

Well, we're told, having heard Mary's testimony, Peter and the other disciple run as fast as their legs will carry them through the still darkened streets to the burial site. And when they get there, they stoop down and peer into the tomb entrance to discover that what Mary has told them is indeed true. Jesus's body is gone. Peter (always a bit of a "belt and braces" man) pushes past the other disciple and crawls into the tomb on his hands and knees just to make sure that it's not a trick of the dawn light or that the body hasn't slid to one side, becoming obscured by the shadows. I'm the type of person who locks the front door of the house, climbs into the car, starts the engine, and is just about to put the car into gear and drive off when, just to make absolutely sure, I put the parking brake back on and hop out of the car again (leaving the engine running) to check that I did actually turn the key in the door before taking it out of the lock. I've even been known to do this more than once on the same occasion. So I can identify with Peter. He wants to be absolutely certain that his eyes aren't deceiving him. But they aren't. Jesus is gone. At this point, John tells us, "the other disciple, who reached the tomb first, also went in, and he saw and believed."[11] Believed *what*, exactly? Do we have here at last a disciple with his wits about him, primed and ready to see what there is to be seen? Well, apparently not. What he *believed* was not that Jesus had been raised by God from death but that the tomb had been desecrated and the body taken away, just as Mary had said. "For," John explains, dealing patiently with his readers as well as the characters in his story, "as yet they did not understand the scripture, that he must rise from the dead. Then the disciples returned to their homes."[12]

What John is describing here is clearly not the response of an excited religious expectation set to burst into fervor at the slightest shred of ambiguous evidence which might confirm rather than contradict its hopes. On the contrary, the bewildered and uncomprehending initial responses of these and other disciples in the Gospels to the fact of the resurrection make it abundantly clear that they couldn't see what, from our perspective as readers of the whole story, was staring them plainly in the face. And they couldn't see it, couldn't see the significance of the empty tomb, couldn't even recognize Jesus himself at first not just because an empty tomb does not a resurrection make (which is true, though it's not a bad start) or because Jesus looked "different" in his new, resurrected body (which also seems to have been true) but because we can only ever "see" what we are ready to see, what we are able to process and make some sort of sense of. Anything that blows the circuits of our minds or refuses to fit onto the map of reality with which we approach its terrain will remain hidden from us, our imagination airbrushing it out of consideration and persuading us that we are seeing something else instead. We know this from a thousand everyday experiences where we have completely failed to recognize something or someone because they cropped up in a strange context, or we were seeing them from an unusual angle, or we were expecting to see someone or something else. Sometimes we can't see what is there in front of us simply because we are not prepared to see it. And the disciples, John is pointing out, weren't ready to recognize what had happened before dawn on that first Easter day—weren't even ready to recognize Jesus himself when he met with them, because they weren't *expecting* to see him ever again. As far as they were concerned, the crucifixion had brought the whole sorry episode to a grisly end because, as Tom Wright aptly observes, "crucifixion meant that the kingdom hadn't come, not that it had. Crucifixion of a would-be Messiah meant that he wasn't the Messiah, not that he was."[13] For the disciples, therefore, he adds, the game was already over. Far from a messianic hope baited and awaiting some presumed-still-to-come miraculous endorsement, their faith in Jesus's messiahship was by now in shreds, having died on the cross with Jesus himself. They were not looking for anything more, not expecting anything more, not hoping for anything more. Instead, disillusioned and afraid for their own lives, they packed up and prepared to head for home.

They couldn't see what was there to be seen, couldn't recognize it, because their expectations were not suitably adjusted, and expectation shapes the substance of perception, giving us, in some measure, eyes to see what is there to be seen. How can this lack of expectation possibly be explained, though, given what we have already conceded—namely, that bodily resurrection was an image alive and kicking in the Jewish religion of the day and part and parcel of how most Jews of the time would think about the future redemption of the world in God's hands? How could it be, indeed, when these same disciples had been in Jesus's company for months and years and heard him say repeatedly things like "The Son of Man must undergo great suffering . . . and be killed, and after three days rise again"?[14] When he did so, though, it threw them into a flat spin, leaving them, in Martin Luther's image, "like cows staring at a new gate"; befuddled; and "questioning what this rising from the dead could mean."[15] Were they, then, we might wonder, exceptionally stupid and cloth eared as well as religiously ill informed? The answer, of course, is no—they were not these things. But the clue to the disciples' difficulty lies precisely here, in holding together the shape and substance of Jewish hopes on the one hand and Jesus's teaching (and, duly, the course of the actual events) on the other. As in so much that proved to be true about Jesus, here too his fulfillment of the religious expectations of Israel was hardly a neat fit, more often challenging and modifying than simply endorsing the form those expectations had come to take—refusing to be contained by them but instead forever breaking out of them and breaking them wide open in the process. There was a painful crunch of gears to be dealt with, therefore, by those who would own Jesus as the Christ, a basic mismatch between the dimensions and contours of the familiar hope and the reality itself that, when it finally arrived, transformed that familiar version radically and in ways that proved too difficult for some to stomach.

Dead Messiahs Don't Rise . . .

THIS IS FAMILIAR stuff, as we have just noted, when it comes to Jesus's weakness, suffering, and death, these not exactly being the traits Jews were expecting or hoping for in one whose job it was to set them free and usher in God's kingdom. The reality of a "suffering Messiah" was always bound to be a stumbling block, or *skandalon*, to those looking for and wanting a redemption more *Game of Thrones* in tone than Gandhi.[16] But it wasn't just his passion and death that threw them. Jesus's resurrection (and the things Jesus himself said about it before his death) was also seriously out of sync with what ordinary Jews like the disciples already understood by the term—so far removed from what they were looking or hoping for, in fact, as to make it difficult even to locate them on the same map, let alone identify the one as the obvious "fulfillment" of the other.

This point is illustrated simply enough again by John's story in chapter 11 of Jesus raising (or, more precisely, resuscitating) Lazarus, summoning him out of the tomb in which he (and the smell of death and decay) has been securely sealed for four days. Before performing this remarkable "sign" (John's preferred word for Jesus's miracles), Jesus tells Martha, "Your brother will rise again."[17] From the reader's point of view, and with the benefit of dramatic irony, the statement is ambiguous, alluding playfully to what is just about to happen. But it evokes from Martha a perfect summary of what *rising again* means and can mean in her religious world and that of Jesus's other disciples. "I know that he will rise again in the resurrection on the last day," she responds.[18] Clearly, though, for Martha, in the immediate emotional aftermath of Lazarus's death, this is relatively cold comfort, akin to being assured by the pastor, with a kindly handshake, that "you'll be united with him again in the next world"—a comforting thought but not much salve for the raw wound of grief. Jesus presses on, using the moment as the opportunity for a bit of peripatetic theologizing: "*I* am the resurrection and the life," he says. "Those who believe in me, even though they die, will live. . . . Do you believe this?" Again, Martha's response is revealing. "Yes, Lord," she says, "I believe that you are the Messiah, the Son of God, the one coming into the world."[19]

What, then, do we learn from this? First, and most obviously, for Martha and the other Jews who had gathered together to see what Jesus was up to now, "resurrection" was on the map clearly enough, but resurrection belonged to a bigger package of things believed about what would occur *on the last day*—that is to say, on the Day of the Lord, when God would bring history to its close, exercise his judgment on the nations, fulfill his promises to Israel, and make all things new.[20] And while bodily resurrection was part and parcel of all this, it wasn't even the most important piece on the board or the particular focus of anyone's longing. It was just one strand in the way Jews had come to imagine what we loosely term *the end of the world* (which in one sense is not its "end" at all but the point of its new beginning—that is, of its "end" or fulfillment in the other sense). The end of the world, though, Martha could safely presume, as we all naturally tend to, was about as far away from the here and now as it was possible to get. And when it came, of course, the end of the world would be something that happened to *everyone*. What no one could make much sense of, therefore, was the suggestion that "resurrection" was something that had already happened, could happen, or was ever likely to happen *before* the conflagration of the end of the world—that is, in the midst of history—and to a particular isolated individual.[21] To think along such lines was a serious religious category error, like a child asking his or her primary teacher, "Where is 9?"—and it simply made no sense. The resurrection of Jesus wasn't so much something *unexpected*, therefore, as something impossible to compute, modifying the rules of engagement so drastically that it became impossible to play the game at all. And, we should note, although Martha reaches naturally for a christological response to Jesus's probing question, it's clear that she's still playing by the old rules and that while those rules certainly associate the Messiah directly with the end of the world (and all that goes with that), they equally clearly do not know anything about "resurrection" (any more than suffering and crucifixion) being something the Messiah himself will have personally to undergo first in order to fulfill his office and prove his bona fides.

Knowing this, we see why it makes perfect sense that the disciples should, on a host of occasions, have demonstrated puzzlement or incredulity when Jesus gestured toward what "must" and was going to happen to him when they reached Jerusalem for that last time. Knowing this, we understand it makes perfect sense, too, that the evidence of the empty tomb should have been met at first with incomprehension and a lack of recognition among Jesus's friends. Knowing this, though, we grasp that what makes absolutely no sense at all is the suggestion that the stories of Jesus's resurrection are likely to have emerged or been concocted by the disciples or anyone else in order to provide imaginative "closure" to hopes, expectations, and messianic claims rudely broken and left hanging on the cross. *They weren't expecting it.* And when it came, therefore, *they didn't recognize it and couldn't see it.* Afterward, and with the benefit of hindsight, they could see (or learned to see) that what had happened was indeed bound up with those ancient hopes, that it was, in fact, in a sense both the fulfillment and the decisive anticipation of God's promises about the "end of the world." And now, at last, they began to find textual traces of it, fragments of foretelling in their scriptural heritage which, hitherto, had remained opaque and unclear. At the time, though, neither its occurrence nor Jesus's predictions of it made any apparent sense at all. Whatever the disciples had expected, it certainly wasn't this, and so when it happened, they just didn't get it. And what they first "believed" to have happened, therefore, was something quite different, more or less in tune, indeed, with what you or I might naturally have supposed had happened.

From the Ridiculous to the Sublime

HOW, THEN, CAN the stories in the form in which we have received them best be accounted for in historical terms? More widely, how might the radically new, unparalleled notion of resurrection demanded by these stories have arisen—involving, as it did, a total overhaul of what first-century Jewish monotheism understood the term to mean, leaving it barely recognizable at first glance? And more challenging still, how are we to reckon with the indisputable and remarkable fact that those whose testimony lay behind the stories themselves had clearly been transformed more or less overnight from a bedraggled bunch of seeming losers, skulking in the shadows and barricading themselves behind locked doors for fear of their own lives, into an energetic and fearless gang of guerrilla preachers, throwing themselves excitedly into the task of sharing the story of Jesus regardless of the threat to personal life and limb? It was almost as if the world itself had shifted on its axis, suddenly looking and feeling altogether differently than it had, bathed now in a radically different light which changed everything—their assumptions; their priorities; their sense of possibility; their understanding of history, God, and God's ways with the world; and of course, their understanding of Jesus. All this had been thrown abruptly into flux, and as it settled again, it dawned on them that the world was no longer the same place. "Reality" was no longer what they had taken it to be.

Whatever it was that had happened to them, in other words, the disciples now finally "got it," suddenly saw for the first time something that had been staring them in the face all along, and whatever it was, it changed everything. At the center of this new, still-coalescing pattern, it seems, two convictions in particular lay: First, despite all appearances, death was in reality no longer to be feared as "the last enemy,"[22] robbing them of their capacity to enjoy all that was good in God's world, or the ultimate weapon of injustice, wielded by those whose might already constrained the opportunities and the aspirations of the weak and the poor.[23] Second, Jesus must in fact have been precisely who he had always indicated he was, which meant that they needed now to revisit all that he had said and done and all that had happened to him and rethink not just their notion of resurrection but their theology as a whole and from the ground up. The dictionary entry for "God" (as in "kingdom of . . .") must now be rewritten. This conviction about Jesus changed everything. It was the news that energized the apostles' acts of "guerrilla theater" from the outset, as Luke's report of Peter's sermon on the day of Pentecost makes quite clear:[24] "This Jesus," he tells the curious, potentially hostile crowd of bystanders (devout Jews from all over the empire who had traveled to Jerusalem to celebrate the ancient religious festival and perhaps were unlikely, therefore, to respond enthusiastically to any new-fangled, revisionist, "liberal" hijacking of it), "God raised up, and of that all of us are witnesses. . . . Therefore let the entire house of Israel know with certainty that God has made him both Lord and Messiah, this Jesus whom you crucified."[25] It may not quite be the longest suicide note in history, but given what had happened to Jesus himself only a few weeks previously in this same place and with the collusion of the same crowds, it's unlikely to have been a claim voiced with anything less than absolute conviction.

Implausibly, It Makes Perfect Sense

HOW COULD THIS death-defying conviction (from which the whole theology of the New Testament slowly but surely emerged) have arisen given all that we have seen? As numerous commentators have suggested, in historical terms, there is no reasonable scope for doubt that the disciples themselves *believed* this to be true. They staked their own lives on it. So what could suffice to account for that unwavering belief? "History" in this sense, of course, is produced as we weigh, evaluate, and interpret whatever evidence we possess about times past. Historians' precise concern is always with the particular events of the human past, but in making sense of that, they will naturally also be bound to appeal to generalities of human experience, operating reasonably enough with the assumption that lots of things don't change much under the sun where human beings are concerned, and the shape of the past is very likely, therefore, in all sorts of ways to have been broadly consistent with the shape of the present. Working on this basis (the so-called principle of analogy), the historical imagination presents us with a reasoned account of what *probably* occurred and why, given the nature of the evidence at its disposal.

Sometimes the results of this sort of historical reconstruction may be acclaimed as possessing a high degree of probability ("What *almost certainly* happened was . . ."), but not even the best historical account can lay claim to the sort of certainty that we tend nowadays, as we have already noticed, naturally to crave and to exalt as an ideal where knowing things is concerned. That sort of "logical" certainty simply isn't available in our dealings with things happening in the real world, and we are bound to fall short of it, therefore, even when dealing with things happening relatively close at hand, let alone at the distance of decades, centuries, or millennia. In reality, the shortfall is often far more considerable (and the scope for differing interpretations and accounts of things greater) than the historians among us care to admit. Nor, of course, being concerned properly only with the patterns and probabilities of things that have happened, are historians in a position at any time *as historians* to pronounce authoritatively on what sorts of things are possible and impossible or to insist that, the world being the sort of place that it is, certain sorts of things "could never have" happened. Such knowledge, desirable though it may be, doesn't lend itself to the tools, methods, and materials of historical study, lying even beyond the purview and jurisdiction of the hard sciences. It falls properly within a different domain of knowing altogether, one serviced intellectually by disciplines such as philosophy and theology and more accessibly in the forms of religion, myth, and story. Historians, though, are human beings like the rest of us, and as such, all of them will tend to buy into some prevailing set of assumptions about such things (what is possible or even plausible) because, as we shall see in a later chapter, human societies and cultures naturally embed and embody beliefs about all sorts of things, weaving them into the fabric of their popular forms for our consumption and digestion. Only when we are aware of what we believe, or what we simply assume and take for granted, about these sorts of questions are we able to monitor the impact such assumptions might have on our interrogation and interpretation of evidence, whether historical, scientific, or some other sort.[26]

I point all this out because Christian belief in the resurrection of Jesus, as part of the wider testimony to the incarnation, occupies rather an odd place where the labors of historians are concerned. On the one hand, it is quite clearly a belief about something *factual*—something, that is to say, which the first witnesses themselves were convinced had actually occurred at a particular time and place and within the flesh-and-blood stuff of their own lives. In this sense, it is certainly a claim about something "historical" and thus cannot claim any diplomatic immunity from investigation by those whose skills lie in making the best sense of whatever evidential traces remain available for scrutiny. In this case, as in most cases lying so far back in the past, those traces are predominantly textual—the written reports and stories of the alleged event itself and what followed on from it. We have considered only some of these traces above, but it is sufficient to give a broadly reliable picture of them. Now, if history itself can, as I have suggested, only ever tell us what is most *likely* to have happened and, in doing so, must draw in significant part on the generalities of human existence and experience, then clearly, when it comes to the alleged occurrence of an event acknowledged from the outset by the eyewitnesses and all concerned to have been wholly unprecedented—a unique interruption of the general run of things (this, indeed, being precisely its point)—historians as such can hardly be expected, let alone permitted, to offer a definitive judgment or "proof" one way or another. Nor in judging the most probable explanation for the evidence should they be allowed to smuggle beliefs about what is possible or plausible (what could or could not have occurred) onto one or the other side of the scale when such evidence is being weighed. As Wright notes, such convictions may duly persuade particular historians to demur to what otherwise seems the most obvious or likely explanation and to prefer to seek another (otherwise less persuasive) one instead, but these same convictions cannot be allowed to masquerade as objective, "historical" considerations on the basis of which definitive conclusions must be reached.[27] And when all the evidence we have alluded to above is put on the table, as Wright and many others have suggested, the most straightforward and obvious explanation for the stories as we have them and for the convictions of the earliest Christian believers that lie behind them is that the disciples had indeed found the tomb empty and subsequently encountered Jesus in person in a form that was undeniably "bodily," even though that body equally clearly didn't belong properly in this world, being instead, as the apostle Paul suggests, precisely the "first fruits" (our technological age might reach instead for the metaphor "prototype") of a coming world that has been renewed by the promise and the love of God.[28]

Clearly, Christian faith will welcome the suggestion that this implausible scenario nonetheless affords the most plausible way of accounting for such evidence as exists, but other explanations are certainly possible, and no amount of historical evidence or argument alone is ever likely to convince someone that Jesus is indeed risen any more than the empty tomb alone led the disciples to jump to that conclusion. In both circumstances, importantly, it is encountering the risen Christ himself alone that suffices to generate faith in him as the Lord. And that faith itself, of course, might perfectly well have accommodated some other, "purely spiritual" version of his "rising" and continued personal existence, had Jesus's friends and disciples not had to grapple instead with the inconvenient facts of the matter—that his tomb was now standing empty and he himself had been present among them repeatedly in a manner that was quite obviously "flesh and blood," albeit flesh and blood not as we know it. Whether we like it or not as Christians, though, those alleged facts thrust the substance of this creedal claim into the forum where matters of "fact" are made sense of by historians, scientists, and others. But given what we have seen, if Christian belief in the bodily resurrection of Jesus cannot claim the intellectual high ground of indisputable historical or scientific warrant, nor has it anything to fear from either history or science as such. Personal beliefs that predispose individual practitioners of these disciplines to claim that "things like that just don't happen" are neither historical nor scientific in the relevant sense, tending themselves, therefore, to fall foul of the same evidential prescriptions and demands wielded by those who quietly rely on them and certainly lacking the endorsement of the academic disciplines concerned. Furthermore, far from enjoying the kudos of peculiarly modern or enlightened convictions, such beliefs have their dogmatic roots and forebears (whether they realize it or not) in religious and philosophical traditions ancient enough for Christian belief in bodily resurrection to present itself—ironically but with impunity—as a relatively novel idea by comparison. And, of course, there are plenty of other historians and scientists whose professional judgments and accomplishments are unscathed by the fact that they do not share or collude with these intellectual prejudices.

Resurrection, Repentance, and Renewal

THE STORY IS told of an Anglican clergyman who, on a visit to a diocese in the United Kingdom from a partner diocese somewhere in sub-Saharan Africa, was invited to lead the Easter Sunday worship in a local congregation and was rather nervous about the fact that his English was not particularly good. But he'd managed to get hold of the liturgy booklet in advance and had done some homework, reading over the material, practicing pronunciations, and so on. What he hadn't quite grasped, though, was the difference between parts of the liturgy in ordinary print and those bits of "rubric" in italics giving instructions and stage directions about one thing and another. And so as the service reached a moment of particular dramatic intensity, his voice was to be heard booming confidently across the church: "Jesus is risen!—*Except in Lent*"!

The fact that belief in the bodily resurrection of Jesus necessarily makes itself vulnerable and lays claim to a reckoning in what we may carefully refer to as both the "public" and the "private" spheres of knowledge in modern Western societies is challenging for those who believe it as well as those who don't[29]—because it raises fundamental questions not just for the sort of worldview that would exclude consideration of God's presence and purposes altogether but equally for one that would happily relegate such consideration to some strictly "spiritual" and private sphere of personal religious concern where it is unlikely to impinge on large tracts of our personal and social existence, not least those bound up with matters of justice, economics, politics, and the pursuit of the common good. A God whose purposes involve raising the dead, though, lays claim to lordship over the whole territory of our lives and, indeed, of creation itself. Such a God will not be contained in any "purely religious" box in which we seek to put him. And those who genuinely believe in a God who raises the dead will not be able to keep that belief hidden away for six days of the week, conveniently disentangled from their activities in the home, in the workplace, in the marketplace, in the polling booth, online, or wherever else.

Jesus is risen!—except in Lent. Or Jesus is risen!—except on those occasions when I'm confronted with an opportunity to take a stand for him in public and so risk rejection and ridicule; or except when I'm filling out my annual tax return or putting in an expense claim; or except when I'm deciding whether to invest in stocks and shares likely to see a significant return but involving companies having ethically dubious dealings; or except when we are urged to act in ways that minimize damage to the planet rather than prioritizing our own comfort and convenience; or except when the answer to the question "Who is my neighbor?" appears, annoyingly, to be someone or some group whose fate and well-being we would rather not concern ourselves with, let alone treat as the rightful object of our love. We could continue in this vein for a long time, and each of us could supply our own uncomfortable examples. Jesus is risen!—but not when it's inconvenient, uncomfortable, risky, or costly for me to face the reality and the implications of his *being* risen.

One way of defining Christian discipleship, I suppose, is as a way of living in which the fact that Jesus is risen cuts identifiably into every situation and every moment of every day and makes an identifiable difference so that how I choose to spend my leisure time, what I do with my income or my possessions, how I deal with other people, and how I think about myself and the sort of person I aspire to be are all affected directly by the knowledge that Jesus is risen. It is the knowledge that compels our constant repentance—the wholesale revaluation of every aspect of our lives during every waking moment of our lives in the light of Christ's own, turning away from whatever contradicts or resists the claim of his humanity on ours, turning to him, and declaring our determination to live instead in accordance with what in him we have discovered we already are and are called to become. No part of our lives can remain unscathed by this knowledge because in his death and resurrection the whole of our humanity, every part of it, was put to death, cured of its unholy alliance with sin and death, and raised up to a radically new sort of life. The *whole* of our humanity. Even the bits which seem mundane and hardly worth bothering God with, the trivial likes and dislikes, habits and hobbies, hopes and fears; even the bits we think are still securely under our control and where our darkest, shameful, and most sinister secrets are, we think, kept carefully hidden from anyone's gaze; even the bits we feel sure God can have no time or place for; even the bits we fear would be bound to provoke God's disgust or displeasure if we were to allow God anywhere near them; even the bits we suppose, if pressed, are none of God's legitimate business and to the title deeds of which we cling resolutely, determined to retain sovereign jurisdiction over them. But in the incarnation, the *whole* of our humanity has been laid claim to and laid hold of by God, putting to death in it everything that is opposed to God and unfit to be in his presence, filling it with his Holy Spirit and fashioning it anew in his own image, drawing it fully into God's own life as the object of his forgiving and transforming love, fit now to share God's joy and to enjoy his glory forever. The resurrection of Jesus from death is the sign that this has happened and will happen, the era of a new creation is upon us, and nothing can ever be the same again.

7

"HE ASCENDED INTO HEAVEN, HE IS SEATED ON THE RIGHT HAND OF GOD THE FATHER ALMIGHTY…"

NOTICE THAT WITH this clause of the creed, our attention shifts identifiably from things past to things present, from things done to things resulting from things done. The narration of God's saving activity in Christ's human history now reaches its end, and a new phase of God's (and Christ's) relationship to the world is embarked upon. The "ascension," as it is commonly called, occurs a whole forty days after the resurrection of Jesus from death, and with it, a watershed is reached. The things that Jesus did, said, and suffered while present among us humanly are now over, and Jesus returns to his Father, from whence, at the story's outset, he "came down" to pitch his tent in our midst.

At once, as intelligent men and women, we stumble over the language and imagery involved and are compelled to wonder whether and how we can take it seriously. All this "up-and-down" stuff doesn't cut much ice in a world where astronomy and geology, respectively, paint a different picture of what is to be found in those directions. That may have been good enough for first-century Palestinians, we suppose, but those of us who shuttle up and down the world's airways know perfectly well that "ascending" increasingly gets you nowhere other than a cramped seat with coffee and UHT milk, plus a bag of complimentary peanuts if you're lucky. But once again, in reality, this sort of objection demonstrates far more naivete than it ascribes to our ancient forebears themselves, who may or may not have entertained odd ideas about the geography of the cosmos but who certainly knew how spatial categories were meant to function theologically and liturgically. They knew that, in one sense, the one we call God is everywhere and not limited by space as we creatures are, but they believed too that God has his own special "place" (How else might one express the matter?) "from" which God comes to be with and alongside us, and it was perfectly natural in speaking of this place ("heaven") to picture it as high-up, a spatial metaphor which still pervades our ways of referring to that which is better, more exalted, and so on. But to ask "How high? How many meters or miles?" is to commit a logical category error; it's the wrong sort of question to ask, whether what is being referred to as "high and lifted up" is God, the queen, the president, or the inflated prices of college fees and designer jeans.

So we needn't and shouldn't get hung up on the choreography or the physics of the circumstance. What Luke tells us, at the end of his Gospel and again in the first chapter of the book of Acts, is that Jesus "withdrew from them and was carried up into heaven" and that "he was lifted up, and a cloud took him out of their sight."[1] Precisely what it was that Jesus's disciples saw and heard we will never know, but it was clearly sufficient to leave them with the clear impression that this was not just another resurrection appearance (notice that all the resurrection appearances end with Jesus's sudden disappearance) but a more final departure from them, and it was of such a sort as to convince them that this particular withdrawal signaled Jesus's return to his Father—in other words, *to be where God is*, a circumstance they would naturally have expressed as "ascending" or being "taken up" (Luke's mention of clouds, of course, having nothing to do with meteorology but being the familiar symbol of God's presence and glory into which Jesus is here translated). So we no more need to suppose a literal elevation of Jesus into midair at this point than we should quietly add a stork, spacecraft, or escalator to the nativity story with which Luke's Gospel opens. It is certainly a story about "coming down," but no vertical transportation was involved in either case, because none was needed.

Proximity, Proclamation, and Presence

THE NEW TESTAMENT writers refer elsewhere to this final departure of Jesus in a variety of ways. Some use the same language of his "ascension,"[2] others of his "being exalted" or being "taken up,"[3] others still of his "going to the Father"[4] or "going into heaven."[5] The language may vary, but the idea is the same one: Jesus, having once come from the Father to be with us, has now been taken back to be with his Father, and the disciples cannot expect to see him "in the flesh" any longer. In that circumstance, we might reasonably suppose that the disciples would be grieved or fearful. After all, having experienced the joy of the resurrection, having had Jesus restored to them after his arrest and death (albeit not quite the same as he had been previously), this second separation would surely have come as a bitter blow. But in fact, the very opposite seems to have been the case. Instead, Luke tells us, "they worshipped him, and returned to Jerusalem with great joy; and they were continually in the temple blessing God."[6]

The reason seems to have been that the penny had finally dropped, and some of the things Jesus had said to them all along about coming from, being sent by, and going back to his Father began to make some semblance of sense. (For a sustained reflection on the theme, see esp. John 14.) And in any case, this departure wasn't really a departure from them at all but an entry into a new phase and a new mode or manner of being with them. "Remember," Jesus tells them in Matthew's account of the same event, "I am with you always, to the end of the age."[7] "With" them and with others not just in the form of happy memories or as some ghostly presence coming and going in the manner of a haunting but *in precisely the way that God is with them*—holding them, surrounding them, sustaining them, closer even than they are to themselves. In fact, Jesus tells them, paradoxically, he must "go away" precisely so that he can always be with them through his Spirit, whom he will send.[8] So, far from leaving them alone, Jesus withdraws precisely so that he need never leave them alone again but can be present to them whenever and wherever they are, the limits and constraints of bodily existence in the world (where, despite the demands that life increasingly seems to place on us, we cannot actually be in more than one place at once) having been suspended by his return to be "with the Father." And if Jesus was now truly with the Father, then what more natural than that they should rush back to Jerusalem and spend their days in the temple, that concrete symbolic focus of God's presence in which heaven and earth were believed to meet and interpenetrate? Again, the symbolic force of all this talk of coming and going and being with is what matters, not the geometry or geography.

We'll return to that thought shortly. But first, it may be worth noting something further about this question of Jesus's presence and absence. It's not uncommon for people to say things like "It would be much easier for me to believe in Jesus if I could actually meet him in the flesh" or "It was OK for the disciples and others who saw Jesus doing things and heard him teaching. It's much more difficult for us, who only have stories about him to rely on." Perhaps we've sometimes felt something similar ourselves. Didn't the disciples have an unfair advantage over the rest of us? Well, they had a particular job to do, which was to bear eyewitness testimony to what they had seen and heard. But the suggestion that being there in the flesh was necessarily any sort of advantage as far as hearing and seeing the reality of what was going on in Jesus ought to be dispelled by the slightest reflection on it. The disciples themselves, who spent hours every day in Jesus's presence, were clearly blind and deaf to that reality much of the time, even when Jesus took them aside and spelled it out for them. What they lacked was precisely eyes to see and ears to hear, and the matter was far worse with the crowds, let alone the Pharisees, scribes, and teachers of the law.

As the Danish philosopher and theologian Søren Kierkegaard pointed out long ago, where the faith that discerns God's presence and activity in Jesus is concerned, a flesh-and-blood encounter with Jesus himself was quite clearly no advantage at all, a fact that compels us to pursue a slightly different understanding of what contemporaneity with Christ and the form of Christ's presence in the midst of history (there and then or here and now) actually means.[9] Such faith (the faith that opens eyes and unstops ears and enables us to grasp what is going on in Jesus) is a gift of God's Spirit. Without that gift, without the work of God *within* us to accompany the work of God alongside or in front of us, we shall never grasp its meaning, and nor would or could the disciples have done so. The simple human realities of Jesus's life as such, odd though they were in all sorts of ways, did not suffice to convince anyone who bumped into or stood and watched and listened to him (i.e., his *historical* contemporaries—those on the scene of gospel occurrences) that this was God himself at work for the sake of the world's redemption. Such things are not patient of explicit, unequivocal, cannot-possibly-be-overlooked-or-denied presentation. They belong to a deeper level of things and require a deeper sort of "seeing" than that provided by the retina and optic nerve. And for that deeper seeing and hearing to occur, what matters is the work of God, of God's Spirit, of the Spirit of Christ himself present in us and at work in us. It is a God-enabled response to the deeper realities of what Jesus did and said and the things that happened to him. For that to occur, of course, we do not need to have been present there in the dust and the sun and the flies of rural Palestine at all. God has engineered things in such a way that, being rooted in the particularities of human history, Jesus's life and work could only be played out in the presence of a tiny handful of the many millions of humans for whom they hold redemptive significance (and of those handful, as we've just reminded ourselves, the vast majority continued nonetheless wholly undisturbed and none the wiser about what they had seen and heard). For those beyond this limited circle of historical occurrence, the challenge and the response of faith comes not by seeing, hearing, and touching the Word of Life—as John tells us the apostles had[10]—but through the less immediate means of human testimony.

Most of our meaningful dealings with reality come to us in this indirect way, in the form of the stories we tell one another about what has happened and what it means, the moment of immediate flesh-and-blood experience itself being in any case both wider than our focal field and wafer thin, forever disappearing imperceptibly but definitely beyond the reach of the present moment into the territory of the present perfect—of that which *has* happened. So testimony—storytelling—is far more dominant and vital in our knowing of things than we tend to recognize. Storytelling selects from the barrage of things in our day-to-day experiences what it takes to be the most interesting and significant among them, and links them in a pattern (a "story line") within which they follow on meaningfully from one another and through which the various characters in the story (ourselves or other people) emerge and cohere. And for everyone except those original eyewitnesses, it is precisely by the story of Jesus being told, by the particular stories about Jesus being transmitted within and by the church, that the knowing of Jesus himself is mediated and occurs, the flesh and blood of testimony, of embodied narration and performance being the means now whereby Jesus's presence among us is manifest and made concrete in the midst of every new time and place and culture and individual life story. It has always been like that, and in reality, few of us would really wish to swap places with the apostles in their peculiar task of getting the storytelling ball rolling. The character of Jesus, unfolded in the various stories that faith tells about him, is the concrete form which his personal encounter with us takes and through which our response to him is elicited. Let's be clear—we are not talking here merely about an imagined contemporaneity of the sort we might enjoy with the character in any well-told story from the past. Imagination aplenty is certainly involved, but if the one we are dealing with here is the *risen* Lord—the same Jesus whose story the Gospels tell—then these stories should be understood as the form under which Jesus himself takes our imagination captive and makes himself present to us, just as he once captured the imagination of those who were his flesh-and-blood contemporaries. Now as then, though, his mere presence alone in this form is not, in and of itself, irresistibly compelling, and as his story is told, our freedom and ability to respond in faith remain securely, as they ever were, in the hands of God's Spirit.

We might unpack all this in more theologically precise technical terms, insisting that the process by which anyone is drawn into the life of faith is thus a fully trinitarian one—the Father sending his Son into the world for all; the Son in his life, death, and resurrection offering our shared humanity to the Father in the Spirit's power; and the Holy Spirit working in the world, in the church, and in us to kindle that faith that alone grasps and responds appropriately to the reality of what has occurred. Such theologically compressed statements can be useful and even important, but we mustn't allow this one to obscure or lose sight of the vital role that the story of Jesus has to play, as though, instead, there were some vague, general "spirituality" summoned forth by God, a religious response for the purposes of which familiarity with the figure of Jesus himself is largely incidental. The Holy Spirit, we must never forget, is the Spirit of Christ, the Spirit poured out upon Jesus by the Father. And the faith that the Spirit enables is always a response to this same Jesus—the one we meet in the Gospels. Another way of putting this might be to remind ourselves again that the risen and ascended Lord was recognized by the disciples as the selfsame Jesus they had shared adventures with for three years or more before he was arrested and put to death. His risen hands still bore the scars of crucifixion, and with that scar tissue the whole story of Jesus's particular life and ministry is carried forward into God's identity and God's future in a defining way, rather than being discarded or left behind as though it were merely an external shell, a husk bearing the seed of an essentially Christless mysticism or generic human religiosity. On the contrary, it is the particular things that Jesus did, and said, and suffered—the "person" we meet in the telling of the stories about these things—that are the very touchstone of Christian faith, for it is in and through and not apart from them that God's character is divulged, and redemption is precisely and only a matter of our being conformed to Jesus's own human likeness. It is this same Jesus, therefore, who is present to us and with us and in us by his Spirit, and "spiritual" experiences which have no direct roots or bearings in the Gospel stories about Jesus are not necessarily "spiritual" in the sense that the New Testament uses that term (i.e., things proper to and summoned forth by God's Holy Spirit, who is also the Spirit of Jesus), whatever else we may wish and have to say about them.[11]

Standing Room Only . . .

LET'S RETURN NOW, then, to the fact that the apostles, in the immediate wake of Jesus's departure to be with his Father, "worshiped him . . . ; and they were continually in the temple blessing God."[12] And let me pick up again the point I made earlier: Jesus was understood not to be absent from them but, even though no longer present with them in flesh and blood (in the time and space of our embodied existence), to be now nonetheless personally present to them and with them and in them *in precisely the way that God was and is.* To grasp this and the implications of what is being said when with the New Testament, we say that Jesus "ascended" and is now "seated at the Father's right hand," helps us see in this creedal claim not an otherwise odd and awkward appendage to the story of Jesus but instead its proper completion and, as the writer to the Hebrews suggests, as having to do with the very sheet anchor of our faith as Christians.[13] If the previous few clauses deal with Jesus's saving person and work there and then, this one has everything to do with his continuing work for us and in us and in the world.

The Jewish Bible, as we have already seen, characteristically pictures God as seated on the throne of the universe, all things being under his dominion.[14] As the creator of all things, God is also the Lord of all things, and as such, God alone is deserving of worship. The imagery of a throne room and a throne on which God sits is borrowed from Near Eastern politics, where kings and emperors held court and exercised their rule. As an extension of this imagery, the idea of someone elevated to "the right hand" of God suggests someone to whom God has granted special status and favor—a dignitary able, perhaps, to exercise some of God's authority on God's behalf as a grand vizier or prime minister might be supposed to do. This image, too, is found in the Old Testament in Psalm 110:1: "The LORD says to my lord, 'Sit at my right hand until I make your enemies your footstool.'" This is a text that clearly became very important in the early church, as it occurs or is alluded to more than twenty times (referring to Jesus's exaltation by his Father), far more than any other Old Testament text. And it is the source, of course, of this image in our creedal clause. Jesus has now been exalted to the Father's right hand. But while this might feasibly be understood as referring to a creature to whom special privilege and status have been granted, the way the New Testament writers actually interpret it is radically different.

Remember, a fundamental premise of Judaism in New Testament times (as in the Old Testament itself) was that God and God alone could be said to have created all things and so to rule over all things. That was what distinguished God from anything and everything else. Angels and even other "gods" (if there were such) were included among the "all things" over which God ruled by right, because God had created them. *Only God* rules over all things and does so from a throne that is exalted above all things. Sitting on this throne and exercising supreme rule is what distinguishes God *as God* (though lots of other things, of course, remain to be said about this God). When, therefore, the New Testament writers, as they often do, appropriate this highly charged bit of Old Testament liturgy and say that, by virtue of his exaltation and ascension to God's right hand, Jesus himself, *seated now* at God's right hand, *rules over all things*, the implication will not be lost on any Jewish reader of the text:[15] one who "rules over all things" cannot possibly be a mere creature, no matter how exalted, because such language situates him on the other side of the vital distinction between creature and creator, between "all things" and God. What is being said, therefore, is that Jesus now *shares* God's throne, *sitting* on it together with the Father rather than loitering alongside it, poised to exercise someone else's authority as and when called upon and "authorized" to do so. Richard Bauckham observes in this connection that in the Judaism contemporary with Jesus himself and the New Testament authors, only God is ever pictured as *sitting* on the heavenly throne, this being a significant marker of God's supreme authority. All others—angels, archangels, and so on—are compelled to stand.[16] For the New Testament to refer to Jesus as "seated at God's right hand" in order to share in this authority, therefore, is as unequivocal an image as we are likely to encounter. Jesus sits on the heavenly throne in order to share directly in God's rule over all things, and that means that he exercises his lordship not just *with* God but *as* God.

So, for instance, Ephesians 1:20–22 states, "[God] raised [Jesus] from the dead and seated him at his right hand in the heavenly places, far above all rule and authority and power and dominion, and above every name that is named, not only in this age but also in the age to come. And he has put all things under his feet." Such texts—together with others that ascribe to Jesus a direct sharing in the creating and sustaining of "all things"[17] and others still that refer to him as the proper object of creaturely worship[18]—make it quite clear that Jesus is not simply being situated "alongside" God here but being identified *as* God, included, as Bauckham puts it, "within the unique divine identity."[19] This is what the writer of the Epistle to the Hebrews is at pains to insist in the opening verses of his first chapter: the one through whom God has made himself known is a Son who is himself the creator and sustainer of all things and so the "heir" of all things, by comparison with whom even the most exalted among the angels pale into insignificance *because he is God and they are not.*[20]

This, then, is what lies behind the terse creedal formula according to which Jesus, having ascended into heaven, is now "seated at the right hand of the Father." It is a theological bookend corresponding to "conceived by the Holy Spirit" and reiterating the identity of the one who enters history as no mere creature (let alone a mere man) but the one already identified as the Maker and Sovereign Lord of heaven and earth, *all things* seen and unseen. This, is the reason for suggesting that in this apparently awkward and recondite doctrine, we are actually dealing with the "steadfast anchor of the soul" where Christian faith and hope are concerned.[21] For in the Jesus story, it drives home one last and decisive time (in case we had blinked and missed it) the astounding truth of just who it is that we are dealing with when we deal with Jesus. The one who "came down" has now "ascended," having accomplished all that he came to do on our behalf and for our sake. And that one is none other than God himself, whose "sitting down" provides a suggestive textual echo, perhaps, of Yahweh's "resting" when the hard work of creation was complete and viewing with satisfaction the outcomes of his labors.[22] Such imaginative resonances notwithstanding, though, as believers, our souls are anchored in our grasp of Christ's continuing *activity* rather than inactivity. What is it, then, that we are to think of Jesus *doing* at the Father's right hand, and just how does this ground our believing and our hopeful living?

Resistance Is Fertile

FIRST, AGAIN, PRECISELY because it tells us in no uncertain terms that Jesus, and no one else, is Lord. In fact, this statement ("Jesus is Lord") is one of the earliest and most basic Christian professions of faith, cropping up time and again in the New Testament.[23] And what it means is clear enough in the light of these other biblical affirmations about Jesus's present status and role: Jesus is none other than God himself. It is Jesus who rules over all things in heaven and on earth. It is Jesus in whose hands the direction and the destiny of the world and its history rest. That's good news for everyone because we know Jesus and we know his character, and frankly, it's hard to imagine anyone better into whose hands we would want all things to be entrusted. Of course, the evidence of history itself often hardly suggests that Jesus is Lord any more than the evidence of the cross suggests that he was indeed Israel's king. His lordship is and remains, for now, veiled and hidden. But all power is indeed properly his, and while for now he has returned to the Father and exercises this power largely unseen, he will return to claim and to reveal it. That is the claim and the hope of those who confess him as Lord. God will eventually bring the world's history to its proper end, and the God Christians believe in is exactly like Jesus, because Jesus is God.

Confessing Jesus as Lord, though, is not simply a matter of imaginative projection into the future, when the kingdom of God (which is precisely the same as the lordship of Jesus the King) will be heralded in. Confessing Jesus as Lord is also a matter of handing over any vain efforts to be sovereign in our own lives, permitting him to rule in our lives and over the whole span and spread of them. It is an acknowledgment that even if for now other powers and dominions have their day, the rightful dominion is already Christ's and should be acknowledged and owned by all who have learned this. Christians are like those who know themselves to be the rightful subjects of a king temporarily exiled by civil war but awaiting his return to claim the throne and the land that is rightfully his. In the meanwhile, refusing to bow the knee, refusing to live in accordance with the dictates and policies of "the powers that be," remaining loyal instead to the statutes of the one whose kingdom is coming, they create pockets of resistance to the status quo and work tirelessly to see the true king's reign restored. Like the King himself, in other words, Christians know themselves, in the imagery of John's Gospel, to be immersed *in* the world but not to be *of* it[24]—their citizenship, their allegiance, their fealty visibly lying elsewhere and with another.

A different but related political metaphor for the church is found in the New Testament and developed by Stanley Hauerwas and William Willimon in their eponymous work *Resident Aliens*.[25] Communities of believers, they argue, are in effect small colonies in the midst of a world and culture quite foreign to them in its beliefs, habits, practices, goals, and priorities, a situation that inevitably throws up all manner of questions and challenges related to believers' sense of identity and belonging and how, in practical terms, they should then live. Tom Wright observes the apostle Paul suggesting precisely this, envisaging the church as, in effect, a colony of heaven found on earth.[26] Paul himself was a Roman citizen, and Philippi, for instance, was an outpost of the Roman Empire in Macedonia that, like most such outposts, was home to not just the locals and barracks full of Roman soldiers to keep them in order but a little colony of Roman men, women, and children who spoke Latin rather than the local mumbo jumbo, dressed in whatever the current Roman fashion was, and generally sought to maintain Roman customs and culture in order to civilize wherever it was they happened to find themselves. For them, too, "home" was somewhere else than "here," somewhere they looked forward to returning to, somewhere, in the meanwhile, they sought to keep alive by every means at their disposal. And so in writing to Christian believers in Philippi, Paul draws on the familiar and enjoins them to do the same: Remember, he tells them, that "we are citizens of heaven, and it is from there that we are expecting a Savior, the Lord Jesus Christ."[27] So don't get seduced by the customs and standards of the locals ("the world") but maintain your citizenship by living it out. And again, to the Christians in Colossae (another Roman outpost, this time in Asia Minor), Paul writes, "Seek the things that are above, where Christ is seated at the right hand of God. Set your mind on things that are above, not on things that are on earth."[28]

So, then, that Jesus is Lord ("seated at the right hand of God") is both a matter of future hope and expectancy and a driver of Christian life and discipleship in the present. It is Jesus—who is himself the concrete approach to us of God's forgiving love and mercy; who bodied God's character forth in the world; who shows us the character human life ought to take if it would be in step rather than out of kilter with the grain of the cosmos; who through his Spirit pours his own life into us, causing and enabling us to struggle with our sins; and who left us a wealth of instruction to wrestle and be getting on with—it is this same Jesus to whom human history and what it has made of the world will finally be answerable and in whose hands its future lies. That, and that alone, is the basis of what Christians refer to as the "good news" for the world, providing faith and hope with both a compass and a mooring that can never fail, no matter how choppy or overwhelming the waters of life may be.

Priesthood, Prayer, and Party Animals

FINALLY, WE NEED to mention something left unsaid so far—namely, that in ascending to the Father, there is no suggestion that the Son of God *sheds* the humanity that he has assumed, as though the incarnation (and the union of God's life and ours that it entails) is merely a temporary episode in God's story. On the contrary, Jesus, and our humanity with him, is precisely exalted to the Father's right hand, and this means we must say the almost unsayable and picture the unimaginable—that the man Jesus is now wherever God is, and in him, our humanity is exalted and sharing in the glory of God that is rightfully his. Again, we need not and ought not to get hung up on the spatial and temporal complexities of this. The words merely point, and point inadequately, to the reality of the circumstance. God has united us to himself in his Son, and that union remains in place, God sharing our human creaturehood now for eternity. But there is more to it than this. The writer to the Hebrews in particular draws our attention to the link between the ascension and Jesus's humanity. And he does so by referring us to an ancient religious ritual of Israel whereby on the Day of Atonement, the high priest entered the holy of holies bearing the names of all the tribes of Israel on the breastplate of his priestly costume and so symbolically carrying the whole people with him into God's holy presence and interceding on their behalf for the forgiveness of their sins. We should understand this, the author indicates, as a symbolic foreshadowing of what was to happen when, having suffered and died for our sins, the one who is the True High Priest not just of Israel but of all humankind bore us with him (being clothed in our humanity, with our names all over it) not into the temple but into the glory of God's throne room itself, ascending to God's right hand not just in order to rule over all things but in order to pray for us, in order to offer worship to the Father on our behalf.[29]

There is enough here to keep a whole gaggle of theologians busy for a very long time indeed. But the basic point is clear and is vitally important. Not only is Jesus Lord, the one who has authority over all things and who lays claim, therefore, to every area of our lives and calls us to dedicate them to him as an act of worship; Jesus is also the one who unites us to himself in order to bring us to his Father, and in the Father's presence, he intercedes for us, commending us to the Father and, clothed in our nature, offering the perfect human worship to the Father that we, with all our sins and failings and weaknesses and despite the workings of the Holy Spirit, can and never will be able to offer. Worship, in other words, is not something that we are called to bring to God in response to all that God has done and continues to do for us, let alone something we do to keep "our side" of some putative bargain or contract with God. If that were the case, pure and simple, we should have every reason to be anxious, and worship would be bound to become the oppressive and joyless occasion that it all too often is. For then awareness of our repeated failure to do it well enough—to "feel" the right sorts of things, to mean what we say or sing without doubt or equivocation, to pray hard enough, to "truly repent and unfeignedly believe his Holy Gospel," as the Book of Common Prayer puts it—would forever hang over us like the sword of Damocles. Worship of that sort, which lies heavy on our shoulders as those whose responsibility it is understood to be to "perform" satisfactorily before God at least once a week, will always leave us suspecting or knowing that our offering, like Cain's in Genesis 4, is in truth not fit for purpose and bound to fall short in God's sight, leaving us in a very vulnerable place indeed. Fortunately, though, that's not how it is.

According to Hebrews, worship isn't first and foremost something that we are called to bring to God. Worship (devotion, adoration, and love) is something that is *already* happening *in* God, as the Father loves the Son and the Son loves the Father in the power of the Spirit. And now, because of Jesus's atoning life and death and his resurrection and ascension to the Father's right hand, this same worship finds its perfect *human* expression not in us and what *we* do (on Sundays or in our lives more generally) but precisely in *Jesus*, who, as our Great High Priest, continually offers his own humanity to the Father in love and devotion and who hears the Father's words (not limited to the occasion of his baptism) "You are My beloved Son, in You I am well pleased."[30] But because worship *is* also something we are called to do (not just on Sundays but from moment to waking moment through the offering of our whole selves to our Father) and because Jesus has united us to himself by taking our humanity, what this means is that, far from being a millstone tied around our necks, the call to worship is an *invitation* extended to us *to join in* the human Son's worship of his heavenly Father, empowered by the Holy Spirit. It's a party already well underway in God when we arrive, and we are invited to get involved and to enjoy it, letting somebody else worry about the contingencies of it being a successful celebration. In such a circumstance, in the light of such a realization, all fear and sense of inadequacy can fall away, and we can worship gladly and joyfully, knowing, as we do, that any shortfall in what we bring or what we do is more than made good by Jesus's own offering made on our behalf. He's our brother as well as our Lord, and he brings us home, like the estranged prodigal son in the parable he himself told, to enjoy being in the presence of our Father and to join in the party.

8

"HE WILL COME TO JUDGE THE LIVING AND THE DEAD . . ."

IT MIGHT BE tempting to see this clause as yet another awkward and slightly embarrassing bolt-on to the basic option of contemporary believing, one that, for one reason or another, we would much prefer to submit to the editor's red Biro or the ~~delete~~ key in any redrafting of the creed for personal use. Doesn't it, someone might well ask, entail frankly ridiculous notions of Jesus descending from the stratosphere like some displaced cosmonaut or homeward-bound drone, hoping for a gentle landing and, in the meanwhile, fielding the attentions of hosts of eager believers all traveling in the opposite direction to "meet him in the clouds"? What's that all about? And how can we even begin to take it seriously? And then, moving on, there's the whole thing about a final judgment, which seems OK as a scene out of Dante or Giotto but is hard to imagine actually occurring and, in any event, makes us uncomfortable in our tolerant, liberal age, it seeming frankly so, well, . . . *judgmental.*

Setting aside for now the inherent dubiety of a circumstance in which, once again, what we are capable of imagining or what we find personally comfortable is appealed to as a reliable index of reality, it must frankly be admitted that the subject of this chapter has sometimes been subjected to unnecessarily unhelpful treatments—literary, visual, and other sorts. And in what follows, I hope at least to provide if not "comfortable" readings then at least ones shorn of some needlessly complicating and problematic aspects and associations and possessed of something resembling intellectual respectability. Nonetheless, as in the previous clause, so too here, I suggest, we are dealing not with an unwieldy hangover from a worldview long since past its use-by date but with something that, properly understood, is essential and close to the heart of a properly orientated Christian faith. Lest that appear a brave or odd claim, let me clarify in what sense it might be so.

This Is How It Ends . . .

WITH THIS CLAUSE, our focus of attention is finally shifted rudely from the past and the present toward the future—our future and God's. And while Christian faith certainly has roots sunk deeply in the soil of the past and while it is without doubt also a matter of supreme relevance to our understanding of and living in the present, it is above all *forward looking* in its take on reality and in its dynamic. Unlike some Eastern religious and philosophical versions of things, Christian faith does not entertain the idea that history is fundamentally a recycling of experience in which the established patterns and options return to be experienced again and again—the same old, same old—with little hope of escape or of anything radically new occurring. It does, of course, recognize that in nature and in the ways in which the patterns of nature shape the patterns of human living (which remain significant even in the age of climate change, global markets, imported foodstuffs, air-conditioning, artificial light, and twenty-four-hour shopping), there are things that go around and come around, and it embraces and celebrates these in the cyclical patterns of liturgy and the Christian calendar. But on the larger scale, it insists that history is linear, not a perpetual cycle without an identifiable beginning or end, and even such repetitions as we experience them are never *mere* repetitions, all sorts of things having moved on and changed in the meanwhile.[1] History itself, therefore, Christian faith insists, can and should be *narrated*—rehearsed as a story that, like all good stories, has an identifiable beginning, middle, and end. And while both the beginning and the end may well need to be handled with care when we come to speak and write about them (necessarily lying way beyond any experience we can have or have had or are likely to have), they can and must nonetheless be spoken of. Appropriate things may be said about them—albeit in ways that stretch our imagination—as parts of a single story involving God as well as the world. And how this story *ends*, how it *will* end, is vital to the shaping of Christian faith and its disposition toward the present as well as the future. At root, in other words, Christian faith takes the form of *hope* and of trusting in the *promise* of God regarding the world's future in God's hands.

And that's what the clause we are looking at in this chapter is about. *This*, it tells us, is how the story will end, and not in some other way—not in some meaningless, purely accidental entropy (the dissolution first of biological, then chemical, then physical systems, forces, and processes) but at a time appointed by God and in an ending that is no mere ending but itself a new beginning, a *transformation* of the cosmos rather than its gradual return to chaos and nothingness, and its transformation in the hands of a good and faithful creator who is sovereign and whose sovereignty manifests itself in goodness, love, and mercy toward what he has made. In the Old Testament, this hope and expectation is cast simply as the Day of the Lord, the day when Israel's God, Yahweh, would finally step in to come and dwell among his people, bringing heaven and earth together and putting the earth right in order to make it fit for that indwelling. As we saw in chapter 7, for Christians, the reality of the situation has moved on and become clearer, as Jesus is now understood to be the one into whose hands all things in heaven and on earth have been committed, and the God who is coming, therefore, is none other than the God revealed most fully and finally in Jesus. In fact, in Jesus, God has *already* come, has already dwelled among his people, has already judged their sins. In Jesus, God has already done the decisive thing that changes everything, and his return will be no radically new initiative, therefore, but the finishing of what God has already begun. So there are no "spoiler alerts" needed where the Christian story is concerned. The ending is already known, already clear, if not in detail then at least in its broad outline and character—because the main player in that ending is to be Jesus, and it is in his hands that the whole thing rests. It is living life daily in the light of this hope and expectation and not some other that shapes Christian discipleship from first to last, or should do so.

Odd Comings and Goings

WE SAW IN our study of the ascension that in an important sense, that event was not the withdrawal of Jesus from the disciples into a remote absence but his transition from one form of presence to another. Having been present with them in flesh-and-blood terms, being where they were, spending time with them, was vital to what Jesus had to do and did do. He participated in our "space-time reality" and shared to the full in the benefits and the costs and limitations of that, not simply for the sake of sharing in it (as though it were an "experience" not to be missed even by God), but in order to redeem and transfigure it from within. But being "in the flesh" had its drawbacks, one of which was, of course, that Jesus could only be in one place at once, only be with a certain number of people at once, only be doing one thing at once. As we saw, what the disciples came to realize was that with his withdrawal to be "with the Father," Jesus was certainly not absent but rather able to be with them in a far more intimate way—in precisely the way that God was "with" them, in fact. So they went back initially to the temple—the most concrete symbolic focus of God's presence—and worshipped him there, and when they were eventually driven out of the temple, they went out into every part of the known world (we shouldn't forget, even though the book of Acts concentrates on the Mediterranean, that the apostles went deep into Africa and Asia too) fearlessly proclaiming the gospel in the confidence that Christ himself was with them "in person" wherever they were and "to the end of the age."[2] And what exactly was to happen at "the end of the age"? Well, all sorts of things; but one thing was, again, that God would "come to be present" with his people.

Of course, God is always present everywhere as our creator, being uncircumscribed by the sorts of boundaries and constraints he has built into our own creaturely existence. But God's presence is not obvious or immediate. It is invisible and intangible, known by faith rather than sight, and easily mocked or derided as unreal by those who choose to do so. And furthermore, even God's lordship, sovereign authority, and power are, for now, veiled and ambiguous rather than apparent or obvious—again, a matter of faith rather than demonstration or deduction. And for Jesus to be "with the Father" means, as we have seen, that his own presence and lordship too are of a similar sort and apprehended by similar means. The analogy has been appealed to, unsurprisingly, of the sorts of "presence" we get these days by means of remote, digital communication—email, Skype, texting, and the rest. It's real enough, and we come to rely on it and live with it, but it lacks the full-blooded reality of engaging with someone face-to-face, someone in the room with us, their body language as well as their words communicating a deeper and richer set of meanings. And what the Old Testament seems to look forward to at the "end of the age" (which is, of course, the same as the Day of the Lord) and what Christians certainly came to look forward to was a "coming" of God to be with his people, in which both his presence and his lordship would be of a quite different sort. It would be an *unveiled* presence which would be apparent to everyone and anyone, and without any concomitant loss of personal intimacy (that way in which God knows us better and is closer to us even than we know and are to ourselves), there would be a more solid, concrete form of God's presence which could be shared and enjoyed by all. For Christians—who already had things to say, of course, about an embodied reality of God—this naturally involved the expectation of a new "coming" of Jesus, now in a way which was more rather than less substantial but which would (in a world transformed in its material as well as its spiritual conditions) be no bar to his being "with us" always, his presence shared and enjoyed by all always.

The fact that we cannot really even imagine such a circumstance is hardly surprising. After all, it could only be true in a world very different from the one we know now, while our capacities for understanding and imagining alike are tied (for the most part, helpfully) to the way things work in the world we know now. So we can't expect to get our heads around it. But this hope—that Jesus would "return" (or "appear") and be present to us in a world wholly transformed by his presence and in which both his presence and his lordship would be known rather than veiled, to be acknowledged and enjoyed by all—was one of the earliest-expressed Christian hopes. In 1 Corinthians 16:21–22, the apostle Paul inserts an odd bit of Aramaic lingo casually (without explanation and seemingly in his own handwriting rather than relying on his scribe) into the middle of his Greek prose: *Marana tha*, "Our Lord, come!" Since Paul doesn't bother to elucidate or further enlighten his (mostly Greek-speaking) readers in Corinth, biblical scholars suggest this is most likely a phrase already perfectly familiar to them, probably a fragment of liturgy or a Christian "meme" dating back to the very earliest years following immediately upon Jesus's death and resurrection, when the church was still concentrated on Jerusalem and largely Aramaic speaking.[3] And while some interpreters suppose it to be a bit of eucharistic liturgy (a prayer for Jesus to "come" and be present in the bread and wine), most understand it to be precisely a prayer for the return of Jesus, expressing a yearning for Christ's reappearance in glory and dominion, which will signal history's end and the world's new beginning and in and amid which Jesus will be known once more "face to face."[4] The Old Testament Day of the Lord at the "end of the age," in other words, has, in this very early Christian hymn or liturgical invocation, already become the Day of Jesus and of his second "coming" or appearing on earth, and longing for it is at the nub of what the worship of these "Christians" is all about.

Of Angels, Trumpets, and Pie in the Sky

IT'S TIME NOW to grasp the nettle and deal with questions about the nature of that return and, in particular, some imaginative and colorful versions based on Paul's own imagining of it in 1 Thessalonians 4:15–17. Here Paul writes as follows:

> *For this we declare to you by the word of the Lord, that we who are alive, who are left until the coming of the Lord, will by no means precede those who have died. For the Lord himself, with a cry of command, with the archangel's call and with the sound of God's trumpet, will descend from heaven, and the dead in Christ will rise first. Then we who are alive, who are left, will be caught up in the clouds together with them to meet the Lord in the air; and so we will be with the Lord forever.*

Let's face it: taken at face value, as it often has been, this does seem to confront us with the prospect of some peculiar (and seemingly implausible) bits of cosmic choreography. But it has been (and remains) the bedrock of some very influential strands of Christian expectation concerning the end times. By way of reaction, meanwhile, others have preferred to assuage their intellectual discomfort by "demythologizing" such verses, insisting that whatever Paul may have *thought* he was talking about, modern readers should understand that what he is *actually* talking about is something else. What we should understand here, it is suggested, is a reference not to any kind of future happening but to aspects of our (and Paul's, and everyone's) recurrent religious experience. Others still (presumably unsure exactly what to do with all this) opt instead for a dignified but theologically problematic silence, pushing the question away and refusing to grapple seriously with it at all. If, though, as I have suggested, an appropriate imagining of and willingness to speak about the world's future (and ours) in God's hands are not discretionary but basic and essential to an authentic and healthy Christian faith, then neither a "recycling" and "de-storying" collapse of the narrative future into the narrator's present nor an embarrassed silence regarding our story's ending can be entertained as an option available to the theologian, the preacher, or the liturgist. So what exactly should we do with these verses?

First, it would be sensible to set alongside them some other things that Paul says elsewhere about Christ's return and see whether they shed any light on the subject. So, for example, in Philippians 3:20–21, Paul writes, "Our citizenship is in heaven, and it is from there that we are expecting a Savior, the Lord Jesus Christ. He will transform the body of our humiliation that it may be conformed to the body of his glory, by the power that also enables him to make all things subject to himself." And then, again, in 1 Corinthians 15:50–53, we read, "What I am saying, brothers and sisters, is this: flesh and blood cannot inherit the kingdom of God, nor does the perishable. . . . We will not all die, but we will all be changed, in a moment, in the twinkling of an eye, at the last trumpet. For the trumpet will sound, and the dead will be raised imperishable, and we will be changed. For this perishable body must put on imperishability, and this mortal body must put on immortality." All three texts mentioned so far clearly encourage and require us to make considerable use of our imagination, and we need to respect their imaginative nature and form, taking care not to force any of them into a "literal" mold and recognizing that these are imaginative pointers to a reality which Paul is certainly trying to evoke for us but that by definition lies way beyond anything in his or our own natural range of experience and understanding. All three texts, though, point identifiably to certain things that we can *grasp*, if not understand: first, Christ will be present in person; second, Christ will be exercising dominion; and third, everyone and everything will be transformed by his presence and dominion from "perishable" to "imperishable."

Now, the Greek term *parousia*, which appears in 1 Thessalonians 4:15, is typically translated there as "coming," which fits the imagery of the context nicely. Christ "comes" in a very visible way, descending on the clouds. As Tom Wright observes in an illuminating discussion of this topic, though, the more basic meaning of this term in other contexts is "presence" rather than "coming," while in other parts of the New Testament still, a different word altogether is used with reference to the circumstances of the Day of the Lord—*phaneroō*, the verb meaning "to appear."⁵ That Christ "comes" and that he is suddenly "present" in a new way and that he "appears" are not, of course, incompatible states of affairs, but the latter two, we should note, do not of themselves necessitate or involve the aerial maneuvers that 1 Thessalonians 4 invites us to imagine. So, for instance, in the first letter of John, we read, "And now, little children, abide in him, so that when he appears [*ean phanerōthē*] we may have confidence and not be put to shame at his presence [*parousia*]. . . . Beloved, we are God's children now; what we shall be has not yet been made apparent [*oupō ephanerōthē*]; but we know that when he appears [*ean phanerōthē*] we shall be like him, for we shall see him as he is."⁶ Again, the themes of Jesus's personal presence and the transformation attendant upon it are central, as is the importance of beginning to live in the here and now as though he were already present—because in another sense, he *is* already present, and what the language of "appearance" reminds us is that what may seem to us like a "coming" or a "return" is also in practice an unveiling or manifesting of something that is already the case. Jesus is already "present," albeit not bodily, and he is already the Lord of all things in heaven and on earth. But whereas for now these things are ambiguous and hidden, on the Day of the Lord, they will be laid bare in the transformation of all things.

Paul himself, too, can use the same imagery. So, for example, in Colossians 3, in urging believers to have their sights set already on things that are "above" (i.e., the things of God and God's kingdom) rather than fixed on the things of this world, he writes, "So if you have been raised with Christ, seek the things that are above, where Christ is, seated at the right hand of God. . . . When Christ appears [*phanerōthē*], the one who is your life, then you too will appear with him in glory."⁷ As Wright puts it, "The promise is not that Jesus will simply reappear within the present world order; but that, when heaven and earth are joined together in the new way God has promised, then he will appear to us—and we will appear to him, and to one another, in our own true identity."⁸ What we call heaven, we should remind ourselves again, is not a "place" within the created cosmos but God's "place" (however we choose to imagine that), the creator's own "place," quite distinct from yet closely related to our world and already intersecting it in all sorts of ways. God's promise, Wright reiterates, is that "one day the two worlds will be integrated completely, and will be fully visible to one another, producing that transformation of which both Paul and John speak."[9]

What, then, are we to make of Paul's vivid account in 1 Thessalonians, with its seeming insistence that Jesus will "come" from somewhere "up there" and believers, furthermore, be taken up to meet and greet him in midair? We've already noted that this account, too, affirms the basics that seem to be consistent across various New Testament texts—that Jesus will be personally present in a new way and that his presence will be the occasion for (or perhaps occasioned by) a radical transformation and renewal of things such as that pictured in other texts as a "new creation," the regeneration of the whole cosmos by a fresh initiative of the one who created it in the first place, one in which God's reality and creaturely reality will come together in a wholly new and unimaginable way. Compared with this, the scooping up of believers (and, in some versions of Christian theology, thereby their removal from the world) to meet Jesus halfway in the sky seems not just odd but strangely unsatisfying as a prospect (even if there's pie). Can we take it seriously? Need we do so?

Well, we might begin by observing that taking a text like this *seriously* and insisting on taking it at face value and reading it *literally* are rather different things. To take it seriously and treat it with the respect due to any text held to be authoritative for faith means approaching and reading it first and foremost as *the sort of text we believe it actually to be* (i.e., seeking what is better referred to as its "natural" rather than its "literal" sense as the product of a human literary endeavor in a particular time and place). Among other things, this involves taking into consideration its proper literary, imaginative, religious, social, political, and other relevant human contexts; the sorts of expectations duly generated by these; and other bits of cultural savoir faire taken for granted by its author as something his intended readers could be relied upon to bring with them to the party, enabling them to complete that transaction between author and readers that we refer to as "meaning." To treat this or any other text otherwise is not to treat it with respect at all or to take it seriously and therefore hardly to grant it "authority," whatever our intention may be. Good biblical interpretation will always illuminate a text by grappling fully with all this, and the most helpful interpretation of this particular biblical text that I am familiar with is that offered by Tom Wright in his book *Surprised by Hope*, which I shall simply summarize here.

Paul, Wright reminds us, was two things: first, he was a Roman citizen, and second, he was a Pharisee steeped in the Jewish scriptures. If we are not going to misunderstand what Paul is doing in these otherwise very odd few verses, we need to keep both of these facts in mind. In effect, Wright suggests, Paul is deploying a form of imaginative rhetoric (something that Jewish interpreters have always loved doing) to refer us to a circumstance lying in any case far beyond the scope of any straightforward, literal mode of description. In doing so, Paul borrows from two biblical texts already known to him (i.e., texts from the Jewish Bible, our Old Testament) and one social and political situation very familiar to his readers, allowing these to intermingle and their meanings to cross-fertilize and ferment until they gesture suggestively toward the significance of the longed-for Day of the Lord, the day when Christ would "come" or "appear" and heaven and earth at last be joined together. First, Wright refers to a particular sociopolitical use of the word *parousia*, the word that, as we've already seen, plays a prominent part in 1 Thessalonians 4 and an equally prominent part in the history of theological imagining of and reckoning with what Paul is talking about. Rarely can a word have been used so often, so confidently, and so problematically in pulpits and Christian publications alike with such little concern for, awareness of, or sensitivity to the connotations and imagery with which it was laden in its author's context.

Parousia, as we have already noted, really means "presence." It is related to the verb *pareinai*, which means "to be present" or "close by" (as distinct from "absent" or "far away") or "to come to be present," "to appear," or "to have arrived." The word *parousia* was used in particular, Wright observes, to refer to the approach or arrival of a royal or imperial dignitary (the king/queen or emperor) on a formal visit to a colony or one of the territories over which they ruled. And when such a visit was imminent, rather than simply waiting nervously behind the city gates, the habit was for the citizens of this royal visitor to flood out of the settlement and meet them before they actually landed, welcoming them and accompanying them on the final stage of their journey, no doubt with much flag-waving and acclamation—the perfect opportunity for celebratory mugs, tote bags, and key rings to be run off the local production line and sold at a stupid price. All this was, of course, basically a mark of respect, of homage, of explicit acknowledgment of the dominion of the one drawing near. That's the first bit of context we need to know about. The second, Wright suggests, is the fact that in the Jewish Bible the classic text associated with the coming Day of the Lord (when God would show up in person to put the world to rights) was Daniel 7, a text which describes "one like a human being" being elevated into the clouds of heaven and given entitlement to sit with God in God's glory.[10] In its Old Testament context, this figure (the "Son of Man," in more traditional translations) was symbolic of the righteous and faithful in Israel, who persevered in their faithfulness to the Lord despite the persecutions and predations of pagan invaders and occupiers. Jesus, in his ministry, applied this same symbolism to himself, as the one true Israelite who would be faithful all the way to the end in his devotion to God. Paul, Wright suggests, is deliberately playing with this text, both evoking its association with Jesus and applying it to the faithful believers of Thessalonica, who we know had been suffering persecution.[11]

So in evoking the image of Christ in the clouds at his "coming" and of believers going out to greet him (just like the citizens of a Roman colony at Caesar's approach) and being drawn up into the clouds themselves, Paul is suggesting several things at once, none of which requires a resort to theatrical smoke and mirrors or even wires and pulleys. First, the one who is to arrive or to appear "at the end" is the Lord himself, the one who has dominion over all things. And even though that dominion may be veiled for now, it will be very apparent when he does arrive, with all the power and authority of empire (the peculiar lordship of the kingdom) in his considerable train. And that Lord is, of course, none other than Jesus. Second, he will come to be present "from" the place where he has been seated at the Father's right hand, a place in the clouds where he shares in God's glory. And those who rush out to meet him will themselves—having been faithful in their allegiance to the gospel, like the faithful of Daniel 7—be "taken up into the clouds," vindicated for their perseverance to the end. But let's note, in terms of the political analogy, the point of going out/up to greet Christ is *not* for him now to lead them away to some other world. It is precisely for them to welcome and accompany him as *he comes to be with us* again in ours and in coming utterly to transform it. This, Wright notes, is no essentially otherworldly vision offering "pie in the sky" but a potent demand to reimagine the implications of Christ's lordship over all things in heaven and on earth once the wraps are taken off. And that means a drastic change to the way we think about the same world here and now, and its value to us and to Christ, and how we should be living in it.

The other piece of very familiar Jewish scripture Wright thinks is alluded to playfully by Paul in 1 Thessalonians 4 is the account in Exodus 19–32, where Moses, having ascended to the top of Mount Sinai to meet with God, comes back down the mountain again—emerging from the smoke or cloud which covered the top, accompanied by trumpet blasts and the deafening voice of God in the form of thunder—and brings with him the law etched on tablets of stone by God's finger. This, we might recall, was the (slightly rocky) beginning of God's covenant with Israel, and perhaps Paul, by alluding to it here, wants to underline the fact that it is the one in whose own humanity the same law has already been etched on "tablets of flesh" rather than stone, both ingrained in his very being and empowered to ingrain it in ours, the one whose life and death fulfills the first covenant and is itself the foundation of a new and lasting covenant, who will eventually "come down" to be present with us.¹² Not a new Moses but the lawgiver himself—God in the flesh, this time here at last to exercise his proper dominion over all things. And if this text about Moses was indeed in Paul's mind as he penned 1 Thessalonians 4, it provides a convenient segue to the second part of our creedal clause—because when Moses came down from the mountain carrying the law, he found Israel already in an ungodly mess, and the first thing he had to do was to exercise God's judgment and get that mess sorted out.

To Judge the Living and the Dead

ON THE WHOLE, the idea of a coming judgment at the end of the age is one the church doesn't make much of today, perhaps feeling slightly awkward and uncomfortable about the whole notion and realizing that, like the church's talk about "sin" (to which, of course, it is directly related), it's unlikely to win friends and influence people even *within* the church, let alone outside it. When it is mentioned, more often than not, there is an awkwardness, a palpable discomfort on the part of all concerned, and a quiet conspiracy to deal briskly with the whole subject before locking it away again in the cupboard reserved for beliefs we're not really sure what to do with and would prefer not to have to deal with at all.

To some extent, this is because, like honest talk about human sin, talk about divine judgment tells us or reminds us of things about ourselves and our world that we would frankly prefer not to hear, things that our culture is certainly ill disposed to hear and unlikely to respond warmly to. It is, we persuade ourselves by way of mitigation, therefore, a missional liability, and to dwell on it might well, we suppose, be detrimental to our efforts to "share the good news" with others and draw them into the church's ranks. To some extent, the discomfort has to do with the choreography and the props attendant on many ways of imagining the whole thing, especially those that coincided with the rediscovery of artistic naturalism in the medieval period, encouraging and enabling some impressive, graphic, and gory "video nasties." Typically pictured is a vast cosmic assize at which the righteous are being filtered out for special treatment in a VIP suite while the rest (usually the vast majority) are ushered through the door marked "Guilty as charged." This hapless crowd, for its part, is being handed over to an unspeakable fate meted out by demons and goblins who appear to have been specially trained in the latest methods of torture. It all makes for some colorful and harrowing paintings, which were often on the west walls of medieval church interiors so that these would be the last things congregations saw as they filed out of the doors and back into the world, with its temptations and trials—conscience stiffeners and warnings designed again quite literally to scare the hell out of people. To some extent, the discomfort has to do, I think, with unhelpful mischaracterizations of the God who, we are led to believe, will wield the judgment. And to a considerable extent, I'm quite sure, it's to do with most of us recognizing that judgment—if it has anything to do with injustice, violence, arrogance, greed, lying, cruelty, oppression, and a whole host of other nasty behaviors finally getting their comeuppance—is not about other people but about us too. None of us has clean hands, and none of us should be gathering stones by way of anticipation, let alone having the gall to throw the first one.

But in Scripture, the coming, promised judgment of God is not something to be feared, mentioned only in hushed tones, and if at all possible avoided. On the contrary, it is something good, something to be yearned for, celebrated, and looked forward to. And it's not just human beings but the whole of creation that is pictured as celebrating the coming judgment. "Make a joyful noise to the LORD, all the earth," enjoins the psalmist. "Break forth into joyous song and sing praises. . . . Let the sea roar, and all that fills it; the world and those who live in it. Let the floods clap their hands; let the hills sing together for joy at the presence of the LORD." Why? Because "he is coming to judge the earth. He will judge the world with righteousness, and the peoples with equity."[13] There's not much sense of awkwardness or discomfort there. The judgment of God is unequivocally good and is seen as a necessary part of what it would mean for God to be present with his people in a radically new way, a way which will involve bringing heaven and earth together so that they overlap and integrate fully with each other—because God is the Holy One and sin and evil of all sorts are things so opposed to him that he cannot bear them in his presence. As I suggested in chapter 5, evil is not a mere irritant to God or something God has simply decided to have nothing to do with. Evil is better thought of as something utterly toxic to God, the very opposite of all that God is and stands for, and its presence is something he suffers and bears for the time being but cannot allow to remain, and it can have no place in God's kingdom—not a trace of it, for even a trace would poison and compromise and foul things, rendering them unfit for God's habitation together with us.

So the belief in a final judgment of sin, an occasion when God will finally set the world right, expunging from it all traces of evil, is essential to biblical faith because what is at stake in it is precisely our understanding of God's own character as sheer goodness and holiness and God's promise that, at the end of the age, heaven and earth will indeed be joined and at one, God dwelling together with us and we with God in a wholly new and unprecedented way. For that to happen, the world itself will clearly have to be wholly transformed, all that is good in it taken up and made new, all that is wrong with it redeemed and made good, and all traces of evil in it purged and made null and void. And that process, however we envisage it, will involve wickedness, exploitation, injustice, and all the rest being "judged," shown in their true light, and dealt with accordingly. Exercising judgment in this context means seeing things aright, setting things right, and making things right—making good the wrongs of our lives, of the world, of human history. And if we still find it hard to sympathize with the idea of judgment as something to be *celebrated*, we need only think of the most recent horror perpetrated upon the helpless or defenseless or vulnerable by someone abusing their power—whether that be cases of historic sexual abuse, or the use of chemical weapons on civilian populations, or the torture ("enhanced interrogation") of prisoners through extraordinary rendition, or whatever (the examples are plentiful)—news of which has left us feeling outraged, crying out (if only inwardly) for someone to be brought to justice and the demands of justice satisfied. In such a circumstance, we might suppose, judgment would indeed be welcome, something to be celebrated rather than feared or avoided, even though the gruesome forms of retribution we cheerily summon up for the perpetrators in our mind's eye (casting ourselves safely in the role of dismayed, albeit secretly gratified, onlookers) may have little at all to do with what God's judgment will finally look like. Putting the execution of justice in *our* hands, we may be sure, would only deepen and perpetuate the problem, fighting fire with fire until the whole earth were scorched and beyond habitation.

Because, of course, in the complicated and messy moral and spiritual world we live in, straightforward lines between good and evil, perpetrators and victims, are not always easy to draw, and certainly not with too thick a pencil. Again, none of us has entirely clean hands, and all of us live in glass houses susceptible to stone throwing. But as an imperfect indicator, that sort of visceral, *sinful* moral outrage at least points us to an underlying moral reality in terms of which the eventual triumph of good over evil in our world, in our institutions, in our lives and relationships could only be a good thing, something worthy of celebration and something to be looked forward to. For the Jews of the Old Testament, such a prospect was good news in a very immediate sense, as they (at one time or another in their history) found themselves the victims of invasion, injustice, oppression, and persecution, whether at the hands of wayward rulers or at the hands of other nations. And their hope for God's coming was one pictured vividly in terms of a courtroom scene where God would exercise judgment over the nations and vindicate Israel, or those within Israel who had been faithful to God's call and commandments. For them, the message that God's coming at the end of time would see God's justice and goodness sweeping through the land and finally established was indeed something to be looked forward to, something to be joyful about rather than afraid of, something to celebrate rather than seek to avoid.

Good news is not always unalloyed, of course, especially when it comes in the form of promise, for there may well be struggle and suffering to be borne yet before and as it is realized. Good news, indeed, is only good at all when it arises alongside or in the midst of something that is bad news for all of us. It is certainly like this where the news of God's coming judgment is concerned—because even as we look forward to the day when God will transform the world so that evil will at last be excluded from it, judged not fit to enter the kingdom, having no place in the new creation, we live with the abiding recognition that we ourselves are caught up in, implicated in, complicit in all manner of things (in our personal lives, in our relationships, in our institutions) that have at least a foot (and perhaps more than just a foot) in the camp of evil and its machinations and its manifestations. And we may suspect that the news that evil is to be judged and dealt with when God comes, that the transformation of the world to accommodate his coming, will and must involve evil being dealt with and destroyed, while *good* news overall may yet have some uncomfortable implications for us and for the world, that the shift from "perishable" to "imperishable," as Paul refers to it, may involve some adjustments that will initially be hard and perhaps even painful to live with. So bold proclamation of God's coming judgment may after all remain in the category of good news that the world plugs its ears to or dismisses with its superior wisdom and more flattering self-diagnoses; but then the baptized are called not to win friends and influence people in order to swell the ranks and fill the coffers but to make disciples—men, women, and children whose lives are marked out above all by the truth as it has been revealed in Jesus Christ, which is the truth that our sinful humanity must be crucified precisely so that it can share in the life of the resurrection.

For Christians, though, the coming of God at the end of the age is not the coming of some unknown, frightening arbiter of abstract justice but the coming of none other than Jesus himself, and it is Jesus into whose hands whatever "judgment" we are speaking of will be placed. Jesus—the one who has himself shared in our immersion in the world, with its trials and tribulations and temptations, and who knows what it is to struggle with those. Jesus—the one who we know is passionately committed to us, who is for us rather than against us, who offers us forgiveness in order that we may go and sin no more. Jesus—the one who has himself borne the judgment for our sins and in whose life of obedience sin itself has already been judged and put to death. Jesus—the one who is the first fruits of the new creation, by being united with whom we are already "put right" with God even though we continue to sin. Jesus—the one who sends his Spirit to convict us of sin's continuing reality in our lives and in the world and to empower us to anticipate judgment here and now as we bear witness to Jesus's lordship and as we seek to conform our lives, part by part, to the shape of that lordship. For as we do so, we begin already the uncomfortable process of putting sin to death, eschewing its seductive approaches, refusing it the handholds in our lives that it craves, denying it opportunities to reproduce and regenerate, and so excluding it bit by painful bit from that small portion of God's world in which our behavior makes any moral and spiritual difference.

III

❦ 9 ❦

"I BELIEVE IN THE HOLY SPIRIT..."

THE LANGUAGE OF "spirit" is back in vogue again, it seems. After half a century or more during which only whatever could be weighed, measured, tripped over, or bumped into was considered to deserve the accolade "real," the occupants of Western societies have at last grown tired of treating themselves as the mere accumulations of atoms—complex mechanical or organic systems susceptible in principle to exhaustive analysis and explanation in the terms admitted by white-coated, dispassionate verifiers of "reality," or as we know them, practitioners in the natural sciences.[1] Having, as they say, been there, done that, and been sold the T-shirt, we have discovered that the shirt is an awkward fit after all and has begun to chafe. So we are ready to reckon seriously again with the claim that our humanity is more expansive and more intricate than any merely material description could ever account for. A more ambitious vision of reality is called for, we now suspect, if we are to avoid the atrophying of our souls, having failed for too long either to attend to or to nourish an entire dimension of our creaturely being in the world. If the material order presents itself to us with an undeniable force and immediacy, we are nonetheless increasingly called upon to acknowledge that we are immersed in, keyed into, and made an integral part of a wider moral, aesthetic, and "spiritual" order too—a depth of reality whose claims and demands upon us will not be ignored or denied except at the cost of our flourishing.

While, therefore, cultural commentary remains fascinated by developments on the front of so-called artificial intelligence (still typically imagined as humanoid in form despite the advent of autonomous vacuum cleaners, self-driving vehicles, and the ubiquitous, dulcet but disembodied tones of "Alexa"²), what drives such curiosity and concern is a desire to be able to say what sets the truly "human" apart, transcending the counterfeiting initiatives of even the most sophisticated robotics, actual or anticipated. We are not (and if we are honest with ourselves, we know we are not) the mere flesh-and-blood "machines" that reductionist naturalism seems to envisage and would certainly have us believe. There is a dimension, or a "mode," or a "field" of human existence and agency that stubbornly resists any such analysis, and with it are bound up most of the things that we value most about our own humanity and the humanity of others. Delineating the scope and describing the nature of this distinctive sphere have always been challenging, and they remain no less so in an age where the mapping of material reality itself has reached such an advanced stage. Yet the primacy and ultimacy of our engagements with it (whether that be the "inner world" of personal consciousness or the mysterious depth of the many different sorts of "things" that confront us, forever resisting and frustrating exhaustive and reductive analyses) drives us to take this sphere seriously, refusing its relegation to the category of the merely epiphenomenal or illusory. And it compels constant resort to the strategies of poetry—as it always has—in order to speak of it, for speak of it we must.³

No doubt many factors (some of them less than appetizing) must be reckoned with in order to account for the resurgence of the institutions of "religion" in the postmodern cultures of the West. Behind the evidence of polls and census results indicating large numbers now content to identify as "spiritual" (even as they eschew the label "religious"), it is probable that we should trace a genuine thirst for depths long since erased from the social imaginaries and attendant public liturgies of societies like ours.⁴ We should be cautious, though, in our evaluation of all this of the significance for Christian mission and ministry in the world. Renewed enthusiasm for the vocabulary of "spirit," "spiritual," and "spirituality" in society at large may or may not be something for the church to welcome with enthusiasm. After all, talk of what is "spiritual" in this context is often little more than a borrowing of language (language, to be sure, with a long religious pedigree) to express the conviction that there are things—"real" things and not the mere objects of illusion or human invention—lying beyond the limits of whatever material stuff we take to exist. But while the reality of "nonmaterial" stuff is certainly part of what many religious traditions, including Christianity, tell us about the world and about ourselves, taking it seriously hardly entails believing in God as such—let alone the God of the gospel—or even being sympathetic to such belief. Christians, for example, as we have already seen, hold the view that all sorts of "things unseen" as well as those things "seen" or engaged concretely via our senses are to be reckoned with in the world God has made for our indwelling.[5] But such nonmaterial entities are precisely creaturely and finite, and the difference between them and God in this regard is as vast as that between God and the basest of material substances or simplest single-cell organic life-forms. "Spiritual" reality as such, then, is certainly neither God nor yet even "divine" but merely a stratum of that complex and diverse reality which God has created. Furthermore, as a moment's reflection should serve to remind us, nonmaterial realities come in any case in all shapes and sizes and flavors, not all of which are harmless or even healthy, let alone good or godly. Evil, in fact, whatever we make of it, does not lend itself to weighing and measuring in either imperial or metric units and so must be classified as "spiritual" in the relevant sense.

There are, of course, enormous goods to be found in the world of "spiritual" reality in this broad sense, some of which, albeit fully creaturely in the forms under which we are familiar with and experience them (love, mercy, compassion, justice, wisdom, joy, peace, and others), seem to render the category of "things unseen" as such an appropriate enough field from which to reap metaphors in our attempts to speak meaningfully of God (or, conversely, God's attempt to reveal Godself to us in terms fit for purpose). Picturing God in terms of spiritual realities of this sort seems less strained somehow, less of an awkward stretch, than the use of available material metaphors. To call

God "spirit," it seems, causes us less of a mental crunch of gears than thinking of God as a rock, or a roaring lion, or an eagle, or a raging fire, despite the enthusiasm with which Scripture itself deploys such down-to-earth images alongside many others and encourages us to do the same.[6] The important thing, though, is to remind ourselves that "spirit" is no less a poetic image in our application of it to God. God is, in a vitally important sense, no more "spirit" than God is a rock or a fire or, in the prophet Hosea's wonderful image, "maggots."[7] No, God is the uncreated creator of all things, both seen and unseen, and, as such, wholly distinct from all else. Again, we should be mindful that the category of so-called spiritual realities includes all that is in creation most thoroughly opposed to who God is as well as those things that, we may think, in some sense reflect God rather more helpfully or are better attuned to the reality of God. And we should observe that this particular poetic image, like most others, even as it fixes reality for us in a meaningful way, nonetheless cannot do so without a playful *surplus* of meaning that thwarts our desire to pin anything down too firmly or too precisely. Thus as we shall see, the Hebrew noun *ruach* can be translated not only as "spirit" but equally as "breath" or even "wind," that dynamic force of nature in which areas of high pressure encounter areas of low pressure and, contrary to Shakespeare's Gertrude and the metaphysicians of ancient Greece, air shifts in ways that—as any sailor, cyclist, or hill walker will gladly testify—prove it to be anything but "incorporal."[8] Sometimes dramatically (and frustratingly) so, in fact; it often manifests itself rather in the form of "a substantial entity with weight, texture, energy, motion and moods all of its own."[9]

So before we get carried away in a sort of theological flaying, enthusiastically pursuing "fleshless" images as those with which to work in our thinking and speaking of God, we should pause and remember that *all* images, including "spirit," have their roots sunk deeply in the soil of our material, embodied existence and experience and will not finally be torn out of that soil without the risk of a significant loss of sense.[10] The interplay between nonmaterial and material connotations in the Bible's talk of *ruach* (whether the *ruach* of God or that of God's creatures) points us, in fact, toward a wider biblical eschewal of any dualism between the bodily and the spiritual aspects of creation. Such a dualism is to be found, for instance, in the dichotomy between a realm of particular material things (*kosmos aesthetos*) and the "divine" realm of universal forms to which the mind/soul properly belongs (*kosmos noetos*), on which most classical Greek philosophy is founded. Whatever *spirit* means biblically and theologically, therefore, for Christians, it need not and should not entail the denigration of the world of flesh-and-blood existence, nor yet the disentangling of something called "spirit" or "soul" from it so that it can fly free and unpolluted into a transcendent eternity. Instead, things visible and things invisible are mixed together unashamedly within the fabric of God's creation, and "soul" or "spirit" cannot be siphoned off or surgically disentangled from the world of our embodied existence any more than they can be reduced to it in the manner attempted by materialists. Rather, the world of spirit (far from being an "airy nothing") is "bodied forth" in a world of material realities, while body has its own reality only when it is granted *ruach* (and, with it, life) by its creator as a gift.[11] Differentiate between these dimensions of our creaturely nature for convenience we may and perhaps must; but separate them out we must not attempt to do, for dissection is bound in this instance to leave both material and nonmaterial dimensions of our creaturely reality fatally lacking what is needed for survival, let alone thriving.[12]

Such unavoidable entanglement of "spirit" with matter, though, does not render the chosen image any less pure or less fitting for our use in thinking and speaking of God. The fact of its being earthed in the world of the flesh just as securely as other more obviously solid and corporal metaphors is not a problem precisely because the God who reveals himself as Spirit among other things is a God who is known most fully and finally not in and through allegedly disembodied "spiritual" realities but in the flesh and blood of our humanity itself. And having made this his own and reconciled it to himself, God then lifts it up to share in "life in all its fulness," a life that is neither biological nor ethereal but *spiritual* in a quite different sense—that is, the fruit of God's own indwelling through the Holy Spirit in a creation renewed by God's love, penetrating materiality itself (together with whatever nonmaterial dimensions or levels creation may be reckoned to possess) with the redemptive presence of God's own life. God, in other words, did not and does not "abhor" the often messy and reputedly "base" stuff of material existence, nor in our attempts to think and speak clearly of God can we.[13] C. S. Lewis, therefore, calls "muddle headed" the sort of Christianity that supposes materiality to be beneath God, and escaping from the body's clutches the highest "spiritual" aspiration. "There is no good," Lewis advises, "trying to be more spiritual than God. God never meant man to be a purely spiritual creature. That is why he uses material things like bread and wine to put new life into us. We may think this rather crude and unspiritual. God does not: He invented eating. He likes matter. He invented it."[14] More than this, he continues, God *invented* it, it seems, precisely so that, in due course, God might make it God's own, sharing in its life fully and personally so that we in our turn might come to share at last in God's life, God's joy, God's glory and do so in a manner that is *bodily* just as surely as it is *spiritual*.[15]

One final note will bear reiteration and reinforcement before we move on: spirit, we have reminded ourselves, is a poetic image, a *metaphor* borrowed from the realm of our human experience and used now to speak of God. All metaphors suggest (and, if they are apposite, draw our attention to) illuminating strands of *likeness* between one thing and another, helping us, among other things, trace the web of interconnectedness between things that is often buried deep beneath reality's surfaces. But metaphors remind us, too, of the abiding *differences* between those realities of which they speak, differences that are considerable and altogether more apparent if we attend to surface appearances alone.[16] If, to alight on a popular example, we are to appreciate the force of the metaphorical assertion that "Achilles is a lion," it matters greatly that we grasp the fact that Achilles is actually not a lion at all and that there are all sorts of things about lions, therefore, that should we seek them in Achilles, we shall be bound not to find.[17] To anticipate finding them would be altogether mistaken and likely, in fact, only to confuse the issue, cluttering the field of perception with irrelevant expectation and so occluding the underlying thread of connection rather than helping us trace and grasp it appropriately. With a metaphor, we must say, there is always a palpable "split reference," a high degree of abiding contraindication in which what is so generously given with one hand is constantly taken away again with the other, a poetic give-and-take that, Paul Ricoeur suggests, is conveniently captured in the tantalizing internal play of the dialectical suggestion that "it is and it is not."[18] Achilles *is* a lion, and yet, of course, he is not; he is a man. If, for the purposes of our ordinary daily discourse, an argument is a container (which may therefore "have holes" and may or may not "hold water"), it does not occur to us to inquire whether it is made of plastic or some more ecologically friendly substance.[19] And if, in the poet's eye, an image can be seen to "lurk behind each word" or our eagerness be "reined in," we recognize perfectly well the companion truth that they cannot, neither having any material form to speak of.[20]

If differences of this sort between *creaturely* realities (whether visible or invisible) demand that the whisper "*It is not!*" be audible at the shoulder of every metaphorical conjunction, who are we to say where metaphors are deployed, as they must be and are, in order to speak of God?[21] For God is, as the great medieval theologian Thomas Aquinas reminds us, "more distant from any creature than any two creatures are from each other."[22] In other words, when compared to the most fundamental difference of all—that between the uncreated creator and that which is created (i.e., between God and everything else that exists)—those readily identifiable between archangels and amoebas, black holes and blackheads, or calculus and cabbages pale rapidly into insignificance. In an important sense, therefore, every use of language drawn from the realm of our creaturely existence (and we have no other language to use) is, when we use it of God, confronted by the challenge of unimaginable difference and involves a surprising poetic leap across a gap that yawns wider than any other we shall ever encounter.

What this means is that even the most familiar and cherished of the words we habitually use in speaking about or speaking to God (i.e., in both theology and liturgy in their widest senses) are, strictly speaking, metaphors—characterized by their being drawn from one context (what Janet Soskice refers to helpfully as their natural or proper "domain of application"[23]) to speak suggestively (and, we trust, *appropriately*) now of a very different reality indeed.[24] Even such mainstays of Christian God talk as "Father," "Son," "good," "merciful," "righteous," and "love" are, on this understanding of the circumstance, stretched to a breaking point over the chasm presented by God's radical otherness—the fact that God is God meaning inevitably that these words (or any others) *cannot* mean whatever exactly they mean when we use them in other contexts. *That* they apply to God appropriately we may trust, but *how* they apply to God we cannot, in the strict sense, grasp, and in an important sense, therefore, we cannot know exactly what it is that we are saying when we use such words of God. In this case, then, the qualificatory whisper attendant on all metaphor needs to be cranked up to a volume that threatens to distract us, lest we ever forget that (precisely because God is God and we are not) God's ways are *not* and never will be our ways and, by forgetting this, slide carelessly into the idolatrous supposition that they might be.[25]

To return, then, to my main point here, to call God Spirit is, at one level, no less striking and surprising than daring to call God Father, or shepherd, or Lord, or a mother, or a friend, or a rock, or a consuming fire, or maggots, or any other of the plethora of biblically sanctioned images offering themselves for our discriminating use and exploration.[26] For "spirit" too has its primary domain of application amid the nonmaterial but nonetheless creaturely sphere of our human world—a fact easily and frequently lost sight of by Western Christianity's tendency to divide reality into the categories of "nature" and that which is "supernatural" rather than identifying the decisive distinction as that lying between creator and creature. More precisely, since Spirit too is a metaphor, the human spirit and God's Spirit (the sense in which God has or is "spirit") cannot, by the very nature of the case, be even broadly the same sorts of things, let alone (as theology has from time to time idolatrously supposed) identical with each other, as though the human spirit were the presence of God within us. As we shall see, God's Holy Spirit and the human spirit are indeed very closely involved with each other in all sorts of ways, but the closeness is one that leaves the otherness of God completely unscathed. Indeed, it is precisely this radical otherness that enables God's "Spirit" to be closer to us even than we are to ourselves.

With this careful qualification in mind, we may now note that with this clause, the creed changes its point of focus. It turns from things which God has done and does and will do *for* us (but that are and remain in some identifiable sense external to us) to things that God does, is doing, and has promised to do *in* us and *with* us and *through* us. Put differently, we turn now to consider our human *response* to all that God has done for us in the work of creation and redemption. But in doing so, we need to notice, we do not simply shift our gaze from God onto ourselves. For what we quickly discover is that this too is the sphere of God's distinctive presence and action, that human response to the gospel is itself part of the distinctive work of God for us and only possible at all on those terms. Nonetheless, here, as a third "I believe" of the creed clearly signals, we are asked to shift our gaze from those territories of God's activity where, we might say, the Father and the Son are the primary agents to reckon now with a third distinct way in which God is God.

Scriptural Glimpses of God's Spirit—the Old Testament

WITNESS TO GOD'S Spirit in the story told by Scripture is plentiful in both Testaments.[27] Mention of the Spirit of the Lord comes, in fact, at the very beginning of the story, as the Spirit of God (or "a wind from

God," in some translations) is pictured "hovering" or "sweeping" over the waters of chaos, from which God will shortly call forth the order and beauty of creation. As we have already seen with reference to the New Testament's ways of speaking of Jesus, to be implicated directly in the work of *creation* is, for Jewish authors and readers, without further qualification to be identified with and *as* God, and in this light, we can say that in the Old Testament, the Spirit is regularly viewed as the agent of God's own personal, creative, and life-giving engagement with the world.[28] So, for instance, Psalm 104:30 envisages God "sending forth" the Spirit to create and to sustain God's creatures, an image that has immediate and suggestive resonances with God "breathing" life into Adam in the creation story itself.[29] As we have already noticed, the Hebrew term *ruach* can be translated as "spirit," "breath," or "wind," but whichever of those options is chosen by the translator in a given verse, the creative interplay among them remains and will have been obvious to the text's first readers in a way that English simply misses. The same play on meanings is very obvious, for instance, in the familiar vision of the "dry bones" in Ezekiel 37, where the blowing of the four winds, the breathing of life into a hapless pile of corpses, and the promise of God's Spirit indwelling the people are all part of the same rich play of images. And because in order to speak we rely on our breath (utterance being a modification by our vocal cords of sounds made in the act of exhaling), there is a natural and close connection too between God's Spirit and God's Word in Old Testament thought.[30] So, for instance, just as the Spirit (or breath) of God is pictured hovering mysteriously at the scene of the world's creation, it is nonetheless by divine utterance—by the Word that God *speaks*—that creation is in significant measure understood as occurring, the whole account being punctuated by the familiar refrain "and God *said*."[31] And if speaking cannot happen without breathing (granted that they are not the same thing), so, the pattern of Scripture encourages us to suppose, wherever God's Word is to be reckoned with God's Spirit is likely to be close at hand, the two being naturally bound up with each other even where their precise prerogatives may be distinct ones. "By the word of the LORD the heavens were made," says the psalmist, "and all their host by the breath of his mouth."[32] The Word and the Spirit are, as Irenaeus of Lyons puts it later, the "two hands" of God's own hands-on creative and redemptive engagement with the world.[33]

The association between the Word (*dabhar*) and the Spirit (*ruach*) of God is reflected too in Israel's understanding of the ministry of the prophets. So while they are first and foremost figures to and through whom the *Word* of the LORD is spoken, prophets are also linked directly with the empowering presence and activity of *ruach*. The association is established quite early in traditions dating back as far as the ninth century BCE concerning troupes of "ecstatic" characters called *nabiim* (seers or prophets), who, having had *ruach* descend upon them, were prone to spells of undignified and even disreputable behavior, including "prophesying." This is the context for the bemused, slightly disparaging question asked by those who observed Saul's frenzied antics immediately after his anointing by Samuel: "Is Saul also among the prophets?"[34] These bands of prophets were clearly not held in high esteem by the paragons of polite society and unlikely to be welcome if they tried to gate-crash a party, let alone turned up in church. In fact, even the kudos of a prophet such as Elijah (with whose remarkable ministry the Spirit is linked[35]) was apparently insufficient to redeem this somewhat unsavory stage in the evolution of the role. So it is that we find Amos in the eighth century BCE eager to disentangle himself from any association with the *nabiim* and their antics;[36] in fact, the preexilic prophets generally remain very quiet about any involvement of God's *ruach* in their activities, preferring to focus instead on the agency of God's Word.[37] As time passed, though, the perceived stain on the reputation of "prophesying" seems to have faded, the Spirit's involvement in prophetic ministry was readily acknowledged,[38] and the benefit of hindsight (rather than foresight) could happily baptize Amos and his preexilic peers into the sphere of the Spirit's operation.[39] After all, the link between "spirit" and "word" is, as we have already had reason to notice, a perfectly natural entailment of both metaphors, and even where only one of the two is explicitly mentioned, therefore, poetic resonances should ensure that the other is never far from consideration. Despite the patchy and at times awkward pattern of scriptural testimony, then, the insistence of the creed of Nicaea that the Holy Spirit "has spoken by the prophets" is one resting on sound biblical as well as later theological judgments.[40]

As well as a wider role in creation as the giver and sustainer of life and implication in the utterance of God's Word (an event necessarily "inspired" in both the giving of and human response to it), in the Old Testament, the Spirit is to be identified elsewhere too as empowering particular figures so that they can acquit key responsibilities within the covenant between Israel and God. As well as the prophets, in other words, others were also held both to require and to "have" (or be "had" by) a generous donation of God's *ruach*. This is the case with some of the so-called judges who led Israel prior to the monarchy's establishment. Thus Joshua, we are told, is identified by Yahweh as a suitable successor to Moses because he is already "a man in whom is the spirit,"[41] while it is by the *ruach* of Yahweh too that Gideon is granted the personal qualities necessary to rout the Midianites,[42] Jephthah to deal similarly with the Ammonites,[43] and Samson to commit spectacular acts of random violence involving the dismembering of (or previously dismembered) animals.[44] As Alasdair Heron notes, what is envisaged in such instances is clearly not "mere innate human capacity" but rather "a violent and temporary possession of a person by a force rushing upon him from without."[45] (Samson's enemies, after all, commission Delilah to discover the "secret" of his remarkable strength, so it's far more likely that he is a scrawny individual rather than pumped up by excessive time spent in the gym.) Other remarkable abilities, too, are associated with the presence of the Spirit. Joseph's salutary ability to interpret Pharaoh's nightmares comes not from dabbling in proto-Freudian theory but, we are told, from the peculiar enabling of God's *ruach*.[46] Qualities which might otherwise be held to "come naturally" to some people—such as a creative skill, a depth of understanding, and a human "wisdom" echoing

God's own—are nonetheless also attributed to the presence and activity of God's Spirit, not just because, as the creator, *all* human ability and capacity must be held to derive ultimately from the Spirit, but because in the relevant cases, they are so exceptional in degree or in nature as to demand instead extraordinary ("supranatural") explanation.[47]

One might say, of course, that much of the time, it is precisely what "comes naturally" to Israel (and to human beings in general) that is the problem, our "nature" itself, ironically, being trapped within and distorted by patterns of inclination and behavior that, viewed in the light of our relationship with God, the Bible knows as "sin." In addressing this too, the Old Testament admits not so much a difference as an apparent *discontinuity* between discrete spheres or modes of the activity of God's *ruach*. On the one hand, there is, as we have seen, the Spirit's generative sustaining of "life" in accordance with God's creative vision.[48] On the other, though, there is the redemptive and regenerative action of the same Spirit in fashioning, enabling, and sustaining forms of life that will *hallow* rather than *profane* God's name—that will, that is to say, by reflecting rather than effacing God's own character, be undeniably "holy."[49] Establishing such holiness in history's midst will necessarily involve contradicting and redeeming rather than simply endorsing (or even turbocharging) the capacities of a sinful humanity. Thus it is precisely in contexts of prophetic *condemnation* that we also find talk of the Spirit of God etching God's law on human hearts, renewing and fulfilling the covenant between Yahweh and Israel by enabling its obligations to be met for the first time (fully and from the heart) from the human side, and as part of a Spirit-filled offering of "holiness" back to its personal source and archetype in which not just the covenant but *creation itself* ("all things") will at last be made new.[50] Then, in a world wholly saturated and shaped by the *ruach Yahweh*, the ancient pronouncement "You shall be my people and I will be your God"[51] will finally find traction, and God will indeed "suddenly come to his temple" (creation itself) and indwell it as God always intended to.[52] Heard within history, such words are bound to reach human ears laden with judgment as well as promise, and the envisioned outpouring of God's Spirit thus be grounds for both hopeful longing and nervous anticipation about its entailments and cost. Being made holy is no picnic. It entails struggle and suffering—even for Jesus, who, Christians believe, bore our flesh and the sin that was in it precisely to *make it holy* and offer it to the Father; who alone, therefore, heard that covenant pronouncement not as a word of personal judgment but as a personal commission, promise, and assurance of at-one-ment with the Father in a shared endeavor; and on whose ears, as the Father poured out the Holy Spirit upon him, it was transformed and its scope clarified further still: "You are my Son, the Beloved; with you I am well pleased."[53] But let's not get too far ahead of ourselves.

In view of the above, the bestowal, abiding presence, and influence of God's Spirit are closely associated in the Old Testament with the figure of the king in Israel—the figure who is meant precisely to be the human symbol and embodiment of Yahweh's own reign among the covenant people, in whom the keeping of the covenant is peculiarly focused, and in whom qualities such as strength, wisdom, skill, righteousness, and holiness, therefore, are generally reckoned to be a good thing. Despite the track record of royal failings that the Old Testament records from the ill-fated identification of Israel's first king onward, the availability of God's Spirit to the institution of monarchy is pronounced from the outset. Thus the one chosen by God can simply be referred to as "the Lord's anointed," a choice that, again, is guided more by what God's Spirit is capable of taking and using than by those natural qualities and capacities that, humanly speaking, might otherwise seem requisite for the role, and that is duly sealed by the symbolic ritual anointing with oil as monarchs embarked on their reign.[54] So, for example, we read of Samuel anointing David as God's chosen king, and we are told, "The spirit of the Lord came mightily upon David from that day forward."[55] Even in David's case (which set the gold standard by which other kings were judged by history), the Spirit's bestowal hardly guaranteed a flawless performance, but it no doubt accounts for the surprising success that, despite his initial physical mediocrity and his moral and spiritual failings, David's reign actually proved to be.

The Swiss theologian Karl Barth describes creation as the "external basis of the covenant" and the covenant as the "internal basis of creation,"[56] an organic connection already signaled in the Old Testament's identification of the Spirit as the agent by which each is to be fulfilled in the fulfillment of the other. This thought gains momentum and comes into sharper focus as there emerges in Israel's life an expectation concerning one whose appearance in the nation's midst will, when it occurs, be not just one more in the motley series of individuals anointed by God as "instruments of the covenant" but, supremely, the revelation of "*the* anointed one"[57]—the *Mashiach*, Messiah, or Christ, whose coming, in fact, will be a complete game changer. So, for instance, there are the familiar words from Isaiah 11 about the Davidic king who will arise and transform not just the political fortunes of Israel but the moral and spiritual conditions of the earth: "The spirit of the LORD shall rest on him. . . . His delight shall be in the fear of the LORD."[58] And again, later in the book associated with Isaiah's name, we find the following vision of an anointed deliverer sent by God to perform unprecedented acts and to secure Israel's salvation: "The spirit of the Lord GOD is upon me, because the LORD has anointed me; he has sent me to bring good news to the oppressed, to bind up the brokenhearted, to proclaim liberty to the captives, and release to the prisoners; to proclaim the year of the LORD's favour, and the day of vengeance of our God."[59] And so it continues. The most expansive vision in the Old Testament's repertoire, though, challenges or complements this concentration of the Spirit's work in a single figure, setting alongside it the hope that on the Day of the Lord, the Spirit of the Lord will no longer be restricted to any individual or group but at last be poured out liberally, and not on the people of Israel alone[60] but on "all flesh,"[61] granting to *all God's creatures* for the first time, that is to say, an intimate "knowing" of (and "being known by") God hitherto only anticipated and restricted to the likes of prophets, priests, kings. Again, this prodigal hope takes shape and gathers force gradually through the course of that history to which the Old Testament bears theological witness and the history of its own assembly, composition, and editing, but we find the hope expressed not only toward the end but in nuce already at the beginning of Israel's story, as Moses—the greatest of all the prophets and the only one, we are told, ever to converse with Yahweh "face to face, as one speaks to a friend"[62]—eschews any jealous protection of his prerogative, expressing instead the desire "that all the LORD's people were prophets, and that the LORD would put his spirit on them."[63]

Scriptural Glimpses of God's Spirit—the New Testament

SINCE THE PROMISED new covenant and renewed creation are identified in the Jewish scriptures as the sphere of the Spirit's promised outpouring and anointing, it is hardly surprising that in the New Testament, we find mention of God's Spirit cropping up everywhere and from the outset.[64] It begins, naturally enough, with the story that the Gospels have to tell about Jesus, the one in whom God's Word "took flesh," became a human being, and dwelled among us as one of us. The Spirit's work in the new covenant—the promised outpouring of God's Spirit on all flesh—does not happen to everyone all at once, nor, as we might think, does it *begin* with the church, the community of believers to whom Jesus promised to send the Spirit. We might suppose so, remembering the excitement of the day of Pentecost recounted in Acts 2 and Peter's enthusiastic appeal to the ancient prophecy of Joel. And, of course, the two are not unrelated—far from it. But the outpouring of God's Spirit on "all flesh," far from being accomplished "all at once" or even by a phased series of individual donations, is in reality accomplished "once for all." It begins with Jesus, the one who came to share our human nature and to regenerate and redeem our nature from within by a continuous offering of his life to the Father on our behalf and for our sake.

The intimate involvement of the Spirit with the Son's humanity thus begins at the outset, with Jesus's conception and birth;[65] takes on a decisive new stage at his baptism;[66] and thereafter is everywhere involved with all that Jesus does, in praying,[67] in struggling with and overcoming the forces of evil,[68] in his ministry of peripatetic teaching and healing,[69] in offering himself to suffering and death,[70] and of course in his resurrection from death.[71] To employ the terms of a nascent trinitarian theology (which begins to emerge precisely in the pattern of Jesus's ministry as the Gospels narrate it): The Spirit is the Spirit of the Father[72] and the Spirit of the Son;[73] the Father sends or pours out the Spirit into the Son's human life,[74] and all that the Son does humanly he does "in the power" of the Spirit who indwells him.[75] The whole life of the divinely "anointed one," from birth cry to last breath, is lived in the Spirit, and the whole is, at the last and in the power of the Spirit, offered up to the Father in an act of worship in which the Spirit herself* too is "offered back," her work in the humanity of Jesus now completed.[76] This last point is nicely made in a suggestive verse in John's Gospel, where we read, "Jesus . . . said 'it is finished.'" Then he bowed his head and παρέδωκεν τὸ πνεῦμα."[77] The last three words are generally rendered into English as "gave up his spirit," but they are equally well (and perhaps better) translated as "handed over (or 'offered up') the Spirit."[78] Just as Jesus's human life begins with the Spirit's overshadowing of the womb of Mary, and his ministry begins with a fresh infusion of the gift of the Spirit at his baptism, so here it all ends, in other words, not in tragedy but in triumph, being brought to its climax and fulfillment ("it is finished") as Jesus, having endured all and done all, faithfully offers the Spirit back to the Father as the gift perpetually and mutually given and received within the dynamics of their love for each other.[79]

This, to reiterate, is why Jesus is everywhere and always identified as "Jesus the Christ" (Jesus *the Messiah*)—that is, Jesus the one peculiarly anointed, endowed, filled, empowered by the Holy Spirit of God. And that's why, having received and responded to the Father's gift of the Spirit for our sake and on our behalf, the Spirit can properly be referred to as the Spirit of Christ, and Jesus, for his part, can and does claim the authority to "send" the Holy Spirit into the church and into the world. Jesus is precisely *the* Spirit-filled human being. The original.

*On use of the feminine pronoun to refer to the Holy Spirit see note 76.

The firstborn. The one who, as the "last Adam,"[80] is not merely also the true Israel, the promised one in whom the covenant is fulfilled,[81] but the firstborn of God's renewed creation.[82] And the Spirit, therefore, is *his*, in his abiding solidarity with and reliance upon the Father, and the Spirit is *his*, in his turn, to offer back to the Father and to give to others.[83] The incarnation, in other words, is as much the work and domain of the Holy Spirit as it is of the Word/Son, and the Spirit can only be poured out upon us because she is poured out first and decisively in the life and death of the human Son himself[84]—that is, within God's own human life. More, though, must be said than this. For the giving and receiving of the Spirit, theologians across the centuries have insisted, is not simply a function of the relationship between God and humankind, or creator and creation but in some sense exists already and in its original, truest, and richest form in God's own life, and so eternally. In fact, "the mutual self-giving of Father and Son in the Spirit," Tom Smail writes, "is of the very essence of the life of God," an interpersonal give-and-take that, when it is earthed in history and in human guise, takes the form of prayer.[85] What occurs in the life of Jesus (which is from first to last the product of a constant dynamic of prayer and self-offering), therefore, is that the close relationship of mutual love and indwelling in God among the Father, Son, and Holy Spirit is knit together securely for the first time with the stuff of our flesh and blood. The life of the man Jesus, that is to say, is itself a creaturely form and expression (and so a "bodying forth" and a revelation) of the love that the eternal Son has for the Father, a love facilitated and mediated by the gift and person of the Holy Spirit and a love into the scope of which, in its solidarity with Jesus and through the outpouring of the same Spirit upon it, "all flesh" is graciously drawn, in which it is now rooted and may participate in its own proper, creaturely way.

In dealing with the Spirit, too, therefore, we are dealing precisely with God present with us in person, present in a way distinct from but closely related to the way God is present humanly in the person of Jesus. This is a claim the breathtaking enormity of which, it seems to me, breaks over us far too rarely. After all, Paul speaks of the Spirit as coming to us and "dwelling in" us as believers and members of the church, of the Spirit taking up residence in our bodies in a manner directly analogous to Yahweh's dwelling in the tabernacle and temple of old and, from within us, making good the shortfall in our praying as we groan under the load of existence in an as yet sin-laden and unredeemed world, by interceding for us and in us and through us, and so opening our hearts, minds, and wills to be offered up to our heavenly Father through the S/spirit of sonship[86]—the very same Spirit whose life was and is intertwined gloriously with that of the one true Son, Jesus. Why is it, I wonder, that Christians have anguished and argued endlessly about the seemingly outrageous claim that in Jesus, God himself became directly and personally present among us in history as the human Son, but have spilled far less ink over the parallel and equally important claim that God was then and is now directly and personally present with and among and *in* us as the Holy Spirit? Is this a claim any less enormous? Any less outrageous? Really? Or do we let it pass unscathed, perhaps, only because we do not have its implications properly in perspective?

In the New Testament, the characteristic way of referring to the Spirit is as the *Holy* Spirit. In part, no doubt, this has to do with what we have seen to be the Spirit's role in drawing the world, and human lives, into gradual conformity to or correlation with God's own character. She is precisely the Spirit of holiness, through whose agency alone creation will finally reflect the holiness that is God's own. But here, of course, is another clue to the force of this description. In Jewish literature and tradition, *holiness* is almost tautologically the defining attribute of Yahweh[87] so that no one else can be referred to simply as "the Holy One of Israel,"[88] and the language of holiness is applied to other things (people, places, times, objects and so on) precisely insofar as they are set apart and drawn within the penumbra of Yahweh's presence and dominion. There can be little doubt, therefore, that reference to the Holy Spirit in the New Testament is intended to underscore the fact that this is precisely the Spirit of *God*, the Spirit of the LORD. The Holy Spirit, in other words, is none other than the Holy One of Israel, a way in which the Holy One of Israel is present among us in person. Paul drives the point home further by referring to the Spirit not just as "the Spirit of the Lord" but simply as "The Lord" (ὁ κύριος[89]), a term charged with theological significance for Greek-speaking Jews as the conventional circumlocution for *Yahweh*, the unutterable (and uninscribable) divine name that, we might note, was held to be unutterable and uninscribable precisely because it was itself so *holy*. This is the one who, in ancient times, could not be looked upon directly and whose very presence literally burned and threatened to destroy mortal and sinful reality. This is the one, Paul insists, who now takes up her dwelling in us and in our church communities, and whose glory our lives are therefore intended to reflect and body forth in the world. At one level, if we don't feel just a tad nervous when pausing to reflect on this, we are probably missing something.

It's important, too, to be clear that the Holy Spirit is God present precisely *in person*, and not some impersonal force or surge of divine energy. In the language of later trinitarian theology, the Spirit is a third "person" (*hypostasis* or *persona*) alongside the Father and the Son in God, and although we need to be careful not to read too much into this technical term (since it doesn't mean exactly what we understand by talk of "persons" or "personalities" today), in the New Testament, the Spirit is certainly pictured as a third distinct center of what we may properly refer to as "personal" identity and activity in God and not simply a way in which either the Father or the Son is present to us "in person."[90] The Spirit, we might say by way of clarification, is *who* is in us, not *what* is in us, and she is so in a way that is her prerogative alone, not that of the Father or the Son. There is, nonetheless, certain anonymity about the Holy Spirit, who is, to borrow a phrase from Yves Congar's magisterial book on this doctrine, the person "without a personal face."[91] The Spirit, that is to say, is never the center of attention in Scripture, never draws attention to her- or himself, but is always concerned to draw attention (and enable our response) instead to the Father and the Son. In this respect, the Spirit has been likened, helpfully, to a well-positioned floodlight, illuminating that which it is the Spirit's task to illuminate and draw attention to while herself remaining hidden and unnoticed in the shadows.[92] Yet unlike an unwieldy, powerful, and efficient bit of hardware fixed to a gantry above us, the Spirit nonetheless acts and wills and relates "personally," both within the life of God (as an identifiable third alongside the Father and the Son) and within the shape of Christian experience. In the New Testament, it has been said, we *meet* God, and in Christian life, we *experience* God not just in three different ways but in three different ways *at the same time*—as the Father, as the Son, and as the Holy Spirit. And if we are to be true to the biblical pattern, we should add, three different ways in which God experiences Godself at the same time. This "triunity" (as theologians like to call it) is evidenced in the patterns of the life of Jesus (in which, as we have seen, the incarnate Son receives the gift of the Spirit from his Father, prays to the Father, is sent by the Father, and offers himself back to the Father in the power of the Spirit). It is also manifest conveniently and classically in the dynamics and language of our prayer and worship, which are typically offered *to* the Father, *through* the Son, and *in* the power of the Holy Spirit; which embrace the whole of our lives (or are meant to); and which are, as I have already suggested, precisely a sharing in the dynamic relational pattern of the threefold life of God.

If, therefore, the Holy Spirit's work in the new covenant begins with Jesus, it certainly does not end there, and the promise of Old Testament texts such as Joel 2 and Ezekiel 36 quickly became picked up by the early church to make sense of its own experience of God in Christ—an experience in which the coming of the Holy Spirit (being "sent" or "poured out" by the risen and ascended Jesus) was focused no longer on key characters in Jewish national life, such as Herod or Caiaphas, but instead now upon ordinary men and women who were believers in and followers of Jesus. Indeed (and scandal of scandals), the Holy Spirit was not even to be limited to Jews but, as the bizarre experience of the day of Pentecost revealed, to be available to gentiles from all over the known world too. In fact, receiving the gift of God's Holy Spirit was, in the apostolic era, part of the basic package of entailments of becoming or being a "Christian" (one identified with the messianic age) at all. Repent, be baptized for the forgiveness of your sins, receive God's Holy Spirit—that was the threefold induction into the community of those who were believers in and followers of Jesus. Far from being restricted to a cohort of particularly important or "spiritual" people, in other words, having God's Holy Spirit dwell within you was the most basic requirement for belonging to the *ecclesia*, or "church," and it was a self-gifting of God available to absolutely anybody who would receive it rather than eschewing or resisting it.

God with Us and God in Us

AGAIN, IT WOULD be good to pause at this point and take stock. I have referred on a number of occasions in previous chapters to the substance of the biblical belief which may be summed up by saying that the world was created so that God and God's creatures might dwell together, a circumstance symbolized in ancient Israel by the tabernacle and the temple but incapable of full realization due to the spoiling of creation by sin and death. But in the new, reborn, transformed world which God has promised, that dream of heaven and earth coming together, of God being with and at the center of "a creation restored by love" (as the Scottish Episcopal Church liturgy puts it), and of God sharing in intimate fellowship with us will at last be realized and the purpose of God's creative project finally fulfilled.[93] So John the "seer" and author of the biblical book of Revelation writes of the coming down of "the holy city, the new Jerusalem" from heaven to earth and of a loud voice saying, "See, the home of God is among mortals. He will dwell with them; they will be his peoples, and God himself will be with them; he will wipe every tear from their eyes. Death will be no more; mourning and crying and pain will be no more, for the first things have passed away."[94] We get the picture. And the very heart of all this is the proximity and availability of God to God's creatures in a radically new way. And so, John avers, there will be no *temple* in the city. After all, what need will there be of a temple? God will be dwelling in *the whole* of it, not in some spatially circumscribed part. And God's glory will illuminate the whole of it.[95]

In the meanwhile, we struggle on, living our lives in the light of that hope and by faith. But while the coming of the eternal Son in the flesh is the decisive anticipation and pledge of that hope, it is not the only concrete anticipation of it. Yes, the Son creates for himself his own humanity in the womb of Mary and comes to indwell it. But in doing so, he also becomes a peculiar locus of the Holy Spirit's indwelling and activity—another way in which God is intimately present and active—in God's world, drawing us back to our creator, transforming and renewing our humanity and thereby the world itself. And to reiterate, this mode of God's being "with us" is not restricted to Jesus, though it has its origin in his coming among us and bearing our nature. But the Holy Spirit is the Father's gift not for the divine and human Son alone but also for *us*, those to whom the Son has united himself by taking flesh, and the Spirit's destiny is, we have seen, to be poured out prodigally on "all flesh," beginning, it seems, with those who now believe in and follow Jesus himself. So the indwelling of the Holy Spirit within us (and if we are Christians at all, Paul tells us, we *have* the Holy Spirit dwelling in us[96]) *is* the personal, intimate coming to be "with us" and "in us" of God himself, the Holy One of Israel (visions of whom had the prophet Isaiah quaking in his boots), the creator of all things in heaven and on earth. And as such, *this*, the establishment of an unnumbered host of "temple[s] of the Holy Spirit" through our union with the humanity of Jesus, is the next step in God's fulfillment of God's great promise, the decisive and visible foothold God retains for the time being in the midst of this messy, broken, sinful, and suffering world.[97]

"Where is God?" people typically rage and demand to know in the midst of it all (especially when things are going horribly badly). The disconcerting answer—or a significant part of it, anyway—is this: God is *here*, here in the Holy Spirit dwelling in and present to the world and all that is done and happens in it, in its pain and sorrows as well as its joys, holding it secure in God's embrace as the object of God's love. God is *here* in the Holy Spirit indwelling the church and the life of every individual disciple of Jesus as a temple; watching, listening, waiting to see how long it will take for us to notice or remember; waiting for opportunities to be at work in and through us in order to manifest God's glory and hallow God's name in the world; changing *us*, changing our relationships to people and things around us, and so changing the world in ways that point beyond the present malaise to its true reality, which is, as yet, still to come. If we dwell on that, chew on it for a while, really believe it and take it seriously, and then call it to mind in the comings and goings, the doings and happenings of daily life, the one thing it surely *cannot* generate is a complacent or casual attitude. Awe, yes; wonder, yes; discomfort and anxiety, yes. But not complacency.

The apostle Paul grapples with some of the spiritual and ethical implications of this directly in his letters to the Christian congregations at Corinth and Ephesus.[98] *You*, he tells them (referring both to individuals and to the church as a community of such individuals), are now the *temple*, the place where God himself dwells through God's Spirit, and the point of the temple is to be a place where God is *glorified*, not horrified, a place where God can enjoy the smell of fragrant sacrifices, not grit his teeth in the face of things that revolt and anger him. The temple is a *holy* place, and to treat it disrespectfully is sacrilege. So, Paul urges his readers, don't treat your bodies (or your minds or imaginations, for that matter) or your relationships with one another lightly or as though they were your personal property, to be done with or done to as you personally please. They aren't. They are places in which God now deigns graciously to dwell in the person of the Holy Spirit, places dedicated to glorifying God and enjoying God. So put away and have nothing to do (in body, heart, mind, or soul) with anything that is bound to *grieve* God's Holy Spirit. In doing so, you aren't grieving God at a safe distance: in effect, you are defiling

God's temple, carrying offensive offerings right into the heart of the sanctuary and dumping them down under God's nose. In that context, as they say, discretion is probably the better part of valor.

The great Baptist preacher Charles Spurgeon says somewhere, "Without the Spirit of God, we can do nothing. We are as ships without the wind, branches without sap, and like coals without fire, we are useless." And yet, it has been suggested, whereas the Holy Spirit's withdrawal from the church that we read about in the book of Acts would see 98 percent of its activity grind to a halt, the Spirit's withdrawal from today's church might easily leave 98 percent of its activity undisturbed. The proportions are exaggerated for rhetorical effect, no doubt, but the point is an important one nonetheless. Christian congregations, Christian denominations, and individual Christian lives tend typically to be the domain of routines, systems, rotas, and religious habits—things that we repeat and do day in and day out, week in and week out, because that's what we do and have always done. Such things can, of course, be incredibly helpful; perhaps they are even *necessary* for the ordering of our inner and outer worlds, enabling us to indwell these meaningfully and get things done efficiently. So there's nothing wrong with routines, habits, and institutions in and of themselves. But such things can also easily become ends in themselves, the ossified remnants on the surface of our lives of something itself once vibrant and pulsing but now enfeebled and withered—reduced to its cherished external forms alone. And the shift between these two states can be and often is so gradual as to be imperceptible, not least to ourselves. Change for the sake of change alone, of course, is something to which most of us are resistant, and perhaps rightly so. But the transformation of our lives, our congregations, our communities, and finally the world itself so that it comes to reflect God's character, to hallow God's name is bound to involve change, and it is precisely this, as we have seen, that the Holy Spirit's peculiar work is concerned to accomplish. So it behooves us constantly to be asking one another whether our routines, habits, and institutions are still the ways in which the Holy Spirit is prompting and calling us to be and to do things, still the ways in which God's Spirit within us is leading us. Or is God nudging us to think afresh, to move on, to step out into the unfamiliar and unknown and inherently uncomfortable? We need, as Paul puts it in his Epistle to the Galatians, not just to have the Spirit within us but to "keep in step" with the Spirit as she prompts and nudges and cajoles and draws us and be careful not to resist or ignore her coaxing and guiding.[99] "Without the Spirit of God, we can do nothing. We are as ships without the wind, branches without sap, and like coals without fire, we are useless." But in truth, of course, it's not that we can *do nothing* without the Spirit; we can *do* plenty and keep on doing it ad infinitum, sincerely supposing ourselves to be putting on a good religious show in the process. But if what we do is *out of step* with the Spirit, if it is no longer the appropriate vehicle for the Spirit's working in us and through us, if it is no longer what the Spirit *would have us* do but we keep doing it blithely anyway, then our doing of it—no matter how sincere or energetic or how impressive the results may appear outwardly to be—will indeed be "*useless*," useless in terms of our growth in Christ, useless in terms of our pursuit of God's kingdom, useless in terms of honoring God and hallowing God's name in the midst of the world around us.

The thing is, though, we can't consciously seek to align ourselves or be "in step" with the Spirit if we aren't even aware of—or have forgotten—the fact that the Spirit is stepping out in our lives. We won't be listening for the Spirit's prompting within us if we aren't expecting to hear it—if, like some of the Christians Paul meets in Ephesus in Acts 19, we have "not even heard that there is a Holy Spirit."[100] Of course, most of *us* will actually have "heard about" the Spirit in Bible readings, sermons, and the like. In fact, we may have accrued quite a lot of *information* about the Holy Spirit along the way. But that's not what Paul is driving at in his interrogation of these Ephesian Christians. "Did you *receive* the Holy Spirit when you became believers?" he asks them.[101] And they have to admit that as far as they are aware, they hadn't. *As far as they are aware.* There's the rub—because in reality and despite our levels of awareness, *receiving* the gift of the Holy Spirit is part of the basic Christian package. Time and again in the New Testament, as we have already noted, we find a threefold exhortation in the apostles' preaching:[102] repent, be baptized, *and receive the Holy Spirit*. And each of those three component parts is hugely important because they belong naturally together. Repent, be baptized, and receive the Holy Spirit. "Did you receive the Holy Spirit when you became believers?" Paul asks them. "Well, no!" they say. "We didn't know we were meant to!" It's perfectly possible to be good, respectable church members; to have been baptized; to have repented and received forgiveness for your sins; to believe that Jesus is Lord—and yet *not* to have received the Holy Spirit. *Receiving* the Holy Spirit is not something that happens automatically or without you knowing it. God *gives* the Holy Spirit, pours the Spirit out in fulfillment of his promise, comes to dwell in our lives, but *receiving* the gift can only ever be an action—something we do and do consciously, intentionally, with full awareness that we are doing so and desire to do so.

Too many Christians—and too many Christian congregations, I suspect—operate with a merely theoretical or "academic" awareness of the gift of God's Spirit poured out in their lives, glugging over them and soaking into them exactly like the ancient oil of anointing. But the Spirit is there. The Spirit is here—in my life, in your life, in the lives of our congregations. But are we *receiving* the Spirit, intentionally paying attention, listening for the Spirit's voice, opening ourselves, making ourselves available to receive ever more of the Spirit's gift to us? Perhaps we haven't done so for a long time. Perhaps we never knew we were supposed to and so have never done so. But it's never too late (and it's never too soon) to start, because without receiving the Holy Spirit, as Spurgeon suggests, we shall necessarily find ourselves stuck where we are—unchanged from day to day, year to year, decade to decade of our lives—and impotent to participate, as God calls us to, in the radical regeneration or "rebirth" of our "flesh," our lives, and our world "from above," of which Jesus speaks to Nicodemus.[103] To return to where we began, the redemptive and sanctifying work of the Holy Spirit is work that takes place *in* us and *through* us, and unlike the work of the Son *for us* (making our humanity his own and offering it to the Father in our place), it will not and cannot happen, therefore, *without* us (without, that is to say, our active involvement) precisely because it is "us" in our entirety—our lives, bodies, imaginations, hearts, minds, wills, relationships, passions, and actions—that is the object of the Spirit's renewing and transforming energy. So *receiving* that Spirit, opening ourselves, no matter how reluctantly or how gradually, to God's gracious approach and desire to anoint and to bless us, drawing and grafting us into a creation that is *being changed*, being restored by God's love, is part and parcel of what our "salvation" has to entail. Again, we find ourselves compelled to reckon with the reality that, far from being a "condition" of salvation—even the *sole* condition as formulations of the gospel message sometimes suggest ("All you *have to do* is . . .")—repentance, faith, and obedience are more helpfully thought of as the forms salvation itself takes and *must take* when our lives are first opened up to become responsive to the Spirit's presence and activity.

The truth is that in and of ourselves, we cannot do anything to put ourselves in that place where "eternal life," "life in all its fulness," that life in which "God lives in us, and his love is perfected in us" becomes ours or we participate in it.[104] What we cannot hope to do *in and of ourselves*, though, God *has done for us* in Jesus and *promises* to do in and through us by the creator Spirit, whose desire and capacity are finally to make all things holy. God in the Spirit gives us the gift of *Godself* present in us, infusing the life of Christ into us; enabling our response to God's call; filling us with joy and peace in our worship; granting us strength, hope, and guidance; liberating us from the things that bind and restrict our living; empowering us to do things we know ourselves otherwise to be wholly incapable of desiring to do, let alone actually doing; sustaining and holding us when the times of pain and suffering come (as they will); and finally accompanying us through death—no longer a fearsome foe whose clutches we resist in terror but the door to a creation restored by love. In short, we are granted a share in the Father's gift of the Holy Spirit poured out upon us in the Son and in the Son's offering of holy love to the Father in the power of the same Spirit. All of life is here, as God draws our creaturely life and its history within the scope of God's own eternal life to share in God's joy and to enjoy God's glory forever.

10

"THE HOLY CATHOLIC CHURCH..."

THE GERMAN TONGUE is renowned for its ability to render entire phrases into single words, cobbling together impressive compound nouns that, one supposes, must present a challenge even for the native speaker, let alone the novice. Take, for instance, the word *Donaudampfschiffahrtsgesellschaftskapitän*, which, at an impressive forty-one characters and eleven syllables, demands a bit of limbering up all by itself, quite apart from any sentence that it may crop up in.[1] German sentences, too, can be long and complex rather than short and pithy, some, as Mark Twain notes, being like a dog that swims the Atlantic with a verb in its mouth. And words such as the aforementioned (which, in case you don't know and are wondering, means "Danube company steamship captain") are so long, he adds, as to have perspective.

On the whole, the English language is much more modest in its ambitions, though there are some notable exceptions to the rule. When I was in primary school, teachers of the day would seek to impress by bestowing freely the adult information that the longest word in the English dictionary was *antidisestablishmentarianism* (twenty-eight letters, twelve syllables), which also looks daunting and as though it might benefit from some punctuation in order to assist those with asthma or other breathing problems. As it turns out, though, this was what nowadays might be dubbed "fake news," since further linguistic modification easily generates an adverbial form (*antidisestablishmentarianistically*, thirty-four letters, fourteen syllables) which pips it at the post, and in any case, neither word found its way into many dictionaries, these tending, on the whole, to be more concerned with words that are actually used in day-to-day conversation. Presumably for similar reasons, *supercalifragilisticexpialidocious* (thirty-four letters, fourteen syllables) didn't figure much either.

Antidisestablishmentarianism is, of course, an attitude of committed resistance to any attempt to dislodge a church established by law from its privileged status relative to the national government and for that reason is even less likely to crop up in daily chat in officially "secular" societies such as the United States or France, say, than it is in the United Kingdom. Mention of it might, nonetheless, seem an inauspicious or provocative way in which to open a treatment of the nature of the church, a doctrine that, as one study reminds us, tends already to be divisive, different understandings of it lying close to the root of the church's gradual fragmentation over the centuries and continuing to drive a wedge between its various communions.[2] In fact, though, I don't intend to talk about ecclesial establishment (or, for that matter, disestablishment) at all, though I may feel the need to mention fragmentation again, at least briefly, before the chapter is over. No doubt the unduly protracted word sprang from memory to mind as one belonging within the relevant ballpark doctrinally, but my use of it was in reality purely for the purpose of plundering its brief suffix, *-ism* (three letters, two syllables). Modern life and reports of it are, as we know all too well, populated plentifully by *-isms* of one sort or another, some more helpful and some more palatable than others.

An *-ism*, we might note, was originally the product of turning verbs into abstract nouns (i.e., ones that refer to something intangible, like ideas, ideologies, qualities, values, feelings, and states of mind). Nouning verbs, of course, is a process unpopular in certain of its clumsy manifestations ("That was an epic *fail*" or "What's the *ask* from the contractor?") with linguistic purists (*purist* itself presumably being the product of nouning the adjective *pure*)—so too is the opposite tendency of verbing nouns (as in *journaling, deplaning, googling,* and of course, *verbing*), much of which, it has been observed, simply weirds language.[3] Nouning verbs, though, goes all the way back at least to the ancient Greeks, who regularly took those of their verbs ending in *-izō* and replaced the final two syllables to create -*ismos*. This practice is reflected directly in our modern English dictionaries in cognates such as *criticize-criticism*, *baptize-baptism*, *commercialize-commercialism*, *anthropomorphize-anthropomorphism*, and so on, though -*ism* has long since spilled over to generate lots of other abstract nouns besides. And so we find our daily discourse cluttered with such words, some striking us as merely nominative and descriptive, others having a decided political edge to them, dependent on our personal preferences, experiences, and points of view: alcoholism, veganism, exhibitionism, fundamentalism, nationalism, nonconformism, capitalism, terrorism, monasticism, sexism, secularism, elitism, tribalism, tourism, and pietism, all picked randomly from the pages of a daily newspaper (eclecticism).

Unmentioned so far are three particular -*isms* lying close to the ideological pulse of modern Western life and thus, thanks to the globalizing impact of media and markets, quietly shaping the assumptions, expectations, and aspirations of people's lives the world over—individualism, idealism, and libertarianism. And these three -*isms* enjoy a peculiar relationship with the very idea of the church (if not always with its actual manifestations), presenting it with both a challenge and an opportunity in equal measure. What the church points us to instead is a very different sort of reality, one in which who and what we are and are called to become humanly is anything but a countless throng of hermetically sealed units of intelligent consciousness, each struggling nobly to transcend the constraints that biology, time, place, and various voices of authority would impose on us, to make of ourselves instead what we will through ambition, ingenuity, and the exercise of individual freedom. The dogma that "You can be whoever you want to be" may successfully sell everything these days from designer clothes, smartphones, and gym subscriptions to online master's programs in creative writing, but you're unlikely to find it either as the strap line for initiatives in Christian mission or front and center in baptismal liturgies. And if you do (or to the extent that you do), beware—because you can be confident that what you are dealing with then is counterfeit rather than authentic Christianity. For whatever grains of truth these ideological doctrines may each contain, their larger commitments need to be taken with a large pinch of salt; otherwise, they feed ruthlessly into the potentially toxic mixture on which the modern world is drip-fed by those standing to benefit most from our addiction to it.

In place of it, though, what the church has to offer by way of a gospel "detox" is a vision of human life as a rich gift to be received freely and thankfully from God's hand rather than individually chosen, demanded (by right), grasped, and "made" bespoke; of embodied persons already grounded and embedded in relationships and responsibilities and bound up with the concrete particulars of a given place and time; of wonder, praise, and thanksgiving as the natural modes of human response to the world rather than a sense of self-entitlement (and resentment whenever the world's determination to be itself takes little account of our personal desires or well-being); of a freedom to be found and enjoyed within various given, creaturely constraints rather than despite them (and most especially in self-sacrifice rather than self-protection or self-advancement); of flourishing and joy to be had in freely sharing with others the riches of commonly held resources rather than grabbing whatever we can for ourselves and our own at others' expense; of power and authority realized most completely in choosing weakness and self-limitation rather than self-assertion or coercion—because it believes "that the power that has the last word in human affairs is represented by a man hanging on the cross" and in a God whose sovereignty is manifest precisely in what the world around us identifies as failure.[4]

It is important that this is not misheard. Like most ideologies, the myth that would construe us as (and turn us into) a marketplace of informed individual consumers is not wholly bereft of insights and goods, and it has been involved, clumsily but positively, in many of the admitted gains of the modern era. No one is advocating a return to a world or a form of society in which each person's unique individuality of potential and value is swallowed up and lost in the interest of "the tribe"; or liberty of belief, thought, speech, and practice surrendered in unquestioning submission to authoritarian institutions of one sort or another; or opportunities for personal flourishing denied de facto by socioeconomic, racial, religious, or any other "accidents" of birth. But the models of freedom and individuality the myth has fostered are, I believe, both false and finally unsustainable ones, encouraging values, ideals, and aspirations that titillate our sense of self-importance and generate unhealthy appetites that, we are led to suppose, we should strive to gratify. And while there have indeed been social, economic, technological, and all sorts of other "gains" that even the briefest comparison with conditions prevailing a couple of centuries ago will quickly divulge, it takes scant consideration of the wider picture of how things stand in the world today to recognize that such gains are of a limited sort, being far from comprehensive, unevenly distributed, and anything but unalloyed in their impacts. A world struggling so obviously, for instance, with an ever-widening gap between the rich and the poor (within as well as among nation-states) and with the nature and rate of our consumption of our earth's resources, in which the demand to choose and choose well (from college course and career to style of coffee and brand of cat food) is so relentless and all-pervasive as to induce anxiety, and where the dominant social ill of the age is now calculated to be loneliness, might be supposed ripe for some reconsideration and deconstruction of its underlying myths and narratives (the so-called "myth of progress" being another[5]) instead of continuing to grant them unchallenged fealty and influence.

Furthermore, history reveals that many of the great gains of modernity were born from the womb of a culture still sufficiently saturated with Christian moral and spiritual vision as to be able to grant them life. Individualism, idealism, libertarianism, and various other dubious *-isms* themselves prove in certain respects, indeed, to have been the malformed progeny of just such a culture rather than intellectual *creationes ex nihilo* or, as often alleged, the surgical retrieval of some untainted, pre-Christian heritage by the humanist and secularist pioneers of the

Renaissance and the Enlightenment. Christendom, of course, had certainly had a checkered and at times horrendous track record to repent of, as the church has often had since. But the so-called dark ages were not as dark in intellectual, cultural, moral, and spiritual terms as some portrayals of them would have us believe, and those of us who continue willingly to bear the yoke of the name "Christian" will, in any case, wish to insist that the reality of the gospel itself—once disentangled from the sometimes unfortunate trappings of the church as a sinful, human institution—is properly generative of a quite different account of the human circumstance and of human capacity and incapacity.[6] The story it has to tell is one that is at once far more negative and far more positive in its estimation of what the human creature amounts to within a cosmos that is the gift and the delight of God. Grounded in the truth as it is given in Jesus Christ—in whom our humanity is "ransomed, healed, restored, forgiven," and drawn into the very life of God himself—it can legitimately lay claim to the status of a "true humanism," in fact, and a truth "by which society can be given coherence and direction."[7]

The myths of humanity supposedly "coming of age" often prove, by comparison, to be tied up in all sorts of ways with the self-esteem, self-interest, and self-justification of both those who tell them and those to and about whom they are told, which no doubt accounts for their popularity and their endurance in the teeth of strong evidence to the contrary. The Christian story is always, on the face of it, going to be less attractive and to "make no sense" to those whose antennae are already attuned to an alternative, superficially more compelling wavelength. As it was in Paul's day—"a stumbling block to Jews and foolishness to Greeks"[8]—so it has always been whenever the church has found itself and its message minority concerns in the midst of a culture at best indifferent and at worst hostile to them. And so they continue to be in modern Western societies, where the dominant ideology (some version of scientistic naturalism and/or secular humanism) enjoys a privileged position at court typically by masquerading as the neutral product of dispassionate, objective, and unmistakably "rational" intellectual procedures. Disavowing anything resembling mere opinion or matters taken on faith or trust and seeking to erase completely the potential distortions introduced by particular personal perspective, its various dogmas are dressed up instead in the guise of empirically established "hard facts," or unchallengeable maxims hardwired into the minds of intelligent persons the world over (the putative canons of "pure reason"), or else some construct built securely and solely on the supposedly solid foundations provided by these. The reality, though, is very different. As Lesslie Newbigin reminds us, "There is no such thing as an ideological vacuum" even in the most avowedly "secular" societies; there are no "hard facts" that have not already been identified, quarried, and *interpreted* as such by someone relying on the tools and the training and the wider vision of their craft; there are no "truths of reason" left unscathed by the personal peculiarities of the one who appeals to and handles them in a particular context.[9] What we know, like what we believe—as individuals, as societies—has our personal fingerprints all over it, and the two are far more closely bound up than we are typically led to suppose.

Officially, modern Western societies are both "secular" and "pluralist," a distinction closely bound up with another which enjoys far less exposure in our day-to-day conversation but exercises a profound influence over the theorizing of those who exercise power and so control the shape life takes in those societies. Significantly enough, this further distinction will be most familiar from its use in the vocabulary of economics, but its ideological reach extends much further into our lives than that. What I have in mind is the sharp distinction typically drawn between the "public" and the "private" domains of life. In economic terms, this distinction refers to that which is owned by the state (or the public as citizens of it) on the one hand and that which is owned by individuals expending their own private income or wealth on the other. Its metaphorical extension in liberal democracies to apply to the "ownership" of truths, ideas, beliefs, and practices instead, though, generates a dualism that rests on an illusion and so, far from being helpful, is unsustainable and finally damaging in its contribution to social and political as well as personal existence.[10] In the terms of this metaphorical conceit, the "public" sector is precisely the sphere of universally "owned" or agreed knowledge—knowledge, that is to say, that is common property, available to everyone by virtue of their nature as intelligent human beings (well equipped to reckon with the indisputable "facts" of a circumstance, the unbiased claims of "cold" reasoning, or even the dictates of "common sense") and their place as responsible citizens of civilized, democratic societies whose policies seek to reflect and embody such public, universally binding truth. To the "private" sector, on the other hand, belong all those things for the truth or reality of which no such public warrant or demonstration can be provided. This is the sphere alone, we are told, in which values, purposes, beliefs, opinions, preferences, and the like may legitimately be entertained and indulged. These are things which may well be the stuff of our personal commitments and investments (if we choose to believe and submit to them) but that, in the absence of any objective, publicly convincing proof for them, we ought not to expect others to take seriously or have to put up with in public contexts. They are not, in short, the stuff of "knowledge," and there is something inappropriate and awkward about parading them before (let alone cramming them down the throats of) others. They are better kept behind closed doors, where ("within the privacy of our own homes," as we habitually say) they can with impunity be lavished with whatever seriousness and respect we choose to afford them. But we are only free to entertain them, express them, and live in accordance with them while ever doing so does not lead us into conflict with the law of the land or with publicly agreed policy and so long as we do not impugn or disrespect the views held "privately" by others by suggesting that ours have a more secure hold on truth than theirs. They may, as we say, be true "for us," but they will not and need not be "true" for everyone.

It's easy enough to see how, in theory, this approach ought to provide for stability and peaceful coexistence in a society that is, as our societies today increasingly are, de facto "plural" in religious, cultural, and other ways. There are certain areas of life where we can all legitimately argue, disagree, and seek agreement and a common mind because about such things everyone is expected to be able sooner or later to identify where truth or reality lies, to have that truth demonstrated to them if need be on commonly accepted grounds, and where matters of public policy are concerned, to agree what it is and determine to abide by it rather than flout it. Where other sorts of things are in question, though, everyone can and must live alongside everyone else, generously tolerating and respecting their privately held views and able to do so precisely because to a large extent and in practical terms, they are left wholly undisturbed and unchallenged by them, unless they themselves happen to choose otherwise.

Another look, though, suggests that this neat division of things, even if it were feasible and accomplished with complete consistency and integrity, is not, in reality, well designed to foster either generosity or respect. The "tolerance" urged upon its citizens in their dealings with "otherness" dwelling next door collapses all too easily into a bland willingness to "let them get on with it" just as long as neither it nor they trespass uninvited into our own space or try to force us to engage with whatever "it" is. Worse still, this "privatizing" of beliefs, aims, presumed goods, and the rest itself creates an expectation that it will indeed all be kept safely behind closed doors and tends to encourage indignation, irritation, or worse, therefore, whenever ideas sufficiently different from our own are allowed to impinge in a manner we find either inconvenient or in any way unwelcome. In a dualistic culture where such things have been respectably privatized, when confronted with the uninvited airing of religious, moral, political, aesthetic, metaphysical, or other convictions (especially if there is an implied challenge to compare them with and reconsider the worth of our own), the impulse of the public-spirited citizen, far from oozing generosity, may well be to cry "foul" and immediately lodge a complaint about having been imposed upon or subjected to intolerant and intolerable initiatives when all we wanted was to be left alone.

Nor, despite the public relations hard sell, is an overflowing of *respect* among groups defined by mutual difference a natural outcome of this sort of ideological pluralism. Such respect, too, becomes a fragile commodity easily broken. After all, especially where minority groups in society are concerned, it is hardly very "respectful" to treat some of their deepest, most cherished, and passionately held beliefs and values as, in practice, wholly undeserving of any claim to the status of "truth" and so irrelevant to the shaping of public life, being better kept hidden away from public view than exposed to its gaze, except where they happen to overlap serendipitously with or reproduce (and so receive a grudging imprimatur from) things that everyone else in that society already knows and believes anyway, these being readily available as the alleged public deliverances of "science," or "reason," or "common sense," things for which no group can lay claim to any credit or distinction. In truth, of course, the "private" sector tends to be populated precisely by the sorts of things that are most deeply held and matter most to people, granting them what we have learned to call their sense of "identity" and belonging—convictions about the sort of place the world finally is, about what it is to be human, what matters most in life, what it is good (and bad) to be and do and seek to become, what it is good to love and to be willing to make sacrifices for, and commitments based on all these. To have such things effectively dismissed as the harmless but practically superfluous and publicly inappropriate flotsam and jetsam accrued by choices we, our families, our communities, or our like-minded associates have at some point made—despite the evident lack of any rational or empirical warrant for doing so—is potentially galling rather than respectful. And the potential exasperation and irritation are only likely to be heightened further by the suggestion (embedded identifiably in so much public discourse, whether spelled out or left unspoken) that in a grown-up, "secular" society like ours, it is far better and more intellectually responsible and respectable to live an existence which bravely embraces doubt and agnosticism about anything that cannot be demonstrated, proved, or certified by publicly acknowledged "experts" to be true, treating the rest as a mere matter of personal taste or predilection (views about the sanctity of human life or our obligation to treat other species and our physical environment with respect and care, for instance, thereby falling, strictly speaking, into the same category as our preferences for dessert or which football team we support—*choice* being the essence of it all).

All this comes to a head, though, as the illusory nature of the proposed public/private divide itself is unmasked and the careful classification developed in terms of it exposed as a ruthless bid for privilege and power by those who hold to certain sorts and certain sets of assumptions, beliefs, and values rather than others. Here's the thing: the distinction doesn't actually hold water. Acts of faith or "believing" of some sort, far from being an inferior or unworthy way of engaging with reality as it confronts us, turns out to be not just unavoidable but a necessary component of every act of human knowing, furnishing the conditions, indeed, under which alone acts of supposedly "cool reasoning" or the "disinterested" handling of facts and data must operate and without which they can accomplish nothing.[11] As the twentieth-century British philosopher of science Michael Polanyi argues persuasively, *all* intellectual activity (including all "scientific" inquiry) takes place and *must* take place within some framework of conviction and commitment or another, "facts" and modes of reasoning themselves being in part the *products* as well as the *basis* of what we believe to be true, being identifiable, classifiable, and usable only by those trained and skilled in traditions of practice and committed to the assumptions, beliefs, and values embodied within those traditions.[12] So a context in which "reason" and the gathering and weighing of "evidence" are exalted will necessarily also be one in which certain unproven assumptions taken on trust or held in "faith" are bound to be alive and kicking, even if (like disreputable habits or dirty laundry) they are kept so well hidden from public view that we ourselves come to disbelieve in their existence. This, Polanyi argues, is precisely what has happened in models and ideals of truth and knowledge adhered to in modern Western societies. And if it is sometimes and in some sense true that "seeing is believing," it is always and in more than one sense true that "believing is seeing"—that is, that even our most basic sensory and intellectual engagements with things are only possible at all because of much more basic beliefs and commitments that, in one way or another, facilitate them and grant them meaning. Where the ideological exaltation of doubt, skepticism, and suspicion is concerned, Polanyi's analysis reminds us quietly that doubting and believing are, in reality, logical equivalents rather than opposites, since every expression of doubt is tacitly a statement of faith in something else. "I doubt P" can always be recast in positive form, either "I believe not-P" or at least "I believe P to be unproven." Such statements, though, invite the question, "On what basis do you believe this?" "The answer, Polanyi argues, invariably reveals some framework of suppositions or beliefs which, at the time and for the purposes of doubting P, are not themselves doubted. They provide the conditions for doubting P (believing not P), but they are themselves not doubted. If they were, then the conditions for doubting P would be removed. And doubting these suppositions would itself inevitably take the form of a belief in some alternative to them, a belief which would in turn be based on some other set of faith commitments,"[13] and so on ad infinitum. In other words, logically speaking, the branch on which every doubt sits is some belief or set of them, and to insist on chopping this branch off in the attempt to attain a wholly objective, uncommitted position is futile and, in any case, results only in the original doubt falling noisily to the floor.

If now, then, we return to the level of the "truths" that shape societies and their public policies, it is unsurprising to discover that neither they nor their putative foundations are the epitome of truthfulness typically sought for and presumed nowadays in awarding the sobriquet "public," consisting instead of just the same complicated and impure mixture of ingredients—fact, reasoning, belief, supposition, value, habit, interpretation, skill, and the rest—to be found (no doubt in various differing proportions and mixed together in different ways) in the recipe for any human act of knowing anything. This certainly does not mean, of course, that all claims to know something (or to apprehend "truth") are of precisely the same sort or of equal validity and worth. What it means, though, is that the playing field on which such claims are reckoned with and contested ought to be a level one and the game played fairly rather than some claims being treated as superior or special and so granted automatic privilege (and hence power) relative to others which are considered to belong in a lower league and hardly worth bothering with or taking seriously at all. If *public truth* means anything, Polanyi suggests, it means that all serious claims to truth and knowledge are deserving of our respectful consideration and critical response, all quite properly laying claim to "universal intent" (and the accountability and responsibility that necessarily accompanies that claim) rather than forced to pull their punches by conceding that their truth may finally only be "private," true "for them" but not necessarily for others.[14] To repeat, the sharp division between supposedly "public," objective forms of knowing and others relegated to a "private" sector will not hold and must not be granted further unwarranted credence. The emperor has no clothes, and to permit him to process his nakedness through the streets any longer is not only an unpleasant nonsense but, sooner or later, to everyone's disadvantage.

Every human society, including our own, Newbigin insists, is in reality "governed by assumptions, normally taken for granted without question, about what is real, what is important, what is worth aiming for"[15]—that is to say, by precisely the sorts of things (convictions, aims, habits, judgments) officially held to have no legitimate public status or permission to speak. That these assumptions are mute and underlying rather than loud and explicit does not mean, though, that they are not there, exercising a powerful influence on all our garnering and handling of "facts" and our application of the powers of reason. On the contrary, precisely because their existence is overlooked or willfully denied, they remain effectively unchallenged, being elevated by stealth to the privileged position of what is publicly accepted and acceptable, becoming embedded in the structure and policies of public institutions (the government, education, science, finance, the media, and others), and so exercising a very profound influence indeed. Such things make up the "plausibility structure" of our society, the shifting but nonetheless identifiable set of assumptions and beliefs that determine what the "public" deems to be plausible or worth taking seriously or pursuing, typically mediated and sustained, as philosopher Charles Taylor has noted, not in secular "creeds" but in the far more persuasive and subtle appeal to our imaginations (and thereby our minds, hearts, and wills as well as our bodies) of "imaginaries" in narrative form.[16] Our culture, that is to say, tells a story about what sort of place the cosmos is, where it has come from, where it is probably headed, what our place within it is, what sorts of things matter and are worth pursuing while we're here, and so on and so forth. The storytelling is subtly done so as to lull us into an unguarded sleep rather than waking us rudely to the reality of things. It is to be found everywhere, woven through the public deliverances of scientists, media hacks, politicians, and all sorts of others as well as in the many forms of popular culture, and although most of us have almost certainly never stopped to disentangle or reconstruct it, it is a story familiar to all of us and quietly shapes us and our behavior as citizens (and not least as consumers). It is, in all meaningful senses, an *ideology* (at the heart of which, we might note, are to be found our old friends the three *-isms* from earlier in this chapter), but it is one that, unlike any other set of beliefs in Western societies, enjoys official authorization and unique, unchallenged access to the corridors of power.

Of course, there are plenty of people who, once alerted to or reminded of the fact that the "secular liberalism" of modern Western democracies is, in reality, neither secular nor liberal—nor indeed "neutral" as it says on the tin but generally undergirded by an unappetizing cocktail of naturalism, paganism, and consumerism—would wish to protest at their own tacit baptism (as public citizens) into collusion with its beliefs, liturgies, and practices.[17] Any attempt to do so, though, or to share the accumulated wisdom and insights of alternative ways of seeing things is quickly swept aside or shut down as the inappropriate venturing of personal beliefs and values, especially if these happen to be associated identifiably with either the outlooks of other (relatively "undeveloped") cultures or the "irrational," "deluded," "discredited," and even "dangerous" phenomenon of "religion." Such marginalizing and belittling of visions that not only are likely to be deeply cherished but some of which may have inspired and nourished humanly rich civilizations and cultures over many centuries are bound to cause resentment and social unrest when they are done not evenhandedly but in such a way as to privilege one particular ideology, the superiority and self-evidence of which is simply taken as read rather than argued for openly and its entanglements with public policy and "truth" occluded rather than laid bare and so made vulnerable to critical scrutiny. The continuation of the West's colonial project (now in the name not of Christendom, to be sure, but of the putative benefits of "modern liberal democracy" and a "free market" global economy) is a version of the same old imperial attitude, ideology being smuggled in again by mixing it carefully into the folds of the undeniable advances made by science and technology in "developed" nations, as if its claims were of the same sort as theirs or wedded inexorably to the package.

Whether at home or on the global stage, we can see easily enough how all this generates affront and resentment among those whose visions and voices are thereby effectively discredited, marginalized, and disenfranchised. We can understand, too, how the legitimate demand for evenhanded, serious, and respectful consideration of their potential contribution as part of a genuinely plural public debate eventually leads some, when ignored for long enough (their views on issues ranging from economics, ecology, the boundaries of human life and death, human sexuality, national and ethnic identity, and others being branded maverick, beyond the pale, antisocial, or even illegal), to disillusionment, a sense of alienation, and the adoption of extreme, publicly threatening strategies in order to gain a hearing or make an impact. There can, of course, be no condoning or excusing of the tactics of intimidation, violence, or terror, though this, it should be noted, is itself a "truth" grounded finally in a moral vision with distinctly religious origins and not the disinterested deliverance of "science" or a purely "rational" approach to reality; furthermore, it is one deployed in a selective manner by governments and regimes the world over (including our own) as best suits the accomplishment of their chosen goals.

Nor, though, can we afford any longer to overlook the deep-rooted ideological divide enshrined in public institutions, policies, and pronouncements that lies behind, generates, sustains, and continues to exacerbate the situation. Nor can we endorse the sorts of responses to such antagonism that seek to exclude unauthorized, "dogmatic," and "undemocratic" voices all the more completely, pointing to extreme instances as proof positive that they are not and never were the sorts of things suitable for a modern, civilized society but continuing anyway ("graciously") to tolerate their existence and expression in the privacy of people's own homes or voluntary associations, one more consumer "lifestyle choice" to be explored only if we choose to do so. The hidden ideology bound up with the "public" world, meanwhile, is deemed neither "dogmatic" nor antagonistic because it needs to be neither, its voice not only being heard by default but having already won the argument (were any argument permitted or encouraged, which it isn't) and holding all the cards of power in its hand. What is needed is not, of course, a revolution in which one set of beliefs is deposed and its public hegemony granted instead to some other, whether religious or otherwise. We cannot go back, for instance, to the unholy and unhealthy alliance of religious belief and political power represented by "Christendom" and sought by every proposal to establish a theocratic alternative to secularism. In that direction lie problems of a wholly different order, as both history and contemporary political realities show us all too clearly. What is needed, therefore, is for the boil to be lanced and the poison drained, not by the establishment of illusory "belief-" or "value-free" zones in which all intelligent people may meet and agree about what really matters, but instead by the unmasking and owning up to whatever elements of belief and ideology are inevitably already shot through public life in our societies, offering these an opportunity to demonstrate their supposed merits and at the same time allowing them to be properly interrogated and challenged, granting others the chance to commend alternatives to them not by brandishing placards or shouting subversive slogans on street corners but as respected participants in a genuinely plural discussion and debate about truth. The result would not, of course, be "secular" any more than the current reality is, but it would arguably be considerably more liberal-minded and democratic.

Regardless, and whatever the political reality and cost of doing so, the church, Newbigin insists, is bound to speak out rather than accede to cultural expectations that it should keep its peculiar views securely behind the closed doors of church buildings on Sundays and safely focused on matters of personal "spirituality" and morality rather than social, economic, or political concerns. But the church, Newbigin reminds us, is called to proclaim a message about God's sovereign claim upon and rule over all things and all peoples (God's "kingdom") and cannot possibly, therefore, "accept as its role simply the winning of individuals to a kind of Christian discipleship which concerns only the private and domestic aspects of life." And since Western societies, like any other, are governed by largely unspoken assumptions and beliefs about "what is real, what is important, what is worth aiming for," the church is bound to find itself sometimes and perhaps often having to offer its own views on these things as a prophetic challenge to the official version of things. "Public truth," Newbigin writes, "as it is taught in schools and universities, as it is assumed in the public debate about political and economic goals, is either in conformity with the truth as it is given in Jesus Christ, or it is not. Where it is not," he adds, "the Church is bound to challenge it," to lay claim to a vision it believes to be truer, more adequate to the nature of reality as a whole and so a more secure basis for a life lived constructively in God's world.[18] It must be ready to bear witness unashamedly to this truth as one advocated with universal intent and to promote and contend for its presumed merits in the marketplace where visions, ideas, beliefs, aims, and ways of living are exchanged and traded. It will not keep its truth to itself, therefore, for it does not own it but is "owned" by it, and nor will it permit society's so-called public truth any longer to masquerade as secular neutrality, but will ruthlessly expose its ideological entanglements, challenging their privileged position of dominance and calling them to account.

In this sense, the nature and calling of the church are precisely those of a congregation of faithful response and prophetic witness bearing, confronting one set of faith commitments with another, different set, speaking up in the name of the Lord against whatever false "gods" or unhealthy *-isms* it discerns enthroned in positions of power and granted unchallenged fealty by an often-unsuspecting public. It cannot do so arrogantly, for it lacks the dubious advantage enjoyed by those in power. Thankfully, even if it desired to do so, it could no longer coerce "conversion" at the point of the sword, and nor can it avail itself of the sort of intellectual strong-arming supposedly granted by evidential demonstration and logical proof, having surrendered such allegedly neutral points of leverage by unmasking their own secret complicity in faith commitments of one sort or another. Even its claim to a divine mandate ("in the name of the Lord") cannot rescue the church from the vulnerable position of being called to testify in a plural and sometimes hostile intellectual environment, for the truth it bears is that of a dominion made known humanly in the form of weakness, shame, and suffering rather than superiority and triumph and so inveighs against the appeal to "force" of any sort in strategies to communicate it effectively rather than contradict it or render it self-referentially incoherent. Nor, though, can the church afford to bow the knee to other gods, compromising with what it knows to be "false ideas about what it is that makes for fullness of life";[19] capitulating, in a bid to seem "relevant" to society's self-diagnoses, aspirations and felt needs; and so becoming a sort of chaplaincy furnishing "spiritual" respectability to the established order rather than challenging it to its roots. The church exists for the sake of the world and its redemption, being, as Karl Barth argues, the *anticipation* and the sign to it of its own redeemed identity in its own midst here and now.[20] But the church's relevance is thus to be found not in comfortable complicity with the world but in boldly issuing a prophetic warning and promise, a word that is at one and the same time one of judgment and of grace.

How, though, can it possibly hope to do this? How should it *seek* to do it? How, in practical terms, can it best be the faithful steward and representative of God's kingdom, God's peculiar "lordship," in the midst of a world teeming with other allegedly authoritative claims on our hearts and minds and wills? Newbigin reminds us of something that is easily forgotten or overlooked and which lies behind most misplaced bids to persuade if not coerce people to "become Christians" and join the church, swelling its numbers, its income, and its public profile as well as being seen to be "successful" in fulfilling its mission. If we allow Scripture to be our guide, then we will know that it is not our responsibility or task to "convert" anyone to anything. Our task is at once much simpler and much riskier: to bear faithful witness to the truth of a message that is a public relations nightmare, a "product" resistant to snappy sales techniques, guaranteed to kill even the most creative marketing strategy dead in its tracks. For the rest, having "delivered" the message as we once received and stumbled over it ourselves, we may and must safely entrust matters to God himself, for God alone is able to open blind eyes, unstop deaf ears, and kindle in hearts and minds the response of faith and obedience. Again, with Scripture as our guide, we shall soon realize that faithful presentation of God's kingdom and God's Word in the midst of a sinful world are more often than not bound, as they have always been bound, to be met with the frustrating response of folk who hear and hear but do not understand, who see and see but do not perceive, and who refuse to turn and be healed.[21] Nothing that we say or do in sharing the gospel of Christ with the world, therefore, should ever be allowed for one minute to compromise that gospel itself, least of all by adopting techniques of persuasion or coercion better suited to the sale of designer goods or secondhand cars, or the measures taken by paramilitaries and mafia bosses to secure popular loyalties on their patch, or driven by expectations and models of "success" that measure it with the world's own metrics—numbers, income, popular appeal, influence. These are the tools and the patterns of influence and power of the world, against which the gospel naturally rubs up and chafes. Where there are converts, where there are resources, where the church is able to be a positive and healthy influence, we should certainly rejoice. The hallmark of faithfulness to the gospel, though, and the church's only secure "brand" must be what it has always been—the sign of the crucifixion and death which Christ himself endured for his faithfulness to the Father's will, and which he calls all who follow him to be willing to embrace as their likely end. It's not success as the world typically understands it, in other words, but "failure" that is the more likely indicator and outcome of faithfulness to the task of proclaiming "gospel truth"—namely, that "the true authority over all things is represented in a crucified man."[22]

How, then, is the truth of such a message to be borne witness to? How can its meaning, its significance for the world most effectively be broken open and communicated? How, in short, are other people ever going to come to "believe" it? Whether they actually do or not may, as we've already noted, be an outcome lying beyond our pay grade and in God's hands alone, but while God is not bound to the church, being free to work exactly how and where and when God chooses (and no doubt doing so), God has nonetheless chosen and called the church to be a primary instrument of his ways of working the truth of the gospel out in the midst of the world. The trouble is that, together with the wider culture of modernity, we have come to see that role primarily in terms of words and ideas, thinking of "truth" itself, indeed, as first and foremost a property of propositions and "believing" as the (more or less well-founded) granting of intellectual assent to the same. As we noted in chapter 1, though, however important words and ideas are, where "knowing" and "believing in" the truth are concerned, in most contexts, they are never the whole story, never the most important things, and (whatever appearances may suggest) never the starting points or bases of our doing so. "You shall know the truth," said Jesus to his disciples, "and the truth shall make you free."[23] Not "the truth shall make you right" or "clever" but *free*—because truth is a quality of living, of the "fit" we encounter among our practices, priorities, hopes, expectations, desires, and habits as well as our "ideas" and the larger, complex, messy reality in the midst of which we find ourselves and are called to exist. Truth, we might say, is a property of our relationships in body, soul, imagination, heart, *and* mind to the world, to other people, and to God—relationships that can be good or bad, healthy or diseased, liberating or enslaving, "truthful" or based on a lie. And truth can, therefore, be "known" or "believed in" not in isolation but only as those concrete relationships themselves are ones that permit, encourage, and enable our knowing and believing rather than contradicting, crushing, or rendering them impossible. Human beings being the sort of beings that we are, what this means in practice is that it is with our belonging to and sharing in the life of various *communities* that our knowing and believing are bound up—because it is the forms of the life of communities that embody, transmit, foster, reinforce, and verify our knowing and believing and thus whatever "truth" we take ourselves to grasp or have some level of understanding of.[24]

In modern Western societies, of course, no one any longer belongs to just one such community but will have their sense of personal "identity" bound up with several and perhaps many such groups. This can be complicated because the various commitments and territories of knowing and believing proper to different communities are not always complementary but sometimes conflict starkly with one another (as, for instance, when students are taught to believe one thing at school or university and another at home, or when browsers online are urged by individually targeted algorithms and advertisements to pursue one set of goals and gratifications and another by the teachings of a religious or philosophical or philanthropic tradition to which they belong or subscribe), conflicts which arise and must be resolved, therefore, not just among the competing "truth claims" of different groups within society but within individual lives and perspectives on the world. Despite such de facto plurality, though, personal fragmentation is generally able to be avoided and some sort of integrity and unity aspired and approximated to because, where the biggest and deepest questions and commitments of all are concerned, our allegiances are not all permitted to function on the same level. Some particular set will typically be granted a more fundamental and determinative role than others, providing the baseline in accordance with which others are duly engaged with, adopted, rejected, or toyed with at the expense of some level of abiding tension and inconsistency in our lives. Such allegiance may be tacit or explicit, unconsidered or carefully reckoned with, and deliberately chosen. And, of course, while our personal beliefs and commitments with respect to all sorts of things can and will change as they encounter others that seem more adequately to reflect the shape of the reality that confronts us, our deepest beliefs and commitments and our belonging to the communities which embody them (whether "religious" or "secular") are likely to change only rarely and because of some major existential crisis in which their truth seems suddenly to give way under the weight of reality itself or to be cast in the shadows by the light of some new and different way of seeing, tasting, and imagining things.

Such drastic changes of the mind (and, more significantly, of the heart, "soul," and practice too) are precisely the sorts of things we typically refer to as "conversion" experiences, though they can happen to anyone and need not involve any specifically religious set of beliefs and practices at all. Such shifts can only occur, though, as people are confronted with and able to evaluate the truthfulness of beliefs and practices very different from their own. They are unlikely to be confronted with these meaningfully, of course, while ever the attempted banishment of such things to the private sector holds, but only as they encounter them in compelling and persuasive forms in the shared territories or "marketplace" of public life. If what I have said above about the role played by communities in bearing, sustaining, and bodying forth truth holds good, then it will be precisely as the lives of such communities are played out faithfully in society that this occurs; not in essentially arcane institutions, gatherings, and rituals, but openly, exposed fully to the public gaze; challenging others with their questions and claims, blessing others with their insights and willing to be blessed in turn by the insights of others; not just inviting scrutiny but offering the hospitality proper to genuine conversation and exchange and the opportunity for imaginative exploration of and provisional, "without prejudice" forms of participation in their particular communal performances of truth—because that is how the truthfulness of any "truth claim" finally dawns on us, taking our imagination (and thereby our hearts, minds, wills, and bodies) captive, replacing the tacit backdrop against which our lives are played out, and so enabling us to see, hear, feel, and taste the world differently.

And so, finally, we come back to the church, about the nature and purpose of which remarkably little may seem to have been said thus far. But in reality, that is what we have been talking about all along. Jesus, Newbigin reminds us, "did not write a book but formed a community."[25] We might well wonder why, especially when we consider the many disappointments, frustrations, and niggles attendant on belonging to any Christian congregation or denomination familiar to us, let alone the shameful lack of faith and complicity in sin that the larger institution has from time to time been guilty of throughout a very checkered history. Surely something more effectual and resourceful could have been devised in order to communicate the truth of the gospel? Well, if God's primary concern were to transmit a set of ideas or "truths" in the most efficient manner possible, God might have waited for the age of online digital communication and global networks to do so rather than "taking flesh" in an obscure Palestinian backwater and entrusting the delivery of the message into all-too-human hands. But the gospel is not just a "message" in that sense, and the salvation it brings is not something able to be transmitted via any form of download to disembodied souls or minds—because "gospel truth," like any other (and perhaps supremely), is personal, relational, and embodied, and it is through dealings with human *communities* that "body it forth" in their shared forms of life that its transformative meaning is bound to be shared or *communicated*. A distinctive community, in other words, was precisely what was required for the sort of truth the gospel itself *is* to take root, grow, and be handed on to others—not just through an encounter with some abstract checklist of ideas or "beliefs" but in the particular personal relationships we form with others whose ways of living together "substantiate" the truth and enable us to indwell it meaningfully rather than simply "assenting" to it (possibly with our fingers crossed behind our backs).

This, then, is the nature of the witness bearing to which the church is called in every time and place. Its "holiness" consists not in any merit, privilege, or superiority it possesses but only in having been called and set apart, like the Israel of old, to be different from "the nations" and what the nations variously stand for. That difference, though, is to be manifest not in the security of splendid isolation but in the midst of the world and for its sake; not by "respectfully" leaving others comfortable in their own beliefs and ignorant of the name of the Lord but by "hallowing the Lord's name" in a manner that substantiates God's character, purposes, and promises in human form and so challenges and changes lives; not crying out as a disembodied voice in the wilderness but embodying and in a sense *being* the very truth it has been given and called to share; and not just on Sundays or privately but 24/7 and in every aspect of the complex lives that its adherents live, both when gathered together and individually in the workplace, the social club, the shopping mall, online, and wherever else they may be. Of course, the church cannot do this adequately any more than Israel could. But this, and no mere rehearsal of verbal formulae and ideas (however central and important those may be as part of the overall package), is the radical and all-involving nature of the church's calling. And, of course, in doing so, it relies on and lives out of resources not its own but, through the Holy Spirit's overshadowing and action, those of the crucified and risen Lord, who is the source and the center of its existence and who lifts it up far beyond its natural capacity to share in his own character and life.

For this reason, Newbigin suggests, the Christian congregation itself is the only authentic and effective witness to the gospel—the true "hermeneutic" or unpacking of its meaning—as particular communities of the baptized believe it and seek to live by it, working out precisely what that means and might look like in the specific times and places in which God has called them and set them apart. Everything else, Newbigin insists ("missions," circulation of Christian literature, "seekers' groups," and the rest), is and must be secondary to this, for unless it is all earthed in and expressive of this same gospel-shaped life together, it will not lead naturally into it. It may perhaps succeed in populating pews by savvy marketing of one sort or another, but its appeal will be superficial and provide no genuine gateway into that cruciform, self-renouncing, thankful, and sacrificial existence which is the truth "as it is given in Christ."[26] When the congregation is true to its calling, though—bodying Christ himself forth in the midst of the world, being, in effect, a colony of those who live according to his "rule" or kingdom rather than the dominion of the various powers that be—"it becomes the place where men and women and children find that the gospel gives them the framework of understanding, the 'lenses' through which they are able to understand and cope with the world."[27] And despite the inherently challenging and "scandalous" nature of its gospel strap line, in God's hands and God's time, it becomes the place where God's will is mysteriously done, God's truth is glimpsed and responded to, and the world's redemption both anticipated and advanced.

11

"THE FORGIVENESS OF SINS . . ."

THERE'S A LOT of talk about forgiveness in Christian circles in one way or another, and rightly so. After all, forgiveness lies at the heart of that "good news" about God with which Christianity is chiefly concerned, and any personal account of salvation that reflects no sense of having been forgiven by God may reasonably be treated with caution and interrogated concerning its lineage. Talk of forgiveness, though, has a much wider currency in our lives than its uses in Scripture, liturgy, and theology. "Forgiveness," in fact, is an idea whose contemporary occurrences are so generously and broadly distributed around various spheres of human concern as to risk its exhaustion and gradual loss of shape. On the whole, we presume forgiveness to be a good thing, whatever it is, but if we ask *what* it is, answers received are likely to be both vague and varied. Since the ways that we make sense of words and ideas to be found in the Bible or used in the language of prayer and liturgy are bound to be affected by the habitual uses of those same words familiar to us in everyday life, such vagueness and variety is a matter of theological concern. Of course, words change their meanings and acquire new meanings and new depths of meaning as they are used over time and in changing contexts. This can be a gain and even a blessing in our approach to their use in Scripture and elsewhere, for it prevents texts from being shackled to the lexicon of any particular time and place and grants them the power to speak constantly afresh. Mostly such rich accrual of meaning involves the creative tension triggered when new uses rub up identifiably against older, more established ones, generating a static electricity that jolts the words into new life. When, instead, it is ignorance or the careless application of words that is involved, meaning is more likely to be distorted, depleted, or lost altogether than enriched, and revisiting the sources of it becomes a matter of paramount importance. What, then, is "forgiveness"?

Forgiveness as God's Business

THE PROLIFERATION OF contexts in which talk of forgiveness is nowadays taken as normal has been accompanied, unsurprisingly, by a developing rash of studies of the idea by philosophers, classicists, social theorists, and others (including some theologians) attempting to clarify the history of uses of the term and so pin down its legitimate range of uses more precisely.[1] Forgiveness is, as one such study suggests, "a very 'in' topic" across a range of disciplines.[2] The striking thing about many of these studies is that they remind the reader unashamedly that, despite its contemporary breadth of use and for all that it remains in need of some clarification and corrective adjustment, the concept of forgiveness we appeal to today originates fairly clearly in the shared religious heritage of Judaism and Christianity, in scriptural texts, and in the ways these have duly been taken up and interpreted in the theologies and liturgical and social practices of Jewish and Christian forms of life. Furthermore, in these contexts, forgiveness is first and foremost an idea belonging to talk about who God is and how God relates to the world, and its application to the sphere of our human engagements with one another, while divinely mandated, is, therefore, secondary and derivative.

Forgiveness, we might say, is properly a divine activity and only a feature of human relationships, institutions, and communities in as much as we are duly called (and seek) to reflect God's dealings with us in our own dealings with others. To this extent, at least, the German poet Heinrich Heine was not being wholly perverse to insist—wittily, provocatively, and (given that the statement was made on his deathbed) boldly—that "God will forgive me because it's his job."[3] The impious presumption of the statement may be religiously dangerous (presuming upon God's forgiveness is certainly not encouraged by Scripture and tends only to foster a spiritually deleterious self-confidence in the face of

God's holiness[4]), but the poet's theological instincts are at least partially on target and more completely so than any suggestion either of wanton caprice in God or of a constant wrestle between two opposing impulses in God's character, one of which must finally constrain, overcome, or satisfy the demands of the other. As Jürgen Moltmann insists, there is indeed a sense in which forgiveness (as the specific form that God's grace takes in the confrontation with human sin and guilt) "comes naturally" to God, God being who God is and we being who and what we are.[5] In this sense, it is indeed God's métier—God's characteristic business, the manifestation of that trait that most fully reveals God's character in his dealings with us—namely, God's love, grace, and mercy. Yet as the Scots theologian P. T. Forsyth saw, such radical grace is precisely a function of God's holiness (God's "holy love"[6]) rather than something held in tension with it, and forgiveness itself, therefore, even as a form of mercy, burns in its implacable opposition to the sin that occasions it, being part of a wider action of God determined to eradicate sin as a form of evil rather than turning a blind eye to it, let alone excusing it.

Forgiveness, then, to reiterate, is in its proper and its fullest sense something God and God alone does and can do, since it is the expression of God's own character in the face of the world's sin. Its possibility reflects the unique moral reality of God and the metaphysical reality of God's unique relationship with the world as its creator. And yet as we acknowledge the uniqueness of this circumstance and the divine prerogatives attaching to it, so we are reminded, too, of the claim that human beings are made and called to reflect the "image and likeness" of this God in the world. And whatever else it may mean, this certainly entails believers (and the church as the human community in which the heart of the "good news" about God is deliberately to be played out) in "imaging," "bodying forth," or performing concrete parables of God's moral character in the midst and for the sake of the world. "You shall be holy to me, for I, the LORD, am holy, and I have set you apart . . . to be my own" is at once both an indicative (a promise) and an imperative (a challenge) lying at the heart of Israel's covenant with God,[7] and the chiastic structure of its first clause echoes another in which the two voices are similarly fused:[8] "You shall be my people, and I shall be your God."[9] To be marked out as "God's people" in the world is precisely to reflect or "image" God's own holiness, and while "holiness" in Scripture certainly refers to more than the moral quality of God alone, it never refers to less.

As L. Gregory Jones, in a penetrating and robust theological discussion of forgiveness, writes, therefore, while "it is God's forgiveness, not interhuman forgiveness, that ought to provide the contours for our understanding of forgiveness," it is also true that "God's forgiveness initiates and sustains, by the power of the Holy Spirit, specific friendships and practices of Christian community and Christian life," in and through which "we learn to embody forgiveness."[10] Of course, for reasons rehearsed in earlier chapters (though, as it turns out, of particular significance in this instance), God's forgiveness and ours are not and cannot be of exactly the same sort;[11] the relationship between them, even when an appropriate creaturely correlation enables human forgiveness to embody and body forth God's own, is, at best, one of analogy. We shall need, later in the chapter, to return more fully to the question of the sorts of discrepancies that might exist between the experience and practice of interhuman forgiveness as we are familiar with it (not least, let it be admitted frankly, in the church) and that reality in God's own unique being and life, which is not merely its analog but its putative archetype. The gap between creator and creature alone means, as we have already seen, that the nature of genuine forgiveness (the "real deal") cannot possibly be discovered by scrutinizing any amount of empirical data gathered from the personal, social, and political realities of human life, since it lies beyond the scope of such realities. More than this, though, we shall see that the transposition of divine forgiveness into forms of creaturely existence resonating with and providing a fitting counterpoint to it is problematic for reasons having to do with morality as well as metaphysics. Put bluntly, far from reflecting anything already germinal in the natural order of creaturely existence, the sort of radical forgiveness to be found in God does not for the most part "come naturally" to sinful human beings at all, and where it arises is always part of that peculiar work of God's Spirit (the Spirit of holiness) that in certain respects interrupts, contradicts, and breaks down the "natural" impulses of an appetite, aspiration, and will at odds with and alienated from God's own and, only insofar as it does so, is able to redeem and regenerate it. Apart from this regenerative work of God at work in and through us, we might reasonably suppose, and despite the fact that it is integral to the authentic form of humanity for which we were created and to which we are summoned, genuine forgiveness, forgiveness resonant with the timbre of God's own, is not a human possibility at all. Or is it?

Fully Human Forgiveness

THIS QUESTION LEADS us to reckon with another point made by Jones—namely, that for Christians, knowledge of God's forgiveness is "centered in Jesus Christ."[12] It is to be seen modeled, that is to say, most fully and clearly in the way Jesus deals with those who encounter him in the Gospel narratives and so, of course, precisely within the horizons of *a fully human life* and set of human relationships. And yet, we must remind ourselves, this is not just any human life; it is the human life of the God who has himself become incarnate, "enfleshed," "enhumanized" for our sake and who has done so in part precisely so that we may grasp and respond to an accessibly "fleshy" manifestation of the essentials of who God is. "Whoever has seen me," says Jesus to Philip, "has seen the Father."[13] In other words, we need have no fear that there may be a God lurking hidden behind the back of Jesus whose character will turn out to be disturbingly different from Jesus's own, a God who is approachable only with abiding anxiety because we are unsure of the likely outcomes of doing so and fear the worst. No—Jesus, as the technical language of theology has it, "reveals" God to us, shows us the very face of God translated into human terms. Of course, this does not mean (How could it?) that in Jesus we see laid bare absolutely everything there is to be known about God. As more than one of those early Christian theologians habitually referred to as the "church fathers" (and they were, mostly, men) observed, to suggest this would be analogous to supposing that when we look up and see the sky, what we see is the *whole* sky, the sky in its entirety, whereas in reality, we do not and cannot. But we do see the sky, even though our perspective and grasp of it are necessarily particular and limited. Similarly, what we grasp or "see" of God in the humanity of Jesus is obviously not the totality of God's reality (as if that could be squeezed into or apprehensible in the reality of a finite human life), but we do see God, not something or someone else ("he who has seen Me *has seen* the Father"[14]), and so what we see and can say about Jesus is trustworthy as a creaturely grasp of who God has shown himself to be. And at the heart of that is the fact that Jesus forgives—he forgives "sinners," he forgives those who hate and seek to harm him, he forgives his friends when they betray and abandon him, he even forgives (and craves his Father's forgiveness for) those who put him to death in the very moment of their doing so.[15]

Because of the unique complexity of Christ's person as one who acts at one and the same time both humanly and as God (or in whom, we might better say, *God acts humanly*), an understanding of forgiveness that is "centered on Christ" is bound to reckon with more than one theologically significant thing going on at once here, a fact that commentators have sometimes overlooked. So, for instance, in her landmark midcentury study *The Human Condition*, social theorist Hannah Arendt suggests that having previously been a purely religious notion referring to a uniquely divine prerogative and action of which God alone was held to be capable, with the teaching of Jesus of Nazareth, forgiveness began suddenly to be thought of as something humanly possible and so as having a role in the social and political realities of human life.[16] Jesus, Arendt suggests, in direct contradiction of the scribes' and Pharisees' insistence that God alone has either the power or the authority to forgive, "discovered" the possibility of human forgiveness, exercised it himself, and urged it upon his followers.[17] In making this bold historical claim, though, Arendt overlooks some important considerations.

First, the "forgiveness" that the scribes and Pharisees suppose God alone to be capable of is forgiveness of *sins*—that is, offenses committed first and foremost *against God himself*, who, as their victim, is, we might suppose, the only one in any position to offer forgiveness to the perpetrators. Furthermore, God is the only one with the power and authority to deal with the potential cosmic consequences of this disruption of the moral order of creation and to grant the covenant relationship between Israel and God new leases of life and energy, holding it secure by anchoring it in God's own goodness and grace. *This*, as Arendt certainly sees, was the primary and proper context of talk about forgiveness in Israel, and the incredulity of the scribes and Pharisees, therefore, was very precisely directed to the heart of the *christological* conundrum: How can this man (or any mere human being) offer to *forgive sin*, something that concerns God alone, that is indeed "God's business" rather than ours because, whatever its manifestations or consequences in the sphere of human existence, "sin" is precisely an attack on God, a serious disruption within the field of God's relationship with God's creatures, and lying beyond the reach of any human (or other creaturely) adjustment?[18] Even though God may choose to *mediate* forgiveness through various human figures and institutions, therefore, only God can possibly be the originating agent of forgiveness where our sins are concerned. For Jesus boldly and frequently to offer forgiveness for sin in "the first person," therefore, naturally and rightly provokes the question, Who on earth does he think he is? God??

This, of course, is the very question that the Gospels and other New Testament writings are intended to address, and sometimes, as here, rather than answering that question directly, the Gospels in particular allow dramatic irony instead to entertain the knowing reader, leaving the answer ("Yes! That's exactly who this is!") to dawn gradually on those confronted with the question for the first time or for whom the penny has not yet dropped. Second, therefore, Jesus suggests *not* that human beings in general are able to "forgive sins" in the way that God can and does but simply that *he himself* has the authority to do so, and since in the economy of incarnation he has "emptied himself" and is to be found in "human form," here of necessity and perfectly properly, he does so *humanly*.[19] Sometimes what he says in this regard links this authority closely to Jesus's specific role as the Son of Man,[20] another office that certainly seems to be one fulfilled *humanly* but which is anything but generalizable. After all, this is a role associated, too, with Jesus's coming into the world to offer his life as a ransom, his ascended glory and rule at the Father's right hand, and his promised return to judge the living and the dead at history's end[21]—all instances of the same conundrum whereby this particular man, *and no other*, shares humanly in actions held by biblically informed Jews to be proper to and possible for God alone. Again, the inevitable suggestion is (whether it be reckoned with seriously or not) that here we have to do directly with God himself, albeit God *humanly* and thus incognito.

So we might say that Arendt's account is at once both correct and incorrect by virtue of its being insufficiently nuanced. It is correct in as much as it recognizes the momentous and, for his contemporaries, mind-blowing significance of Jesus's repeated offer of forgiveness of sins to those encountered in his public ministry. It is incorrect, though, in its supposition that this constitutes the announcement that all human beings have the power and authority to forgive sins. To suppose this is to misunderstand what sin is and to fail to reckon with its cosmic gravity. What Jesus's forgiveness of sins shows us is simply that when God takes flesh and becomes a human being, God is still able to exercise his unique authority to forgive sins and does so here in his (equally unique) human dealings with others. This point is well made by another historical, philosophical, and theological study by classicist David Konstan. Arendt, he argues, is simply mistaken in her inference from Jesus's behavior and words. "Jesus," he writes, "is not arguing . . . that forgiveness of sin lies within the competence of ordinary human beings; rather he is demonstrating the legitimacy of his claim to be God's son . . . with authority to act in behalf of his father."[22]

Konstan makes this observation in support of his wider argument that no clear idea of "forgiveness" as a distinctly and generally realizable *human* reality emerged with Jesus at all and would not emerge at all, in fact, until much later in the development of postbiblical, Western societies. But this too, I think, is a needless and a mistaken inference from Jesus's words and actions if we consider these more widely and in the light of theological reflection upon who Jesus was and what he came to do. As I have already suggested, we should always reckon with the likelihood of more than one thing going on at once in anything that Jesus says and does and suffers, and seek to avoid the risk of grasping one significant thread only to lose sight of others in the process. In this instance, while Konstan is right to maintain that Jesus's forgiveness of sins points primarily to his authority as the (human) Son of God rather than any wider human capacity to share in this unique divine prerogative, arguably, he does not do sufficient justice to the fact that Jesus urges upon his followers the idea that part of the challenge of their discipleship will indeed be to learn to forgive others who "sin against" them as God has first forgiven theirs. This parallelism, contained at the heart of the Lord's Prayer and echoed clearly elsewhere in Jesus's teaching, resists Konstan's attempt to drive a decisive wedge between God's radical forgiveness of human sin on the one hand and various forms of human forbearance shown in response to debtors and the perpetrators of offenses and crimes in human societies on the other, constantly insisting instead on the discrepancy between the two.[23] On the contrary, without conflating the two circumstances, Jesus points consistently to an *analogy* between God's disposition and action and what, in turn, God expects and demands of us.

We must, of course, concede that God's power to forgive sins is necessarily wholly different both in nature and in scale from anything arising in human relationships. While the latter may also be related to sin against God as, say, an indirect manifestation or consequence of it, we do not experience the misdemeanors and hurts committed by others (or have the power to tackle them) as attacks on our very being and threats to the very moral fabric of the cosmos, as God does and must. But the point of *analogies*, as we have seen repeatedly throughout this book, is exactly to look such admitted differences or "discrepancies" fully in the eye while yet insisting that they not be overplayed, some traces of a suggestive likeness remaining nonetheless to be glimpsed. To be sure, even an appropriate creaturely "forgiveness" may prove to be something human beings struggle ordinarily or "naturally" to evince (the evidence suggests that we do). But it may nonetheless be something *God is capable of fashioning* in our humanity. In fact, at the heart of the gospel lies the promise that, together with much else besides in our humanity, such creaturely likeness to himself is something God has determined to fashion, as the Father works regeneratively through the incarnate Son and the Spirit of holiness to purge all traces of evil from our nature, raising it up finally with Christ and drawing it into the interpersonal dynamics of God's own life and so fulfilling that ancient covenant formula that stands over against us as both a demand and a promise: "You shall be holy . . . as I the LORD am holy."

We might sum up the foregoing by saying that here, as elsewhere, in his declaration of radical forgiveness to sinners, even as Jesus shows us who God is, so, simultaneously, he shows us too what it is to be truly human. In him, our humanity is laid hold of and, by a sustained, lifelong act of obedient self-offering, wrestled into its true shape in relation to God and the world. In him, God acts *from within* our humanity in order to conform its shape and substance to the pattern of its true creaturely end, living out *humanly* what it means to be the eternal and only begotten Son, filled to the brim with the Spirit of holiness, in relation to the one who is the Father. In him, God's own eternal holiness now finds its true creaturely counterpart and response. In him, in other words, the covenant between God and Israel (and through Israel, humankind) is for the first time fulfilled from both sides, and while it is God who acts here from both sides at once (humanly as well as divinely), the promised likeness or analogy between creator and creature is wrought and underwritten with Jesus's full human involvement and laid bare in him for us to grasp.[24]

"Forgiveness" Broken and Made New

THIS MEANS, OF course, that Christian theological anthropology more broadly should always be christologically informed rather than a merely empirical or introspective exercise, its proper object lying precisely in this unique and unrepeatable instance alone. In the case of forgiveness more obviously than elsewhere, perhaps, this methodological consideration is vital if we are to avoid two equal and opposite errors. Beginning elsewhere than with the humanity of Christ, we may either take those human manifestations of forgiveness with which we are familiar from day-to-day existence as the genuine article (and, worse still, project them onto God) or—recognizing that it is not, that the sort of "forgiveness" associated with God is in fact radically different from anything we are typically capable of—slip instead into supposing that (since we for our part are, after all, "only human") it makes no legitimate claim on us and so has no direct personal, social, and political relevance in human affairs, being God's métier, and God's alone. Keeping our eyes fixed firmly on the figure of Jesus, on who he is, and on what he does, says, and suffers should preclude our falling into either of these errors. Failure to do so or failure to grasp the significance of what we see opens the floodgates to errors of both sorts.

The first sort of error is by far the more common in theology. Hearing the word *forgiveness*, we reach naturally for uses of it embedded in various social realities around us, taking these, at their best, as normative and abstracting from them a picture of what forgiveness is and ought to be and how it works. When, then, we hear that God forgives sinners, we naturally suppose that some version of this all-too-human modeling of forgiveness must be indicated and proceed to project it (with suitable qualifiers such as *divine* or *heavenly*) confidently onto God without pausing to consider how, in this peculiarly theological conscription of it, the word may need to be broken on the rock of divine difference and made new. As we have seen, none of our words can ever mean exactly the same when used appropriately of God as they ordinarily mean in their day-to-day mundane uses. That is exactly what is meant when it is insisted that theological language functions *analogically* rather than either *univocally* or *equivocally* (the latter suggesting that when used to refer to God, our words must mean something completely different from whatever we ordinarily understand by them, which would seem to reduce our talk about God to either meaninglessness or something even worse).[25] This consideration extends to all language drawn into the circle of specifically religious and theological use. Interestingly, though, it is precisely in connection with the presumed differences between divine and human *forgiveness* that Scripture makes its clearest and most sustained allusion to the circumstance. So in Isaiah 55:6–9, we read,

> *Seek the* Lord *while he may be found,*
>   *call upon him while he is near;*
> *let the wicked forsake their way,*
>   *and the unrighteous their thoughts;*
> *let them return to the* Lord, *that he may have mercy upon them,*
>   *and to our God, for he will abundantly pardon.*
> *For my thoughts are not your thoughts,*
>   *nor are your ways my ways, says the* Lord.
> *For as the heavens are higher than the earth,*
>   *so are my ways higher than your ways*
>   *and my thoughts than your thoughts.*

While this hardly constitutes a philosophically nuanced appeal to the doctrine of analogy, it makes the basic point clearly enough—namely, that the difference between uncreated creator and creature (even human beings as those created in God's "image and likeness") is of an order that makes any direct movement from familiar creaturely realities to grasp some purported counterpart in God misguided and theologically risky. And nowhere, it seems, is appropriate theological caution called for more than in the case of God's dealings with the wicked and the unrighteous. Here, as elsewhere, we must stop, and look, and consider what sorts of dealings these actually are, for here, as elsewhere, our typical ways of doing things are *not* God's ways, and our expectations of God ought not, therefore, to be constrained by the patterns of our dealings with one another. Indeed, these same patterns themselves, as part of our humanity, are under bondage to sin and in need of redemption. An appropriate human analogy to God's ways, here as elsewhere, in other words, remains to be fashioned in us by the work of God's Spirit of holiness, tantalizing glimpses of it being available for now only as we look to the one in whose flesh and blood alone it has already been wrought and won—through obedience, suffering, and death—the *pneumatikos* man Jesus Christ, our Lord.[26]

Notice now, though, what happens when such caution is not deployed and "our ways" are unhelpfully projected onto God on the assumption that they will in all relevant respects be "God's ways" too. The result is bound to be not just clumsy poetics but also bad theology, a characterization of God distorted by eliding the differences both between the uncreated creator of heaven and earth and his finite creatures and between God's holy love and those "fallen" modes of human existence in which even our created "likeness" to God remains, for the time being, occluded or unrecognizable. A God made substantially in our own image, we must realize, is bound in the end to be a God in whom we shall discover—to our dismay rather than by way of solace—traits all too familiar from whatever self-knowledge we possess and from our dealings with other people, even the very best of which are blighted by misjudgments, conflicts of interest, and imperfections of character. In fact, though, Christian theology has not consistently drawn its unregenerate anthropomorphisms from a pool of the best available exemplars, a fact with a cost that has from time to time been very high. Not only has God been pictured as a figure presenting with many of the symptoms of unregenerate humanity at its most unpleasant, unstable, and unconstrained (legalistic, capricious, ill-tempered, violent, merciless, brutal, partial, vainglorious, self-absorbed, self-serving); such images have, in their turn, been fed straight back into the system to grant supposedly "divine" warrant for institutionalizing "man's inhumanity to man." Put bluntly, bad theology grants permission for and results in damaged and distorted human relationships—personally, socially, and politically[27]—not in the church alone but, because of the influence of religious ideas on the formation of our culture, far more widely in the supposedly "secular" societies of modernity. And nowhere is this more apparent, it might be argued, than in the models of "forgiveness" we find in play all around us, most of which tend, finally, either to endorse or smuggle into play some form of a self-serving or self-gratifying transaction between a victim and a perpetrator.

Forgiveness and the Sphere of the Personal

HAVING RAISED THE question at the outset of this chapter, the foregoing methodological excursus, while necessary, has rather delayed our actual answer to the substantial question at issue: What *is* forgiveness, anyway? And despite all that has been said thus far, the most straightforward way to embark on an answer is probably, in the first instance, to consider some ideas about forgiveness formulated largely empirically—that is to say, on the basis of its manifestations and our experiences of them on various levels of our existence as persons in human society.

Perhaps the place to begin is with the widely made observation that forgiveness is indeed precisely a *personal* matter. It is something that has to do directly, that is to say, with our dealings with one another as persons, our "personal relationships." That's a flexible category, of course, but the further from its natural center of gravity we get, the less relevant and useful the language of forgiveness as such seems to be. Uses of the idea in legal or political contexts, for instance, often seem to require such a stretching of it that it becomes baggy and loses its proper shape. Such metaphorical appropriation of the language is common enough, but it is imprecise and, rather than illuminating, tends instead to blur or obscure the reality of what is being spoken about, eliding significant differences rather than drawing attention helpfully to hitherto overlooked resonances between contexts.

In studies designed to pin it down, forgiveness is often linked in one way or another to *anger*, another supremely personal response that has no place, for instance, in the public dealings of the law or political process. Judge and jury may well find the alleged perpetrator of a crime guilty or innocent in the law's terms, but we would not ordinarily think it either relevant or appropriate to ask whether they feel anger toward them. For anger, we naturally suppose, is properly felt only to the extent that one has been affected directly in some way by the wrong that has been committed, as a warranted reaction to a *personal* hurt or affront. Were it to be discovered, though, that the judge, an attorney, or even an individual member of a jury in a legal case were also, in their private lives, a party affected even indirectly by the circumstances of the crime under consideration, in any system worth its salt, we should expect this to disqualify them from any further involvement in the case—not, let it be noted, because such an emotional response is not warranted personally but precisely because as a public institution, the operation of law must disentangle itself as fully as possible from anything that might prejudice or exercise undue influence on a "fair hearing" being afforded to the evidence, let alone on the verdict or sentence delivered in due course. The spheres of personal relationships and legal processes must, we take it for granted, be kept as far apart as possible precisely in order to secure the maximally "dispassionate" nature of the latter and the impartiality of their outcomes.

By exactly the same token, of course, forgiveness too is a misplaced category when applied to the impartial agencies of due legal process, since none of those involved in such process as officiants or representatives should ever be in any position to *offer* forgiveness. For whether or not we remain entirely satisfied with definitions of it as the conscious waiving of anger or a deliberate foregoing of anger's natural demands, forgiveness nonetheless belongs properly to the same irreducibly personal nexus of relational actions and reactions as anger itself[28]—a world that should, as philosopher Jacques Derrida insists, be "inaccessible to law."[29] It has nothing and *must* have nothing to do with the apparatus of due legal process and its judgments, from which, in theory at least, all personal considerations must be expunged. As a matter of principle, therefore, the categories of any penal system (punishment, exoneration, pardon, and so on) must both be and remain distinct from those pertaining to the level of our personal dealings with others, lest, through loose talk and conceptual confusion, the integrity of one or both be compromised. The contemporary tendency to extend the range of the language of forgiveness, transplanting it into territories of meaning where it does not belong (law, economics, diplomacy, politics, etc.), is thus, Derrida observes, decidedly unhealthy in its implications.[30] Forgiveness, he insists, can, properly speaking, only ever involve two personal singularities: the perpetrator and the victim. No third party, let alone the third party of a public institution, can ever meaningfully offer forgiveness, having neither the right nor the power to do so.[31]

It is true, of course, that often more than one person may be in a position to be angered by and/or to offer forgiveness to the same person for a particular action committed, but they may do the latter, strictly speaking, only insofar as they themselves are identifiably a "victim" and not for the suffering borne by someone else. So, for example, the parent of a child abused by another family member, while not the primary victim of the crime, certainly counts as a victim in their own right and is thus in a position to offer or withhold forgiveness, but they may forgive the perpetrator for the hurt caused only to themselves, not on the child's behalf. Forgiveness, precisely because it is irreducibly personal, is also nontransferable.

Finally, before moving on, we should notice that because forgiveness pertains properly only in the sphere of the personal (being, again like anger, a mode of personal reaction to actions undertaken by others and harmful in intention or impact, or both, in relation to "me"), its being offered or withheld is perfectly compatible with the due processes of law being executed. They cannot be incompatible because, as we have seen, they are incommensurable. The judgments and penalties of law are not and ought never to be about *personal* reactions but precisely about the *impersonal* responses whereby society seeks to order and protect its own well-being by regulating the behavior of its citizens. Neither is the scope of concern of the two coterminous, of course; they simply overlap. As yet, for instance, we do not place people on trial for behavior that, while potentially damaging to our relationships with others, is not classified as illegal, such as lying, betrayal, deceit, sustaining grudges, and the like. Yet all of these and a host of others are things that, when they arise, make the question of forgiveness (and alternatives to it) highly relevant and sometimes urgent.

In that region where the two spheres of consideration do overlap—where actions that hurt us personally (whether the perpetrator is someone known to us personally or not) are also things proscribed by law and so committed "against" society too—because the levels of the personal and the legal must nonetheless remain properly distinct, it does not follow at all that a victim inclined personally to offer forgiveness should or may not be perfectly content for "justice" to be done and the criminal tried, judged, and (if found to be guilty) punished by due legal process. Indeed, as Derrida observes, the inverse is also true. "We can," he writes, "imagine, and accept, that someone would never forgive, even after a process of acquittal or amnesty."[32] And it is, of course, common enough too for those tried, convicted, and duly punished for their crimes to remain nonetheless unforgiven by the victims of those crimes. Such refusal or failure to forgive may be undesirable for all sorts of reasons, but it cannot be held to be inappropriate or incompatible with the legal verdict. The two belong to distinct and incommensurable spheres of consideration, and nothing is actually violated or contradicted when personal and legal responses fall in different directions.

This, we might notice, bears directly upon discussions of God's ways of dealing with human sin, where it is sometimes suggested that a logical contradiction exists between talk of sin being judged and its penalty borne on the one hand and the insistence that God forgives freely on the other. The confusion here, it seems to me, is not on the part of those who (following biblical precedent) wish to maintain both sets of imagery as important in theological terms but rather those who see a contradiction where none exists even at the human level. Whatever we actually wish to say about the status and implications of such imagery for our thinking about God, the fact is that the categories of punishment and forgiveness are compatible rather than contradictory, belonging as they do to quite different levels of consideration and, therefore, to incommensurable clusters of imagery.[33]

Can a Gift Be Given?

IN PURSUIT OF a useful working account of forgiveness typical of the word's contemporary uses, in her own recent study, Martha Nussbaum turns for convenience to the one proffered by Charles Griswold in 2007.[34] Like many other writers on the subject, she observes, Griswold understands forgiveness in relation (and by way of contrast) to the emotion of anger. Thus, according to Griswold, "forgiveness . . . is a two-person process involving a moderation of anger and a cessation of projects of revenge," not entirely gratuitously or unilaterally, but rather "in response to the fulfilment of six conditions."[35] Thus, Nussbaum summarizes, a candidate for forgiveness and the healing of a personal relationship must do the following:

1. *Acknowledge that she was the responsible agent*
2. *Repudiate her deeds (by acknowledging their wrongness) and herself as their author*
3. *Express regret to the injured at having caused this particular injury to her*
4. *Commit to becoming the sort of person who does not inflict injury and show this commitment through deeds as well as words*
5. *Show that she understands, from the injured person's perspective, the damage done by the injury*

6. Offer a narrative accounting for how she came to do wrong, how that wrongdoing does not express the totality of her person, and how she is becoming worthy of approbation.[36]

Laudable though the reformative outcome envisaged in all this may seem, and while elements of the account proffered may well ring true and resonate with our actual experiences of the phenomenon, we are nonetheless, Nussbaum points out, bound to ask whether what is described here is in fact really "forgiveness" at all. Is it not actually at best a thin substitute for the genuine article, a counterfeit beneath the surfaces of which lies something quite different in nature and significance and, in its specious species, altogether less radical in its impact than *true forgiveness*? Insofar as our understanding is theologically informed and adjusted, I suggest, we have good reason to insist so. The issue, of course, has to do with the unashamedly transactional dynamic involved in what Griswold portrays. If this sort of "forgiveness" is to be offered or granted—and *before* it will be offered or granted—there are tasks to be satisfactorily completed; the perpetrator, we might say, must first become a serious *penitent*. The religious roots of this image are not lost on Nussbaum, who proceeds to trace elements of teaching on forgiveness in the sacred texts of both Judaism and Christianity (including the teaching of Jesus himself) that seem, on the face of it, to reflect this same conditional logic[37] and that are taken up and codified by strands of development in the life of the patristic and medieval churches.

So, for instance, Nussbaum refers us to the example of the early Christian author Tertullian (ca. 150–ca. 225 CE), a Tunisian lawyer who wrote several practical and moral treatises on the importance of the ministry and ritual of the church in mediating the individual believer's relationship with God.[38] Tertullian's accounts were centered chiefly on the question of how first to obtain and then hold on to God's forgiveness of sins, and in them, he unfolded a theological model of "penitence" (*poenitentia*) that would go on to enjoy huge importance on the thought and practice of the Western churches in particular.[39] The scheme he outlines (the so-called process of *exomologesis*) is precisely a conditional one, at the heart of which lies the satisfactory and meritorious performance of prescribed works. It begins, naturally enough, with the sinful person owning and coming to terms with their actual need of forgiveness, expressing their desire to receive it and their determination subsequently to turn their behavior around so as not to repeat the sins that have occasioned the situation confronting them in the first place. This process of confession and repentance, though, is insufficient in and of itself. It must be followed by a phase of faithful penitential living or "penance" decreed by the church, typically the completion of certain moral and/or spiritual tasks understood variously as the reparation of a debt or fulfillment of an obligation defaulted upon, the provision of supererogatory compensation for the offense caused, and the purgation of sinful influence from the muscle memory of the flesh. Such performances (fasting, virginity, self-inflicted chastisements, suffering, and martyrdom are examples held to be particularly meritorious in this regard, though less imposing exercises were no doubt also approved) are held to be required before God's forgiveness can be offered and received through the sacrament of baptism.

Just how Tertullian understood all this in relation to Christ's role as the one who has "borne our sins" and (in familiar language derived directly from his penitential theology) "satisfied" God by standing in our place is not entirely clear and need not detain us here.[40] For our purposes, we may simply note the unashamed contamination of the idea of forgiveness—which we have seen properly to be a function of personal relationships—with a calculus drawn identifiably from the world of economic and political contract (Tertullian was, as I have observed, a lawyer before he was a theologian). Parallels with Griswold's purely secular model of forgiveness abound, following a pattern in which forgiveness is something offered not freely but only once rightful anger is assuaged by some performance of sufficient merit. Indeed, the picture of God entertained by Tertullian's penitential theology is, Nussbaum suggests, precisely of "a demanding and angry God, who, nonetheless, if sufficiently supplicated, may opt for forgiveness, in the sense of turning from anger and not exacting the merited punishment."[41]

The chicken-and-egg relation between religious/theological and "secular" notions here is one we have already touched upon and do not have space to pursue further, but it does seem that our unregenerate humanity struggles whenever it is encountered by genuinely free and unconditional acceptance, whether divine or human in origin. It's as though we cannot live comfortably with the knowledge that we are accepted by someone not for what we have accomplished or what we have to offer but only for who we are and, more unnerving still, despite the many things that ought (according to the standards we ourselves would apply to others) to make us unacceptable. Such knowledge robs us at once of any bargaining power, any ability to control the relationship by putting the other person in our debt, and so leaves us without any security other than the sort that is based on relationships of trust. The genuinely unconditioned and unconditional, therefore, is unbearable to us in its contradiction of whatever shreds of self-esteem and self-determination we cling to, and we find it more or less impossible either to receive it or to offer it to others. This, perhaps, explains why human models of forgiveness so rarely enshrine a genuinely unconditional offer by victims or receipt by perpetrators and why, instead, some element of bargaining, of a self-enhancing or self-asserting exchange of benefits, is generally to be found in practice, no matter how slight or how well hidden. The victim and the perpetrator alike feel the need to control the renegotiation of their relationship (no matter how close or how distant it may be), and in order to exercise any degree of control at all, each must have something to broker with, something they might withhold, and something that, when contributed, leaves some shred of their sense of dignity intact. The vulnerability of a gift freely given and equally freely received is, it seems, simply too much for us to deal with, a personal encounter impossible to get our hearts if not our heads around.

In religious terms, this means that no matter how often or how carefully the disarming and humbling gospel of God's unconditional forgiveness confronts us, the temptation is always to end up smuggling something of the transactional back into our approach to it. The penitential scheme advocated by Tertullian is a stark example of this, and categories such as *merit* and *satisfaction* borrowed from the world of Roman jurisprudence stayed in the bloodstream of Western theology like a virus and would come to shape not just its typical ways of picturing the work of Christ but its broader impression of the character of God's dealings with us. When left unchecked or unqualified, this tacit transactionalism led mainstream strands of medieval theology and religious practice to place an identifiable emphasis on human "works" of various sorts as needful in order to render God gracious toward us. "How can I"—that is, what must I *do* in order to—"get a gracious God?" was the very question that plagued the soul of the sixteenth-century monk Martin Luther, finding his answer eventually during a careful rereading of the apostle Paul's Epistle to the Romans.

Indeed, it was precisely the rediscovery of a Pauline emphasis on *grace* as the most fundamental thing in all God's dealings with us, of course, that led the theologians of the Reformation to renounce all suggestion of the kingdom of God as a meritocracy. They insisted instead that favorable standing before God could never be "merited," not simply because unregenerate humans are quite incapable of the relevant quality of moral and spiritual performance (though that is true enough), but because salvation does not *need* to be earned, being held out to us freely, gladly, and without condition, to be received as the overflow of God's forgiving, fatherly love for us, which in turn calls forth from us a reciprocal, filial love equally unconditional in nature. Here, if anywhere, the personal finally trumps the transactional, whatever place legal and pecuniary images may still have usefully to play in our thinking about God.

This was arguably the most important theological point driven home by the Reformers and the one around which various other significant points of reform coalesced. Salvation is not accomplished "by works" but to be received solely "by grace ... through faith," as Paul puts it.[42] It is the logic of gift that applies here, not the logic of transaction.

And yet, true to form, even those styles of Christianity most obviously indebted to the theological heritage of Paul and the Reformers have managed regularly to smuggle just a smidgen (but a spiritually deadly smidgen all the same) of the transactional into their various formulations of the gospel of grace. They have, in other words, reintroduced the logic of the "conditional offer" into their thinking, as though the possibility of sheer, unconditional grace were simply unthinkable. "If you only repent and believe," we are told, "God will forgive your sins and adopt you as his sons and daughters." It sounds like a reasonable trade-off at first blush. All we have to do is "repent" and "believe"—whatever that means. By comparison with the pre-Reformation insistence that the debt of our sins must be paid for by morally and spiritually meritorious performances of a sort we suspect we should never be able to achieve, surely this is good news? "All we have to do . . ."—or (as I have sometimes heard it put) "All that's *left* for us to do . . ." And yet, of course, with this, the pass has been sold, and the really radical thing about the gospel is already compromised.

Because the point is that there is still something here that *we* must do first, something that if left undone or else done unsatisfactorily may leave God unmoved, under no obligation, unwilling, or unable to forgive us at all, the terms of the transaction (for a transaction, in this version of things, it still essentially is) not having been sufficiently fulfilled from our side. Be these terms ever so easy, ever so undemanding, ever so slight, therefore, we had nonetheless better make quite sure we *do* fulfill them and do so in a manner sufficient to meet whatever God's expectations concerning them are. But there's the rub—Can we be absolutely sure exactly what *repentance* means or just how far-reaching or expansive or genuine that repentance needs to be in order to measure up? And what, when all is said and done, counts properly as "believing"? How much must we believe? How fervently or determinedly must we believe it? And can we ever be sure, therefore, that we have succeeded in doing either of these things thoroughly enough to know ourselves to be forgiven?

Extenuation and What Remains "Unforgivable"

IN THEOLOGICAL TERMS, this tendency to loiter in the corridors of the transactional, despite having heard a word of unambiguous grace, is what one of my own theological mentors, James B. Torrance, bewails as (in a telling phrase) "legal repentance"[43]—repentance that still supposes its own adequate performance of some task to be the thing on which our forgiveness by God finally hinges, translating us at last, as it were, from the category of those as yet remaining "unforgiven." "All that is left for us to do. . . ." "*If* you repent and believe, *then* God will forgive you." It is no different in principle from Griswold's "six extremely difficult things to do before breakfast" model or the religious progenitors of that in various more full-blooded versions of "salvation by works." And it shifts the burden of responsibility for getting ourselves right with God back onto our own shoulders in a worrying and potentially crushing manner, as a task to be accomplished, a status that must in some sense actually be *merited*.

The "if-then" logic of too much proclamation of the gospel today leaves a shard of transactional thinking buried deep in the heart of many people's faith, festering and gathering to itself the pus of fear and perpetual anxiety—the gnawing fear that, knowing ourselves as well as we do, the quality of faith and repentance that God has in mind might just be something more intense, more sincere, more adequate than anything we have yet managed to summon up. The fear that we may yet be found among those whose sins have not been forgiven, despite having sought such forgiveness in acts of penitence and faith (possibly, in some traditions, having been urged to do so publicly more than once just to be on the safe side), is a spiritual infection that spreads hidden beneath the surfaces of too much Christian profession and practice, slowly but surely diseasing and deadening that love, joy, and peace which otherwise grant faith life, and life in all its fullness. Those less inclined to self-doubt are no better served, the same transactional logic tending in their case necessarily to engender a form of self-righteousness ("It may not be much, but I have done that which God commands") equally toxic to the proper enjoyment of the forgiveness and life that come only as free gifts received unconditionally from the hand of a father who has first loved us unconditionally and always.

Ironically, motivated as it is chiefly by nagging fear, "legal repentance" of this all-too-familiar sort can never be *true repentance* at all, being more a self-interested survival strategy than a loving, devoted determination to align our being with God's own holiness, whatever that may cost us. It shares, too, the very problem that some secular theorists have identified in Griswold's version of things—namely, that whether we are assured or uncertain about the sufficiency of our performance, what would be procured by satisfactory fulfillment of the stipulated terms and conditions would not be *genuine forgiveness* anyway. For as long as a shred of transactional thinking remains in place, as Derrida observes, we cannot avoid the conclusion that the perpetrator or sinner is called upon to render themselves "forgivable" and that having done so successfully (no matter how much or little is presumed to be the price or payment required to accomplish that shift), they are no longer "guilty" in the law's eyes, no longer the defaulter on a debt.[44] The terms of the transaction or contract have now been adequately met, and there is thus no longer anything left to be forgiven.

The paradoxical thing about true forgiveness, though, Derrida muses, is that whatever may reasonably count as "forgivable" is in fact irrelevant to the circumstance. Forgiveness, he insists, is actually only required at all when we are concerned with whatever in an action remains *unforgivable*—something for which, in other words, we judge there to be no reasonable justification, explanation, or excuse.[45] Conversely, in certain moral and legal situations, an appeal may be made to notions such as "diminished responsibility" and "extenuating circumstances." When, say, someone commits a crime or offense not entirely freely but under the compulsion of an internal or external force ("voices" in their head, perhaps, or a gun held against it, or after years of cruel abuse and maltreatment at the victim's hands) or they act in genuine ignorance of the likely consequences of their actions, it may be judged that *to this extent*, their action lends itself readily to explanation, understanding, and imaginative sympathy, and warrants neither the full penalty available under the law nor the deliberate withholding of personal forgiveness. It is precisely, to this same extent, explicable, pardonable, and *forgivable*.

There are clearly differences between "extenuating circumstances" of this sort and the various "conditions" of forgiveness elucidated by Griswold and others, but we should not overestimate them. The two lists blur easily into each other at points, and one might argue that the most significant difference between them is finally a matter of chronology and the order of events. Both are concerned with the identification of extenuating considerations, whether these lie in moral realities preceding and accompanying the perpetrator's action or in the post-factum performance of actions (confession, remorse, repentance, restitution, or whatever) specified as meritorious and so adjusting the overall moral ledger of gains and losses. In both cases, furthermore, some sort of inner change is effected in the "moral identity" of both the perpetrator and the victim.[46] The offender either is revealed to be morally other than was hitherto supposed (as in cases of diminished responsibility, for instance) or else furnishes sufficient evidence after the fact of a moral capacity and willingness to change. In both cases, the victim's perception of the offender's moral identity is thereby altered in a favorable direction, effecting a change in the way the victim her- or himself now sees, feels, and reacts to the larger moral circumstance. The satisfactory performance of "terms and conditions," in other words, functions just as effectively as "understanding" to extenuate and to render *forgivable* the commission of even the most serious crimes and offenses and does so by recalculating the larger distribution of moral merits and deficits surrounding the action in question. Indeed, we might note that compliance with the transactional logic of conditional forgiveness is itself precisely a matter of a sort of "understanding" being arrived at between the victim and the perpetrator.

"To understand all is to forgive all" may be an attractive commonplace at first sight,[47] but in reality, Derrida suggests, to understand *all* is again, in effect, to judge that there is no longer anything remaining that requires to be *forgiven*.[48] That which is "understood" is granted a certain respectability, thereby possessing an agreed meaning and a legitimate place in the orderly scheme of things, the shared moral calculus in terms of which intentions, actions, and outcomes are weighed and measured and their cost dealt with reasonably. Where *understanding* exists between the victim and the perpetrator, the necessary adjustments can be made, and a smooth transition to an agreed reconciliation is already not only possible but in practice already well underway. But it is not that in human actions which can readily be explained or excused and so mitigated to which the moral response of forgiveness is relevant at all. It is only the surd, unjustifiable, outrageous, inexplicable, and meaningless element in a person's behavior (what we might finally be driven to classify—cautiously if we are wise—as "wicked" or "evil" in origin and affiliation) that either requires to be or *can* be forgiven. For it is whatever remains without excuse, whatever cannot easily be laundered in moral terms, and whatever to which we can and ought never to be content to become reconciled that creates the deepest and most abiding fissures in our personal relationships. In the face of this and this alone—and thus with the evil, the guilt, the sin of the perpetrator clearly in its sights and despite it—*genuine forgiveness* is called forth, offering, as it does, the only real prospect of hope and healing. Like evil itself, Derrida avers, true forgiveness, where it occurs (in God or in us), is thus in an important sense "meaningless"; it can make no appeal to explanatory or extenuating considerations; it is no product or necessary requirement of the ordinary nature of things (the "order" of God's good creation) but is precisely a "madness of the impossible,"[49] an interruption of all moral cause and effect or the logic of "desert," and summoned into being against all expectations (seemingly ex nihilo) precisely and paradoxically by its logical antithesis—that which, on any reasonable account of the matter, stands over against it as "unforgivable."

Love, Actually

THE RADICAL, COSTLY, and risky nature of what it means truly to forgive is an unavoidable consequence of its restoration to the sphere of the personal. This is a sphere of existence most fully recognizable and most fully realized where relational realities such as trust, promise, and self-giving are in evidence and where the logic of transaction is introduced and appealed to only where these break down or cannot be relied upon. None of these things themselves, though, are commodities that can be either purchased or used as the coinage of contractual exchange. Their nature is such that the very mention of price or payment already compromises their proper integrity. It is because forgiveness, too, belongs in this same category, both Derrida and Nussbaum insist, that in its genuine form, it can never contain even a shred of conditionality, being completely unconditioned by anything in the one forgiven.[50] To speak of "forgivability" is thus a category mistake. Forgiveness is only genuine, indeed, when it issues forth freely from the victim to the perpetrator *as such*—that is to say, as the guilty one, stained horribly still by the very worst of whatever he or she has done, remaining perfectly "capable of repeating (the same action), unforgivably, without transformation, without amelioration, without repentance or promise."[51] This inherent vulnerability of forgiveness (risking rejection, betrayal, and humiliation to antagonize further the already existing wound) makes it costly indeed, but not in terms of any sort of transaction. It is costly to the victim in the offering of it and, as we shall see shortly, to the perpetrator who will receive it.

It was, the apostle Paul reminds his readers, *while we were still sinners* that Christ died for us[52]—not waiting for us first to display any signs of inherent forgivability, to ask after the existence of extenuating circumstances, or even to show the willingness or desire now to turn our lives around, but taking the concrete, costly step in which God's forgiveness was laid before us, freely and unconditionally, in flesh-and-blood terms, although we were and remained at the time very clearly God's enemies.[53] Were we to resort to the technical terminology of Christian theology at this point, we should have to insist that, far from being something that *persuades* God to forgive us (as some theologies seem to suppose), the "atonement" that comes to a head in the death of Jesus is itself precisely the form that God's forgiveness takes—reconciling to himself these sinful, alienated creatures while they are yet still hostile to all that God is and stands for. Forgiveness, divine or human, if it is indeed genuine forgiveness, does not wait, and it does not barter; it takes the first, supremely costly step, and it is always offered to *the as yet unforgivable*. It comes to us as an impossible gift, interrupting our despairing determination to do something to pay our own debts (and the fear attendant on knowing deep down that we cannot), and it presents us with the challenge of accepting it with no conditions attached on either side.

According to Paul's account, this unsolicited initiative of radical forgiveness on God's part is the action and thereby the revelation of the *love* that, as Scripture tells us elsewhere, God not only has but *is*.[54] In God, it seems, forgiveness is the form that love naturally takes when confronted with the indefensible and unforgivable. And this same radical love together with all its costly implications, far from being something God guards jealously as a unique divine prerogative is, as we have already seen, something God longs to see reflected in the life of every human creature too. In the self-offering of Jesus to the Father and for our sake, a decisive bridgehead has already been established in history's midst so that this same radical quality of love may now make inroads into our relationships and communities, being, in fact, as John reminds us in his first epistle, the very form that the life and presence of God take humanly when they begin to flow into us and, through us, the world.[55] What this means, of course, in a world so thoroughly blighted by sin and evil as ours, is that *forgiveness* (authentic forgiveness rather than one of its counterfeits or approximations) is, where it arises, chief among the signs of those same inroads having been made, marking out the various fronts on which the battle for occupation is being fought vigorously and won.

Without appealing to this overarching religious and theological framework, Nussbaum also concludes that forgiveness, arising as it does only in the context of our dealings with one another as human persons, has directly to do with what it means to love. In her account of the matter, though, the two are related finally by what she sees as the differences between them as *alternative* moral responses, love or "generosity" being privileged even over the sorts of unconditional forgiveness Nussbaum herself has helpfully disentangled from transactional variants of the species. Even the purest "forgiveness," she suggests, is in reality not so virtuous as we tend to suppose.

The problem (and what sets love's reflex apart from mere forgiveness) is, she contends, the latter's definitional entanglement with *anger*, its nature as a decision to "stay the hand," and so *not* to do what our impulse of anger tells us it is reasonable to both wish to do and (should we choose) actually do to the perpetrator. In other words, the forgiving person only reaches the point of forgiveness (and *can* only reach it) via a route that itself already fosters and perpetuates an unhealthy "narcissism of resentment"[56]—an inquisitorial mentality, moral fault-finding, list keeping, and an imaginative reckoning with what forms of personal vengeance might be warranted by this or that misdemeanor. For only having first traveled some distance down this psychological and emotional path can the victim apply the moral brakes and decide meaningfully *not* to follow it to its end, thereby deliberately eschewing the gratification promised (falsely no doubt) to those who do so. No doubt this is a better outcome for all concerned than pressing on vindictively. But this inner journey itself, Nussbaum avers, is one we ought to aspire to transcend altogether, craving instead a higher form of moral response, one that remains untarnished by having embarked upon the journey at all. "The personal realm at its best," she suggests, "is characterized by a generosity that gets ahead of forgiveness and prevents its procedural thoughts from taking shape" rather than clemency having to be wrested at the eleventh hour from the opposing clutches of a demand for vengeance.[57]

In Jesus's familiar parable of the waiting father in Luke 15, Nussbaum observes in passing, it is not the son's appalling behavior that is the truly prodigal thing at all but the father's love for the son, who, while he is "still far off," is glimpsed by the father, who is driven by the gut-wrenching passion of love to run out to meet him, embrace him, and carry him home for a huge family celebration.[58] The question of forgiveness simply never arises. The son does not expect it, knowing that his behavior has been disgraceful and without excuse, and so resorts instead to transactional logic in a bid to secure what would, at best, amount to a very partial restitution ("Treat me like one of your hired hands"[59]).[60] And the father's reaction to the son's return has nothing in common at all with any of the versions of "forgiveness" we have considered thus far in this chapter. The terms and conditions that the son supposes himself able to offer are rendered pointless as such by the father's speed and exquisite timing—the son already being held in the embrace of paternal love long before he has a chance to rehearse his penitential litany. So is this, then, "unconditional forgiveness"? No, says Nussbaum, because even to classify it thus, "we have to imagine the father dwelling on his resentment, before choosing freely to give it up. But, of course, there is no such thought process in the story, and no reference, even, to anger. Such a thought process would have been that of a different father, more calculating and controlling. This father is taken over by love."[61]

It is love or generosity and not "forgiveness," therefore, according to Nussbaum, that we should aspire to as the moral response best suited to healing and holding out hope for our human relationships—intimate, social, and political. For love of this sort has no need to struggle in order to deny anger its violent pound of flesh. It is single-minded, paying not even the slightest heed to thoughts of vengeance or recompense, concerned only to do whatever lies within its own power to sustain the relationship which has been damaged and endangered by whatever hurt has been inflicted and suffered.

* * * * * * * *

THIS ACCOUNT OF the relative virtues and vices of nonretributive reactions to personal hurt may initially seem to have much to commend it. After all, the benefits of "anger management" in various contexts are well known, as are the corresponding dangers of allowing untempered indignation, resentment, or moral outrage to shape the way we behave toward "those who sin against us," whether they be our long-term life partners, the "neighbors from hell" living next door, or inconsiderate fellow commuters during peak rush hour. Ill-tempered tantrums and cold, calculated strategies of payback alike are, experience itself suggests, if left unchecked, only likely to wreak further damage rather than effect those satisfying adjustments to the moral order of the cosmos that our sense of outrage initially suggests they might. In fact, if we take *experience* as our guide in these matters at all, then we might well be inclined to think that where our personal dealings with others are concerned, taking "anger" out of the equation altogether is indeed something to be aspired to, even if we can rarely accomplish it. For anger of one sort or intensity or another can itself easily become a *source* of wrongdoing as well as a response to it, perpetuating conflicts rather than resolving them, raising the stakes rather than lowering them, and so fueling the mechanisms whereby relationships and communities (and finally societies) break down and fail.

It is no doubt for reasons of this sort that the past few years have witnessed the publication of a flurry of books in the category of "popular philosophy" all urging upon us the benefits of the emotion-curbing strategies advocated by Marcus Aurelius, Seneca, Epictetus, and other ancient Stoic philosophers.[62] Training ourselves to be able to face even the very worst of life's pressures and misfortunes in such a way as to leave our peace of mind largely unscathed by them is, it seems, an attractive proposition to the average stressed citizen of late modernity. So too a best-selling work to be found on the "self-help" shelves of your local bookshop offers an appetizing digest of the teleological psychology of Alfred Adler, classifying anger as an emotional tool that we habitually reach for in order to accomplish a goal or purpose that we already have in our sights. Like all tools, far from being uncontrollable or overwhelming, the authors suggest, anger can actually (when it suits us) be put away just as easily and quickly as it is picked up and wielded, a realization that leaves us free to choose not to fabricate and wield it in our interpersonal relationships at all, and thereby furthers the cause of the authors' promise to help us "change our life and achieve real happiness."[63] Not only is anger frequently to be identified at the root of all manner of personal disequilibrium, interpersonal ills, and reciprocal wrongdoings, in other words, it's not actually necessary for our dealings with one another at all. Whether by eluding its alleged grip on us or (if we suppose it to be an artifice of our own making and sustaining) simply pressing the "Off" switch, anger can and should be transcended in our relationships and the disturbance and distress occasioned by it avoided. The message is clear: Anger bad. No anger good. So get rid of anger. What, as they say, is not to like?

In her disavowal of anger as a moral pollutant capable of rendering even *unconditional* forgiveness impure by fleeting association, then, Nussbaum puts her finger on something of significance. She too sees anger as something best avoided, morally tainted, and antithetical to the project of securing our common personal, social, and political good. (Her account, to be sure, makes no appeal to the possibility of us either surgically emasculating anger or voluntarily sheathing it via tricks of the heart and mind; instead, she pictures one powerful emotion waning and being eclipsed by the waxing of another. But be that as it may.) Our own experiences of anger and its often messy (sometimes tragic) manifestations and consequences are likely to make the classification of it along some such lines attractive and persuasive—initially, at least. I respectfully suggest, though, that to understand "forgiveness" in this way, as a moral reality locked into a zero-sum game with anger's claims upon us, and "love" as a morally superior disposition which need not reckon seriously with those claims at all is problematic even in human terms. It is all the more so when we consider, as faith is constrained to, the ways in which these same moral realities are apprehended as related to one another in God. Once again, in other words, we need to reckon with the probability that the most secure mooring for an understanding of these characteristics lies not in any number of familiar human incarnations of them but in what we are shown of their divine origin and exemplar.

One problem with Nussbaum's account might be said to be that it fails to reckon seriously enough with the moral price tag of evil or the nature of its impact upon morally attuned creatures such as ourselves. Is the sense of outrage we sometimes feel in the face of appalling wrongs committed against others not, we might reasonably ask, both natural and proper—a reliable gauge of moral realities and thus a perfectly "rational" emotional response rather than the symptom of an underlying affective disorder requiring to be offset and finally overcome by other morally superior impulses?[64] Differentiating carefully between the ordering of public life on the one hand (jurisprudence, politics, economics, etc.) and personal relationships on the other certainly permits an account to be offered of a "cost" attaching to certain sorts of actions, how those costs might best be paid, and by whom. But a translation of matters into the dispassionate metrics of legality or some other strictly amoral discourse, while needful, is hardly sufficient, and where the moral realities of things are concerned, it seems, "anger" of sorts is sometimes a warranted response to evil without which we should show ourselves to be less rather than more completely human and humane. That such anger itself is, in its human guises, too easily conscripted and twisted to further the ends of evil rather than resisting or thwarting them need not mean that the entanglement is a necessary one. Nor does it indicate that, rather than an admittedly fragile emotional register of an enormous moral truth that it cannot yet fully bear, "righteous anger" is as such an oxymoronic notion, "anger" being intrinsically unstable and destructive unless and until it is successfully muzzled and tethered by the impulse to forgive or, ideally, taken out of play altogether by the power of love.

The sort of duality that Nussbaum posits between the demands of love and the impulses of anger has, to be sure, been projected onto God and has played a significant part in Christian "theories" of the atonement in particular. Theologians wishing to maintain a significant place for God's anger (or "wrath") rather than allowing it to slip quietly and embarrassedly into the shadows have thus sometimes found themselves compelled awkwardly to envisage either a transaction hammered out or a marginal victory won in a struggle between two evenly pitched and opposing sets of characteristics and concerns in God's own being, each having legitimate claims on the lives of sinful humans. But this is highly problematic in theological terms and does not do adequate justice to the larger pattern of the biblical use of these creaturely analogies. Someone who makes this point helpfully and points us beyond the apparent dilemma is the Congregational theologian P. T. Forsyth.[65] We must not think of any "settlement" having been reached between God's mercy and God's wrath, he argues, nor of any final overwhelming of one by the other because love, wrath, mercy, and justice are in God all manifestations and forms of one and the same thing—God's character as the Holy One—distinct from one another only in the artifice and abstraction of our speaking and thinking of them but eternally one and the same moral reality. Thus, Forsyth insists, there is no "zero-sum game" to be reckoned with; the concerns of God's love and the concerns of God's wrath are always one and the same—namely, the utter destruction of evil and sin and their replacement in the creature by a goodness and holiness correlative with God's own and able to enjoy that filial love and joy in communion with God which is its proper end. Such things may well be fractured apart and conflicted in our typical experience of their fallen human approximations, but that is not where a serious theological account of them can begin. Instead, Forsyth suggests, we learn from the undivided moral reality of God's own "holy love" how we should think of those various moral responses in us that reflect and echo it, realizing not least that they often do so very poorly indeed.

Such a theological account will not differ from Nussbaum over her insistence that genuine forgiveness is always the fruit of love, but it will resist her claim that anger must therefore either be suppressed or ideally swept aside as irrelevant to the context, the offense that provokes it thereby being left unaddressed in *personal* terms, whatever legal or other processes may duly be played out. In God, Forsyth would remind us, anger or "wrath" is precisely the form love itself takes when confronted by evil and the distorting and toxic effects of evil on the creature. It is the passionate and unstinting opposition to evil of a God whose love cannot and will not permit it to continue to harm or desecrate the creature and whose concern is always to make good the fatal injury that evil does and threatens forever to do to God's promise to dwell together in fellowship with the creature. Far from a zero-sum or inversely proportioned relationship between the two, therefore, Forsyth insists, for the considerations of God's anger to be assuaged or set aside would not be more "loving" in its implications but less so. Questions about the "costliness" of forgiveness where God is concerned cannot be addressed here, but we should at least note the insistence in biblical and theological treatments that it *is* costly and that it is God who *bears* the relevant cost in himself. Humanly, we might properly observe, it is precisely the abiding root of "anger" as a rational response to evil that makes forgiveness costly and difficult rather than easy for either the one offering it or the one called upon to receive it.

The Condition of Forgiveness

FORGIVENESS DOES, OF course, have to *be* received as well as offered if it is to be transformative of our relationships and thereby our communities and our world. And while it is of the essence of true forgiveness that it can lay down no prior conditions without sliding back into the transactional logic whose dangers we have already reckoned with, it bears its proper fruit only when, as we might say, *forgiveness* on the part of a victim meets with and perhaps in some measure generates *forgivenness* in a perpetrator—a response of reception and acceptance of the moral realities at stake in the circumstance.

This may well take the form of some of those things listed earlier among supposed "requirements" of forgiveness: acknowledgment of guilt, contrition for the harm done to the victim, repudiation of the action committed, commitment to nonrepetition of such behavior, and so on. Notice now, though, that these are not performances upon which the disposition and offer of forgiveness itself are *conditional*. Forgiveness as such is, as we have seen, far more radical and costly than that and logically precedes any such response. *Forgivenness*, as the act of receiving an unexpected and undeserved gift, is precisely always a *response*, akin to whatever may be involved practically in the genuine acceptance of a gift of any other sort. Some gifts are more costly to receive than others because the act of receiving them involves some change in the recipient and commitment to an open-ended pattern of change in the future. A bunch of flowers is less costly in this respect as a gift than a puppy or a hive of bees, presuming that the gifts are indeed appropriately received rather than put quietly on eBay or "regifted" at the earliest opportunity. Fortunately or unfortunately, forgiveness cannot be put on eBay, but as gifts go, it is among the most costly of all to receive, since making room for it in our lives will involve quite considerable adjustments. Such adjustments, though, are wholly misunderstood if we construe them as "conditions" of forgiveness. They are not. They are simply what the "condition" of *forgivenness* itself (the state of having been offered and received the gift of forgiveness by the one against whom we have sinned) naturally, logically, and inevitably entails.

This is vitally important to grasp where God's forgiveness is concerned, since misunderstanding of it is bound to turn forgiveness back into a transaction demanding of us meritorious performances of one sort or another with pastorally disastrous consequences. If biblical injunctions to "repent . . . for the forgiveness of your sins"[66] or petitions invoking God to "forgive us our sins, as we forgive those who sin against us"[67] are not interpreted in the light of this distinction, then we shall not finally be able to avoid slipping into the sort of "legal repentance" against which Torrance warns and be plagued constantly by either self-doubt or the equally obnoxious condition of self-righteousness. Instead, Torrance urges us, we should grasp the logic of "evangelical repentance"—repentance, that is to say, that is only ever a response to

God's prior offer of unconditional forgiveness, forgiveness born precisely of God's love, the same love that burns ferociously to purify the world from the sin and evil that besmirch it. It turns out, therefore, that receiving this forgiveness equally unconditionally may end up costing us everything, for to do so is to open ourselves to God's promise to transform us from the inside out.

Human forgiveness, too, insofar as it approximates to its divine source and exemplar, is bound to be transformative of the web of human relationships. For although forgiveness cannot be put on eBay, there is an important sense in which it not only can but must involve a sort of "regifting" if it is genuine. As Arendt notes, the gift of forgiveness is, in effect, that of a new beginning offered and received within a relationship between persons. It is, she suggests, in human terms, the only "reaction" to events that, within the moral ordering of things, does not "react" by playing out familiar patterns of behavior in which actions and their consequences remain locked into an *unforgiving* causality. Instead, remarkably, forgiveness chooses to break the natural cycle of vengeance and retaliation, which distorts and finally destroys our relational and personal being and which, left uninterrupted, might conceivably never come to an end for as long as victims and perpetrators are there to be identified in moral terms.[68] In terms of the causal patterns discernible at various levels of human existence, Arendt suggests, radical forgiveness of this sort cannot easily be accounted for, and even approximations to it are profoundly costly and demanding.

Too often, such approximations prove to be unsustainable. The "free" gift either proves after all to have a price tag discreetly attached to it or else, being genuinely without a price, is never properly received, both its inability to be purchased and its promise to change us alike making acceptance of it too costly to our sense of dignity and self-worth and too risky. Where it is to be found and to the extent that it is to be found, therefore, the operation of genuine forgiveness is a *novum*, a regenerative act which is, strictly speaking, humanly impossible but which nonetheless occurs and is from time to time to be found at work in the teeth of both natural expectation and explanation. Insofar as its existence and transmission can be plotted at all, it is so only when our dealings with one another have succeeded in leaving behind the logic of the transactional and are overwhelmed instead by the radical, costly, and subversive logic of gift or, in theological terms, "grace." "Freely you have received," says Jesus, "so now you give to others freely."[69] It sounds simple enough, but in reality, it's absolutely nothing like quietly regifting the unspeakable pair of socks or "useful" box of perfumed coat hangers reluctantly received from an elderly maiden aunt at Christmas.

Plotted within the causal and other explanatory frameworks of the world and our own humanity as we know it, radical forgiveness of the sort we have been considering in this chapter makes little sense at all. It crops up, in Derrida's words, only as "a madness of the impossible,"[70] as surd, unintelligible, and therefore strictly "meaningless" in terms of any rational account available to us. We cannot, as we say, "make any sense" of it either when we encounter it or, more disturbing still, when it draws us in and we find its unnatural impulses taking root and cropping up awkwardly from time to time in unpredictable and inexplicable ways within us so that we are hard-pressed to furnish any meaningful account at all of what we are forced to admit are excessively gracious and self-abjuring dispositions and actions on our part.

We might use a bit of heavy-duty theological shorthand at this point and refer to such genuine forgiveness as "eschatological"—an adjective indicating that its possibility and explanation do not really belong in the present moment at all but come to us from a future in which God has already made all things new and in which creation now reflects and corresponds to God's own character. Put differently again, we might say that where genuine forgiveness arises in the midst of historical time, it always does so as a sign pointing beyond itself to the God in whose hands the future of creation's story lies, being made possible only by God's own gift of forgiveness and amounting, in fact, to direct participation in the forgiveness and the love of God as such. Of course, God is in no position to forgive someone for an offense committed against me or you or anyone else, and in that sense, whatever forgiveness I am able to offer will and must always be my own. And yet what God *is* able to do and constantly does is to introduce fresh infusions of his own forgiveness into the system. As God forgives us for those sins we personally have committed against him and as we are enabled to receive that forgiveness and begin ever more fully to manifest the quality of *forgivenness*, so we discover that this takes the form (among other things) of wishing that we in our turn were capable of passing this selfsame costly gift to those who "sin against us." As God grants us this gift too, so God's kingdom gradually takes root and grows and spreads, always fragile and yet always subversive and powerful, as it liberates people both from the accumulated baggage and inexorable moral causality of their past and from the destructive possibilities which that bears into every new present, and so opens us and our communities up in surprising ways here and there to receive the unimaginable gift of God's promised future and to enjoy just the merest taste of what it will be like when, at last, we shall be truly and fully human.

Belief in "the forgiveness of sins," therefore, is no mere recondite or theoretical conviction regarding an adjustment in the moral ledger of history, likely to work out in our favor rather than to our detriment. It is to believe and trust in the regenerative power of holy love, a power already secretly at work in human lives, relationships, and communities, rippling out from the generative event of the cross by the creative energy of the Spirit of holiness and love, drawing those who realize that they have been "forgiven much" into a radical dynamic of forgiving much in their turn. Their call is to acts of "guerrilla theater" whose willing vulnerability, fragility, and seeming foolishness, far from being indicative of weakness, are in fact the power and wisdom of God unto salvation, pointing us to moral realities that we can confidently expect to pertain in "a creation restored by love," where God will be "all in all."[71]

12

"THE RESURRECTION OF THE BODY, AND THE LIFE EVERLASTING..."

THE CREED ENDS, naturally enough, by looking to the future, and articulates in a nutshell the shape and the substance of what it is that Christians look forward to. Or at least, it sums up neatly the shape and substance of what the Bible *expects* Christians to look forward to. My guess, in fact, is that many Christians would actually find it hard to construct even a coherent sentence or two sketching what it is that Christians believe about God's promise concerning the world's and their own futures, and that among any who ventured boldly to do so, some would give a very misleading account indeed. It must surely be admitted that, relative to its presumed importance, the substance of our future hope is something we rarely give our minds to in any careful way, remaining content to leave our grasp on the matter vague, impressionistic, and largely inarticulate. The reason for this is not that the subject is, by its very nature, a profound one lying beyond the proper limits of human imagination, thought, and speech. Actually, it isn't—not wholly so. No doubt the *fullness* of future salvation lies way beyond the reach of our finite understanding; but that's not the problem, and it's not really the issue here. Those who have things to say about such matters in the Bible—the Old Testament prophets, Jesus himself, Paul, and other apostolic writers—may not suppose that we can sum it up and pin it down satisfactorily, but they do provide us with plenty to work with by way of provisional images, parables, pointers—indications of what *sort* of thing it will be (or, drawing on our current experience of the world, what it may be *like*) and, by implication, what sort of thing it will not be.

On the basis of such biblical pointers, we may take it, for instance, that God's promised future for the world will not be an uninterrupted endorsement and celebration of all the gross stupidity, selfishness, greed, cruelty, and wanton carelessness that human beings have indulged in across the millennia of history. Rather, it is consistently pictured as a time when, among other things, justice and peace will finally be established, the high and mighty brought low, and the lowly lifted up. Whatever that means. And again, the point is that we don't need to know *precisely* what it means to be able to say *something meaningful* about it, something that most of us would, if asked, wish to affirm rather than to deny. So the vague agnosticism or awkward inarticulacy of some Christians on this front and the erroneous and misleading impressions trotted out with undue confidence by others are not to do with the difficulty of the topic at hand. They are due to an apparent unfamiliarity with the things that the Bible actually has to say about it on the one hand and an uncritical reliance on bumper sticker distillations of it that, while having scant biblical warrant, nonetheless probably reflect and reinforce what the public (within the churches as well as outside them) takes Christians to believe about all this on the other.

Bumper Sticker Salvation

HOW, IN NUCE, might we sum up what it means for someone, as we habitually say, to "be saved"? Confronted with this question in a street poll, it's probable that many folk inside and outside the churches alike might respond with something like the following: "People profess personal faith in Jesus, repent, and receive forgiveness for their sins and then go to heaven when they die." Now, no doubt there are numerous ways in which this admittedly brief digest of events might be tested and found wanting. For our purposes in this chapter, though, the problem lies here: "and go to heaven when they die."[1] Both in what it suggests and in the ways in which that is typically imagined, and notwithstanding the refrains of some of our best-loved hymns (and even, it must be admitted, some of the prayers in our authorized liturgies[2]), this is, in truth, a version of things that sits ill with the larger shape of Christian belief and hope insofar as these are adequately grounded in Scripture.

It's hardly very inspiring either, "heaven" all too often being pictured as some dreary, interminable, wraithlike state where disembodied souls sit around waiting for something exciting to happen, but nothing ever does. So while Christians know well enough that we ought to be looking forward to "heaven," having been assured that whatever it is will be "beatific" (which sounds desirable enough), we are actually prone not to pay it too much detailed imaginative attention, lest in doing so we both disappoint ourselves and dampen our ardor for eternity altogether. Such fleeting imaginings of it as we do permit ourselves tend to be so vague or dull edged as to render it rather a dull and flavorless prospect—literally as well as metaphorically flavorless, in fact, our taste buds, we imagine, having no more place in the midst of a state of "spiritual" beatitude than any of the other bodily bits and pieces that presently plug us into the joyously rich world of sight, smell, sound, taste, and touch. Older readers may even be inclined to picture it as bearing a disconcerting likeness to the endless Sunday afternoons of childhood, where heading outside to play football, ride bikes, or build dens was still proscribed in favor of sitting demurely behind chintz curtains in our "Sunday best" and pretending to read an "improving book"—all enjoyment of creation's sensuality deliberately stripped back by parental injunction to "respect" the Sabbath and attend instead to the well-being of the "soul." It's hardly surprising, then, that instead of living our daily lives consciously in the light of "the hope that is in us," we spend our time instead creating bucket lists of 1,001 exciting things to experience before we die—determined to drink the cup of this-worldly experience to its dregs before heaven robs us of the opportunity. Somewhere we have lost sight of the sense that what lies in store for us is *more* and not *less* real, more and not less exciting, more and not less glorious than anything this world has to offer so that, as the apostle Paul insists, for the believer, "to live is Christ, and to die is gain."[3]

Placing the Hope That Is in Us

HOW, THEN, MIGHT we go about recovering a proper sense of Christian hope and joyful expectation as distinct from holy resignation to a future that, like medicine, we believe will be "good for us" but at the cost of being less than pleasant? We might begin, I suggest, by committing this clause of the creed to memory and, whenever occasion or opportunity arises, substituting its authentic phraseology for any vague and misleading iterations about "going to heaven": "I believe in the resurrection of the body and the life everlasting (or 'eternal life' or, better yet, 'the life of the coming age')." For the reality is, as Tom Wright observes, that the Bible rarely speaks at all of "heaven" as a place to which believers are supposedly translated to dwell in peace, felicity, and beatitude with God when we die, a place by definition *removed* from this earth and the sort of life we live and have lived in it.[4] That's not an idea that Jesus or his disciples or any of the early Christians would have recognized. And if, when we do open the New Testament and dig in, we think we find it there, then we are almost certainly importing it from other sources.

For Western readers, the classic influence in this regard is almost certainly the medieval poet-theologian Dante Alighieri, whose epic *Divine Comedy* is structured around the depiction of three distinct and exotic locations (paradise or heaven being one of them) to which the souls of the dead may find themselves translated when death arrives to interrupt their sojourn in this material world.[5] And, of course, Dante in his turn is simply reflecting a widespread medieval vision of things which was a popular inspiration for painting, sculpture, and drama as well as poetry.[6] But despite its enormous and enduring influence on the Western Christian imagination, this idea of the redeemed as transiting from the present world to enjoy a paradisal existence *somewhere else* has next to no biblical warrant. It both occludes and distorts genuine biblical expectation and threatens to enervate proper Christian hope.

When the Bible speaks of "heaven," it is not picturing some exotic, postmortem, all-expenses-paid holiday destination for the recently-retired-from-life-in-this-world. In the Bible, heaven means wherever God is. Heaven is God's place—or, as Wright suggests helpfully, that peculiar *dimension of reality* in which God exists.[7] In the New Testament in particular, the word *heaven* is often used, in effect, to refer to God himself, a way of avoiding direct reference to God or God's name, in accordance with the devout Jewish practice of the day. So, for instance, in Matthew's Gospel (which typically reflects that same practice), the phrase "kingdom of heaven" is always used by Jesus where other Gospels have "kingdom of God."[8] The words mean (and say) exactly the same thing; they are just different ways of saying it. And neither of them has anything to do with a "spiritual" (disembodied) Nirvana far-flung from our current location in this material cosmos, to which redeemed souls will happily depart after death. If, though, we open the New Testament at its beginning with this skewed spatial notion already lurking in the back of our minds and, only a few pages in, find Jesus talking enthusiastically about things that might affect our future prospects of "entering the kingdom of heaven," it's natural enough to hear in his words an allusion to strict border controls and to begin wondering where exactly this fabled domain is and how long it might take to get there as the crow flies.

But that's *not* what Jesus was talking about. "What must I do to get to heaven when I die?" was not a question on his agenda or even one he would have recognized as meaningful. Entering the kingdom of heaven is all about the same reality that Jesus taught his disciples to pray for: "Your kingdom come, your will be done, on earth as it is in heaven."[9] Your kingdom *come*, on *earth* as *it is* in heaven. In other words, "entering" the kingdom is a matter of entering into God's sovereign rule, submitting to that rule, and seeing it played out *in the world in which we live*, whether that is now, already, or in some presumed future lying beyond death—our own and that of the world in its current unredeemed condition. And the kingdom (of heaven or of God) is precisely *not* a "better place" that we go to in order to leave this world behind but that exercise of God's sovereignty which we are taught to pray will *come to us* so that the realities of heaven and earth might cohere and coincide. It is about *God's coming to be with us*, rather than our translation to be with God, so that God's will may finally be done "on earth as it is in heaven" because heaven and earth will at last be established and disclosed as one and the same place.

On Earth Because It Is in Heaven

ONE PROBLEM WITH Dante's *Paradiso* notion of heaven is precisely that it shifts the focus of "salvation" *away* from this world, away from its distinctive and complex mix of environments and ecologies, away from its wealth of biodiversity and its fragile balance of forces and processes, away from the blessings of nature and culture and all that reality and possibility of which, even now, we have only begun to scratch the surface in terms of our appreciation and understanding. And salvation becomes, instead, about the translation of individual human souls to a better place. It is hardly surprising, then, that ecological concerns to celebrate, respect, and protect our natural, material environment as an enduring gift from God's hand have sometimes struggled to find adequate theological traction in the church's life. For if the "better place" that is to be our final destination is by definition somewhere other than the place we now find ourselves in, we may well suppose that active concern for the well-being of *this* world, for both inanimate nature and the teeming array of life-forms that share it with us as a home, is energy that might be better expended in other ways. It does not follow, of course, that even a temporary residence with no abiding place in God's purposes may legitimately be treated by its occupants with anything other than humane respect and care, but the supposition of the world's transience and eventual consignment to the state of nonbeing out of which it, like we, was originally summoned probably makes such carelessness more likely and may, for some particularly ungodly tenants, even furnish sufficient warrant actively to exploit and maltreat it for the sake of their own pleasure and convenience.

That, needless to say, is not the Bible's vision but a dangerous counterfeit that has too often been substituted for it. As we have already had reason to observe in earlier chapters, the *biblical* hope from first to last (already anticipated in the accounts of the creation of the world by God) is in a future when God himself will at last find himself fully at home in his creation and dwell in the midst of his creatures, when "heaven" will come down to earth, and when God's life will be played out "on earth as it is in heaven" because heaven and earth will be one. The biblical hope is in the coming of God to redeem, to make good, to bring to its proper fulfillment this world in which we live, in all its brokenness and its beauty, in all its woe and its wonder. The biblical hope is in the transformation of this world in all its fullness, in "a creation restored by love,"[10] a world "ransomed, healed, restored, forgiven"[11]—and we only together with and as part of it. The biblical hope is in a world suffused by the kingdom of heaven, a world with God's glory situated at its heart and radiating out from every part of it, a world, as the prophet Habakkuk puts it, "filled with the knowledge of [God's glory] as the waters cover the sea."[12] The biblical hope, in other words, is in the bringing of God's whole creative project to its glorious fulfillment—and we only together with it and as an integral part of it. A world reconfigured and refurbished, fit at last to be the dwelling place, the temple, the home of God himself—and we together with God. By comparison with this, the notion of the translation of a queue of individual "spiritual" entities to some disembodied location notable chiefly for doing a good line in pearly gates, clouds, and harps is vapid, thin, and insubstantial—both literally and metaphorically so.

Grappling with the Hard Reality of Things

AND HERE IS another problem with the commonplace notion of "heaven" as a desirable afterlife abode, of course. It tends naturally toward a *dematerializing* of things, typically being cast in terms of the salvation of *souls* by their translation to somewhere uncontaminated by the concerns, constraints, and complaints associated with our entanglements with flesh and blood. That's an idea that has a long religious and philosophical heritage—that human beings are essentially spiritual, that the material world (and our bodies as part of that) is a prison house to be liberated from, a mortal coil to be shuffled off so that our souls can fly up to be absorbed into a beatific spiritual ether. That notion of what "life everlasting" or "eternal life" entails goes back a very long way indeed (and with it, of course, a tendency to denigrate or grant little value to the physical world in which we now live). It is the vision of salvation, versions of which we can find admirably presented in much classical Greek philosophy and in many of the Eastern religions—Buddhism, Hinduism, and others. And because these same traditions fed into Western culture early on, it has all too often found its way into the church too, not least in versions of "going to heaven when we die." But again, there is little warrant for any such expectation in the Bible, and it has nothing whatsoever to do with what Jesus appears to have expected or what any of the New Testament writers lead us to expect or to look forward to.

In fact, it's the *very opposite* of what they expect. So, for instance, far from desiring to escape from bodily existence into some purely spiritual paradise, the apostle Paul writes of our current existence as one of "groaning" in the body and longing not to be "unclothed" (stripped of the body, which would leave us naked, in a thin, insubstantial, wraithlike existence) but clothed by God with a new body, one suffused with "life" from heaven.[13] And, of course, we can see why once we grasp the vision of salvation that Scripture as a whole holds out to us, of a world redeemed rather than relegated; a world transfigured by the fullness of God's presence rather than left behind; a world fulfilled and suffused with God's glory rather than superseded and discarded; a place more substantial, more solid, more real than the world we know now. The latter point is made powerfully by C. S. Lewis in *The Great Divorce*, his quasi-allegorical novella of postmortem, afterworld existence in which residents of Grey Town are granted an excursion by bus into the foothills of heaven, where, the bus driver tells them, they may choose to remain if they wish.¹⁴ Finding the reality of the place so remarkably solid by comparison with their own thin existence, though (the grass being too hard for their feet and painful to walk upon, the stem of a daisy impossible for their hands to break), most decide that too much reality is actually more than they can bear and remain close to the bus so as to be sure not to miss their journey "home."¹⁵

If the venue for "the life of the coming age"—or "life everlasting," as the creed has it—is to manifest some such density and splendor of being as Lewis's biblical imagining gestures toward, then who on earth would want to be left "unclothed," with bodies more spectral than solid, and so unable to bear the weight of that new world's glory? To be left thus would be to be bereft of eyes to see, ears to hear, fingers to touch, noses to smell, and tongues to taste and so to *enjoy* the glorious, more-than-sensory goodness and reality of God's new creation. For a faith that believes in a redeemed cosmos rather than a fleshless sphere of spirits, that sees creaturely sensuality as but a shadowy pointer to the richness and blessing of the world's coming fulfillment in God's hands, that is to say, "groaning in the body" *now* is a perfectly natural thing to do (knowing that the sin and pain and suffering and transience and decay of this life are not how things are meant by God to be and not how things, in God's hands, will eventually be). And longing instead to be clothed with a *new*, redeemed body, one fitted out to share in and to enjoy to the full the renewed creation, is the most natural desire in the world. *That's* the Christian hope, "the *redemption* of our bodies," as Paul puts it in Romans 8:23 (emphasis added), as part of a creation restored by love.

Unapologetic about the Taste of Fresh Strawberries

I ONCE ATTENDED a formal university dinner to mark some grand occasion and found myself seated next to an elderly woman who was both a major benefactor of the institution in question and, it turned out, a person of considerable opinion on all sorts of subjects, whose idea of polite small talk was evidently to embark on an unrehearsed, no-holds-barred intellectual sparring match at the earliest opportunity, determined to show no mercy in the contest even if the object of her sport hammered audibly on the canvas in order to indicate willing submission. By the time the soup course was over, this garrulous interlocutor had long since ascertained, to her obvious delight, that my academic discipline was Christian theology. This, I have found, is a conversational epiphany typically resulting in one of three outcomes: (1) the conversation, after an awkward silence, takes a sudden and complete—and frankly very welcome—change of direction ("So erm . . . did you see the big game on TV this past weekend?"); (2) conversation as such comes to an abrupt and permanent end, one's putative partner in the venture clearly having decided instead that the person seated on their *other* side merits undivided attention for the rest of the evening (again, often not unwelcome); or (3), and this can end well or badly, the conversation receives a sudden injection of energy courtesy of which one is compelled to endure a litany of personal views on matters religious (informed or otherwise, pro or contra) and quite possibly a forensic examination regarding one's interlocutor's particular doctrinal hobbyhorse. So it was that, true to form, just as dessert was being served, my companion went in for the kill, deciding to skewer me on the substance (or lack of it) of the afterlife. "How on earth can you believe in something so silly as bodily resurrection?" she demanded in a tone that called for little other than an apology offered up meekly to her offended intellect. She was clearly an intelligent and thoughtful person, and I suppose it's possible that she might have been a card-carrying Platonist or an idealist of some other stripe. My suspicion, though, is that she was simply voicing the concerns and prejudices of a culture wedded to the crude idea that to be human must either be finally to transcend the body altogether or be reducible to its terms, rather than being grounded in it, wedded to it but nonetheless resistant to any analyses in terms of it alone.

To be honest, after-dinner apologetics is neither my forte nor my favorite pastime, tending rather to spoil the anticipation of cheese, coffee, and mints, but I thought I should do my best, initially adopting what may, I suppose, have seemed a rather oblique angle of approach. "How are you enjoying your strawberries?" I asked her. It turned out that she was enjoying them very much, that fresh strawberries were, in fact, a great favorite of hers, so that she rhapsodized for several minutes about the way their taste burst upon the tongue and then lingered as a delicious accompaniment to a crisp white wine. The possibility of a conversational body swerve at this point was certainly there for the taking had I wished to exploit it, but my ire was by now kindled, and I decided to tackle her instead. So I explored with her the suggestion that an afterlife lacking in the taste of fresh strawberries might reasonably be reckoned less desirable than one in which their flavor was not only there still to be enjoyed but perhaps now even *surpassed*, strawberries in a creation "made new" by God promising to be tastier than any supplied by the university caterers (a bowl full of which she was nonetheless still demolishing with considerable gusto). On reflection, I wondered aloud, is it not generally the case that among those things we typically enjoy and value most fully as human beings (things that, as we say, make our existence in the world worthwhile), the majority are identifiably things we should not be able to enjoy at all were it not for our bodies and the larger material reality that they key us into? Now, for creatures for whom goodness, enjoyment, and blessing are tangled up to this extent with the facts of our embodiment, I continued, might it not be supposed reasonable rather than risible to picture fullness and fulfillment of life in terms of qualities consistent with such goods rather than denying most of them (or anything analogous to them) any possible form of future existence?

Furthermore, I continued (by now warming to my theme a little), a number of recent, highly regarded studies by philosophers and psychiatrists with no religious ax to grind at all have argued convincingly that the "inner" world of consciousness and the mind's operations is not only integrated with but *utterly dependent upon* the ways in which our bodies situate us and function in our material environment. The categories of thought and language themselves, that is to say, are born from the ways we human creatures exist and what confronts us as embodied participants in a material world and presuppose the existence of that world so completely that any attempt to disentangle them from it would be bound to fail. Put differently, far from being essentially minds or spirits temporarily incarcerated in bodies, a truly "human" existence becomes something impossible even to imagine, let alone make much sense of, as we strip away the identifiable layers of involvement and distinctive contributions made to it by our bodies.[16] The attempt to imagine a "purely spiritual" afterlife, too, thus runs quickly into the ground if we take at all seriously the facts of how, as "psychosomatic" unities, human beings actually function in experiencing the world, reflecting on, and speaking meaningfully about it.[17] Indeed, this same fundamental unity is drawn attention to by the very fact that imagining *anything* already involves "clothing" it in some, at least, of the stuff of material existence (line, shape, dimension, and duration seem feasible minimums); otherwise, we are unable to picture any "thing" in our mind's eye or "think about" it at all. Why, then, should we strive to attempt the impossible, straining to picture the hereafter as a reality flayed to the point of becoming immaterial and thus lacking in human meaning?

Finally, for my bravura performance was indeed now approaching its swan song (or running out of steam, depending on how you look at it), might my well-fed antagonist not consider whether perhaps the notion of a future "bodily resurrection" of creatures such as ourselves, far from being tangled up inexorably with clumsy, macabre, and frankly ridiculous scenarios involving the recomposition and resuscitation of myriad individual corpses—most of them necessarily already reduced long since to mulch or ash by worms, bacteria, or crematoria, and their atoms redistributed by the vast cosmic recycling program from which they originally came ("for out of [earth] you were taken; you are dust, and to dust you shall return"[18])—need not be so crudely understood at all? What if, instead, the symbol of bodily resurrection were precisely that, a necessarily imaginative attempt to insist as straightforwardly as possible that whatever human existence in God's promised future might actually prove to be like, it is bound to entail realities *more solid, more real*, more "bodily" in fact, and better than the very best of those things that bring us joy and pleasure in the world we inhabit now? More, not less. And certainly no colorless, tasteless, silent, intangible alternative from which everything resembling the sensuality of creaturely existence has been stripped away by the fleshing knife. Not only is any such "spiritualizing" notion distinctly unattractive, impossible to imagine, and finally meaningless; it is hardly worthy either, surely, of the God who presently gives life to a world rich in fabulous colors, shapes, sizes, sounds, textures, and fragrances and who promises his sentient creatures the contented, peaceful, and joyful indwelling together of "a new heaven and a new earth"?

In the light of all this, I submitted, the fact that Christians believe God to have promised not to rescue "souls" from an unpleasant entanglement with bodies but to redeem human beings by granting them new life ("life in all its fulness") in the midst of a new heaven and new earth might begin to seem less unreasonable to anyone concerned about being and remaining truly "human" at all. And the possibility of such a promise being kept was something to be glad rather than grumpy about. The strawberries were all gone by this time, and my companion was at least willing to admit that their absence from whatever (if anything) lay beyond death would be a regrettable loss. It wasn't exactly a Damascus Road moment, but perhaps it was a start.

"It's Flesh and Blood, Jim, . . . but Not as We Know It"

ONE WAY OR another, "resurrection of the body" is indeed part and parcel of what Christians expect "life everlasting" to be characterized by so that the two phrases in this final clause of the creed turn out to refer us to two aspects of the same thing rather than providing us with a pair of postmodern, consumer-friendly alternative endings to the story of human existence. If there is a choice on which the shape of our personal hereafter hinges, this certainly isn't it. Eternal life, the life of the age to come, will, we should suppose, be in some identifiable sense an *embodied* existence (*more* than bodily, of course, but not less) in a redeemed materiality that Scripture sums up under the rubric of a "new heaven and new earth" as yet still to be "created" by God.[19] Again, of course, we cannot imagine in any detail what that life will be like except in the most broad-brush of terms. But then we don't *need* to do so in order to grasp and hold on to it as something well worth waiting for.

As I have already suggested, though, we are not without points of reference from which to embark on our attempts to imagine this "life everlasting" in compelling concrete ways, as long as we realize that these are bound to be provisional rather than prescriptive and that we shouldn't seek to build too much upon their foundations. This is the categorical error committed by the Sadducees in Matthew's Gospel, appealing to the logic of the world we know now in order to argue, via a proposed reductio ad absurdum, against the coherence of believing in resurrection of any sort at all.[20] Jesus's response is precisely to point out that God's promise of a resurrected "flesh-and-blood" existence does not imply any straightforward continuity between the conditions and institutions proper to such an existence and those pertaining in the here and now. On the contrary, in a world "made new" by the creative action of God (and "creation" is the image deliberately appealed to in Scripture to evoke the essential newness of any such world, suggestive as it is of both a radical new beginning and a common genesis with that other radical beginning spoken of in the Bible's opening sentences, in the creative purposes, power, and possibilities of God alone[21]), we may suppose that things will necessarily be different in all sorts of ways from the circumstances of life in this world—unimaginably so, in fact.

And yet we must also suppose that the fulfillment of God's promise of "all things made new" will result in something continuous with our current experience in meaningful ways too because it will be precisely the life of *this world* that is to be made new and not some other world. Unlike God's original act of creation, in other words, this one will definitely not be summoned into being ex nihilo or ab initio as a "novel" creation, but consist instead in the radical *qualitative renewal* of that original world, taking it as a given starting point with and upon which to work.[22] "This world" redeemed, we might say, will certainly be "this world" transfigured, and transfigured drastically, but not beyond all meaningful recognition. And part of that undergirding continuity, Christian hope in the resurrection of the body insists, will be the entanglement of our existence with materiality of some description. Of course, the properties of matter themselves are likely to be rather different from those we currently know (a prospect likely to both excite and frustrate physicists, whose ventures may find themselves compelled to go back to basics), but the point is that life in the new creation will at least be *analogous* to our experience of life in the world now, a life in which it is *bodies* that key us into reality, enable our action and our engagement with others, and so on. So while for the time being imagining may be the only mode of knowing available to us in our apprehension of the new creation, inasmuch as we are called by God to anticipate and bear witness to it, acts of imaginative *poesis* are precisely what we must be prepared to perform. In light of all this, I think, we can and should look forward (analogously but nonetheless confidently) to something even better than strawberries.

Imagination — Does It Stretch and Will It Break?

IN ITS OWN performance of this task, Scripture begins (as it must, there being nowhere else for it or for us to begin) with elements in our experience of the cosmos in its current fallen state. It then modifies these imaginatively so as to provide suggestions, clues, and pointers to a redeemed, qualitatively new world that lies as yet beyond the range of our mundane powers of speech and understanding.

Scripture does this in different ways. Sometimes it pictures an earthly idyll that, given the weight of experience, certainly demands of us a stretch of the imagination but does not yet stretch it all the way to the breaking point. So, for instance, the prophet Micah kindles a vision of a time when God's justice will finally prevail, violence between nations ended (swords being ecologically repurposed as plowshares and spears as pruning hooks), and everyone free at last to rest peacefully in their gardens, shaded from the sun's heat by the vine, fig tree, or whatever other species of generously proportioned vegetation happens to be growing there.[23] As idylls go, this may not, of course, be designed to whet the appetite of the modern, urban, air-conditioned reader. But it is a text addressed originally to a small nation of farmers whose cultivation of their particular plot of the "land of promise" was forever under threat of interruption by yet another round of military conscription, they and their hired workers being compelled to leave the crops untended in the fields in order to attend refresher courses on "the Military Deployment of Agricultural Implements" and sent off into the heat of battle knowing that they might well never see home again, razor-sharp pruning hooks or plowshares notwithstanding. For such readers, what Micah depicts is a state of tranquil, joyous well-being (*shalŏm* in biblical terms) barely imaginable except as a dream fit to elicit deep longing and desire. Another such image is the familiar one of God's coming messianic kingdom and of "life in all its fulness" as a huge party enjoyed in God's presence, a joyful celebration where feasting, dancing, and good company will all be available in plenty, as at a Jewish wedding banquet.[24] Again, while such parties are hardly an everyday occurrence (and, when they do occur, are rarely quite as enjoyable as they promise to be), no actual blowing of our imaginative circuits is required to grasp the basic idea here. But we need to recall that these are precisely images and not literal descriptions, and as such, they refer us beyond the realities they depict to something even better and more fulfilling. Holding out pictures of some of the very best experiences available to us as dwellers in this world, they nonetheless seek not to constrain our imagining but to give it an orientation and an impetus that will enable its exploration further into the mystery of God's promised end. What they say to us is not "This is it, folks—nothing more to see" but "Yes, it will be *something* like this but *unimaginably more and better*, compared to which even this is but the merest shadow." The suggestion is that "the new creation will fulfil the authentic utopias of every generation, and still more and still better. Its transcendence is of an inclusive rather than an exclusive sort."[25] Whatever in the present world is consonant with "life in all its fulness" will, we might say, be taken up and transfigured to find its proper place and fulfillment as part of God's promised future, while whatever is contrary to it will be judged, purged, and destroyed, having no possible place there.

The biblical imagining of this future works in other ways too, though it is sometimes disturbing in its departure from anything we know now "by presenting the unfamiliar and the surprising, and more disjointed and bewildering visions whose negations and symbols strain our imagination to the limits, leading us to the brink of the unimaginable, peering into the brilliant darkness beyond."[26] So, for instance, "Isaiah 65 offers a concrete utopia which we can imaginatively inhabit. We can harvest the grapes, play with the children, chat to our two hundred year old neighbours, put down straw for the oxen to eat and enjoy watching the lions eat with them. Only with respect to this final image might we begin to find our imagination stretched in such a way as to force upon us the anxious suspicion that, while this appears to be the world we know and are at home in, it just might not be."[27] Passages such as Revelation 21 and Isaiah 25, meanwhile, cross the Rubicon and bite the bullet at the same time, presenting an image in which is recapitulated the weight of numerous hopeful glimpses scattered more widely through Scripture and forcing us up against the most unimaginable thing of all—that when God at last makes all things new and makes his home among mortals, *death* will be no more, and with it will be destroyed all those things that, as death's henchmen, blight life as we know it and can have no place in God's presence eternally: weeping, sorrow, pain, transience, decay, fear, selfishness, greed, violence, disgrace, shame, guilt, self-loathing, and all other denizens of the regions and legions of hell.[28] Instead, with God dwelling immediately in our midst, we must look forward to a fullness of a life of which qualities such as goodness, beauty, peace, and justice, where we find them in this world, serve as worthy parables, a life that will be a creaturely sharing of this world with God in God's own life, sharing in God's joy and enjoying God's glory forever.

Looking Forward to What Was, and Is, and Is to Come . . .

CHRISTIAN HOPE, THEN, is finally invested in not an extension of the present order of things or a development from its conditions, actualities, and latent potentialities, nor even a divinely undertaken repristination or "upgrade" of it, but a complete overhaul from the foundations up, a project to be undertaken as a new work by the same God who in the beginning called it into being and resulting in an altogether new and different order of existence.[29] This being so, our expectations and hopes must be constrained or circumscribed not by the capacities and incapacities of the world as we know and experience it now but only by the capacities of the God with whom "all things are possible."[30] The resurrection of the crucified Jesus from death, cropping up incongruously in the midst of history as it does, is God's sign and seal to us that this radical renewing of the cosmos (and of our humanity as part of that) is indeed coming and, in certain ways, has already begun by way of anticipation. Christian profession of belief in "the resurrection of the dead and the life everlasting," therefore, is both an expression of trust in this promise and surety and an act of commitment to involve ourselves actively in all those incongruous ways of living in the world that "life in all its fulness" already demands of us.

Finally, therefore, we should notice now how reimagining "life everlasting" in terms of the new creation and bodily resurrection transforms our understanding both of responsible living and of the breadth of the church's mission in the world here and now. Curiously, what this means is precisely that the quality of "everlasting" or "eternal" life, or "life in all its fulness," is not and cannot be confined to the new creation at all but reaches back from our promised future into our present moment, interrupting the patterns of fallen, historical existence by summoning us to act in ways that testify to the reality of that future, having their explanation and their true warrant in it alone, not in the familiar. Such hopeful acts of "guerrilla theater," as I have referred to them in earlier chapters, are bound sometimes to be disruptive acts of resistance too, as the discontinuous elements of the new and the old cause friction and chafing and even some violent crunching of gears as they are obliged to rub up directly against one another.[31] Lives lived already in the spirit of filial devotion and obedience to a heavenly Father are bound to that extent both to experience and to be the cause of such friction. Drawing life and energy not just from the constantly depleting and contaminated supplies given by their biological, social, and spiritual heritage but equally from their inheritance as those united now to the humanity of God the Son whose own life courses through them by the action of the Holy Spirit, such lives will by definition be places where the old and the new are to be found locked in a furious struggle, as fallenness is gradually superseded by holiness and God's kingdom finds ever more traction "on earth, as in heaven." And the shock waves caused by this radical heart transplant in individuals, relationships, and communities will be felt not only in the spheres of the moral and the spiritual but in our "hands-on" dealings with the material world too.

Once we grasp the fact that "life everlasting" is going to take the form of *life in this world*, albeit a world filled at last now with the goodness, peace, joy, and glory of God—whose plan and promise, it turns out, was always to dwell in it together with us as our shared residence—it is more probable that we shall find and invest more rather than less value in it and seek to treat it with far more respect and care. After all, discovering that, contrary to what we had supposed, it is precisely *this world* and no other that God loves, and that God has determined to overhaul it completely so that he and we can share and enjoy it together, we can hardly continue to view it or treat it (as, it must be admitted, Christians sometimes have and still do) like some now outdated gadget that exists only for our own convenience and gratification and comes with the same "built-in obsolescence" on which capitalist economics depends so completely. Confident that market forces will in any case soon summon into being an even newer, shinier, better, and costlier version to replace whatever the particular gizmo in question is, we readily slip (with what we take to be reasonable impunity) into treating those we already possess with indifference, scant care, or even shabbily, preoccupied already with imagining the delights of possessing their glamorous replacements.

The cosmos, though, is no mass-produced widget designed for early replacement and neither capable nor worthy of being "made new." It is much more akin to a singular work of art in which the artist has invested everything of him- or herself, unique in its beauty and in its potential to give joy to all who will receive what it has to offer. Knowing it to be the undisputed product and object of God's love and concern and grasping it as a precious gift that God's love has bestowed upon us (a place to dwell with God not just for now but forever), we shall treat it with the love and respect to which, even in its current broken and desecrated form, its nature as gift (in theological jargon, "grace") lays claim. And viewing it not so much in its current disfigured condition but in the light of its true identity and destiny in God's heart, God's hands, and God's promised future, we may discover that even "waiting" for the Lord to fulfill his promise cannot possibly be a passive thing. For those whose belief is in the resurrection *of* the world of the body rather than delivery *from* it, "waiting" is all about how we live in the meanwhile, and it demands of us the concrete action of lives that begin *already* to manifest the characteristics of the kingdom and the Spirit in our living here and now, personally, socially, politically—striving for justice, making for peace, pursuing goodness and joy in all created things (in our dealings not just with other people but with the wider creation too), and struggling actively against the myriad forces which would oppose it.[32] It's all a million miles away both from "pie in the sky, bye and bye" and from its unholy (but not, alas, always unreligious) counterpart "grab as much as you can get and do whatever you like with it while it's still available and you're still capable of enjoying it." But it is the form that authentic witness, authentic discipleship always takes, set apart and dedicated to function as a sign to the world of the world's own true identity and destiny.

This is what believing in the resurrection of the body and the life everlasting looks like. Like the other articles of this creed, this one has "self-involving" force, so to profess it in public is publicly to announce our willingness to involve ourselves actively in this scandalous agenda. It is thus what in the chapter "Memorizing Mere Christianity" we called a "speech act."[33] It is, that is to say, no mere recitation of centuries-old, harmless theological mumbo jumbo, but tantamount to a promise or declaration of allegiance made and refreshed weekly in the midst of the congregation and before the world and to which, therefore, we may reasonably expect to find ourselves held accountable. Together with all the preceding clauses of this creed considered in this book, in fact, we should definitely take care never again to utter this one carelessly or without consideration, lest, like the casual attendee at an auction room, we find ourselves taking home something very costly that we had no serious intention of buying into at all. After all, God works in mysterious ways.

NOTES

Preface

1 Eccl 12:12 NABRE.
2 Jude 1:3.
3 This is a phrase associated with the fifth-century French monk and theologian Vincent of Lérins (✝ ca. 450).
4 Trevor Hart, *Faith Thinking: The Dynamics of Christian Theology*, 2nd ed. (Eugene, OR: Cascade, 2020), 3–7 passim.
5 Isa 45:18.
6 Luke 10:27.
7 1 Pet 3:15.

Memorizing Mere Christianity

1 This familiar term—which in current popular discourse applies to whatever happens to be the prevailing doctrinal consensus in politics, economics, and other fields as well as in religion and theology—is simply a rendering of the Greek word *orthodoxia*, meaning "right opinion." To be orthodox in this sense, therefore, is to conform to the sorts of views and assumptions prevalent and held to be true by some group or institution, whether formally and explicitly or merely tacitly. To be heterodox is to align oneself instead with some different belief or beliefs.
2 *Ecumenical* is another word borrowed from Greek via Latin. In ancient Greek, the adjective *oikoumenikos* meant "of the whole world" (i.e., in practice, the known and civilized world of the Greek and then Roman Empires), a use borrowed by the Latin transliteration *oecumenicus*, meaning "general" or "universal." So an "ecumenical council" was one convened among representatives of the whole church in its geographical spread across the East and West rather than merely part of it.
3 See further chapter 3.
4 In fairness to the theologians of Nicaea, it must be admitted that the complexity of their formulary pales into insignificance when compared

with the so-called Athanasian Creed, or *Quicumque Vult*, contained, for instance, in the Book of Common Prayer of many Anglican provinces for occasional public recitation.
5 Because it is contained in the eucharistic liturgy, though, in actual fact, this particular creed often *is* used as the basis or a part of the preparation of candidates for baptism and confirmation. Indeed, my own experience as a young adult convert to the faith some forty years ago was of preparation that, while certainly enjoyable and helpful, included some slightly abstruse and intellectually strained grappling (over coffee and dessert) with "light from light" and "who proceeds from the Father and the Son."
6 C. S. Lewis, *Mere Christianity* (London: Collins, 1952), 5–12.
7 1 Pet 3:15.
8 Disclaimer: Other presentational software packages are, it should be noted, readily available and lend themselves equally well to either highly imaginative and rich or else unimaginative and soporific modes of use.
9 Some such instances are thought likely to have been "hymns," a suggestion reminding us of the power of what we *sing* together to form and reinforce the theology of any Christian congregation, as well as what we say together and whatever is said to us from the pulpit.
10 The aforementioned Nicene Creed refers to the church as "one, holy, catholic, and apostolic," epithets sometimes referred to as identifying four "marks" of the church.
11 The distinctive nature of performative utterance and its dependence on the precise context of saying is illustrated helpfully, perhaps, by observing that any of these things said by an actor on stage or as part of a scripted performance would not normally be expected to count as a speech act (other than a fictive speech act) in this sense. Indeed, in theory (though one suspects for all sorts of reasons that this would be unlikely to enhance the quality of the performance), the words themselves might be uttered while lacking not just the coefficient of personal commitment or investment but even the most superficial understanding of their ranges of meaning as language.
12 Michael F. Bird, *What Christians Ought to Believe: An Introduction to Christian Doctrine through the Apostles' Creed* (Grand Rapids, MI: Zondervan, 2016), 40.
13 Baptism typically takes place today in the context of public worship, where there is a proper emphasis on accountability on the part both of the candidates and of the Christian congregation as the local manifestation of

the body of Christ into which they are being baptized. Baptism, though, is also a powerful witness to the reality of God's working in the lives of individuals and congregations alike, and there is perhaps an argument to be made for its deliberate relocation from the safety of the sanctuary to far more identifiably public contexts, as most occasions of worship in our current culture are "public" more in theory than in practice.

14 For an accessible discussion of this contested topic of truth (and suggestions that we live now in a "post-truth" world), see Hart, *Faith Thinking*, esp. chs. 12–15.

15 The notion of "relevance" can be misleading if it is permitted primarily to suggest conformity to the concerns of wider social and cultural agendas and assumptions. Arguably, it is more often when it is compelled to challenge or criticize such agendas and assumptions that the church is at its most relevant rather than merely obscurantist or isolationist. See further chapter 10.

Chapter 1

1 Drawing again on the language and thought of an earlier ecclesial era, theologians often follow the fifth-century African theologian Saint Augustine in distinguishing between "fides quae creditur" and "fides qua creditur"—the particular set of things that faith holds or believes to be true and the disposition or act of faith by which it holds or believes them. Both are forms of "faith," and as we shall see, they belong properly together.

2 Rom 4:1–12; Heb 11:8.

3 See, for instance, Karl Barth, *Dogmatics in Outline* (London: SCM, 1949), 15–21.

4 Mark 12:29–30, 34.

5 Jas 2:26 NET.

6 Lewis, *Mere Christianity*, 127.

7 The Red Queen to Alice in Lewis Carroll, *Alice's Adventures in Wonderland and Through the Looking Glass* (London: Penguin, 1998), 174.

8 Mark 12:30.

9 As Thomas F. Torrance reminds theologians repeatedly, to be "scientific" is to proceed in ways that are appropriate to the nature of the object concerned, thus allowing reality itself to dictate and to shape our ways of knowing it, the sorts of tools and measures we deploy, and what sorts of things we subsequently dare to say about it, rather than vice versa. See, e.g., Thomas F. Torrance, *Theology in Reconstruction* (London: SCM, 1965), 53–54.

10 Peter Rollins observes that such overweening claims amount to nothing less than the sin of idolatry—i.e., the mistaken identification of our cherished images, ideas, and words with God's own reality, which leads in practice to our "deifying" of them, granting them status and value that are not just inappropriate but dangerous. See, e.g., Peter Rollins, *How (Not) to Speak of God* (London: SPCK, 2006), 5–19.

11 For an account of all this by an eminent research chemist and philosopher of science, see Michael Polanyi, *Personal Knowledge* (London: Routledge & Kegan Paul, 1958). For a helpful overview and evaluation of Polanyi's thought, see Drusilla Scott, *Everyman Revived: The Common Sense of Michael Polanyi* (Lewes, UK: Book Guild, 1985). We shall have further significant dealings with Polanyi in chapter 10.

12 Heb 11:1 NRSV reads, "Now faith is . . . the conviction of things not seen."

13 Nicholas Lash provides an illuminating exploration of such questions as, What makes a thing a "thing"? How do we know things? What kinds of things should count as "things" at all? See his short essay "On What Kinds of Things There Are" in his *The Beginning and End of "Religion"* (Cambridge: Cambridge University Press, 1996), 93–111.

14 Where questions of morality are concerned, for instance, this is the case argued in a popular classic: J. L. Mackie's *Ethics: Inventing Right and Wrong* (London: Penguin, 1971).

15 Readers interested in exploring these ideas at more length and in greater depth will find them treated accordingly in Trevor Hart, *Making Good: Creation, Creativity, and Artistry* (Waco, TX: Baylor University Press, 2014).

16 For those of a philosophical disposition, this claim is developed persuasively and at length in Nicholas Wolterstorff, *Divine Discourse: Philosophical Reflections on the Claim That God Speaks* (Cambridge: Cambridge University Press, 1995).

17 On this metaphor, see helpfully H. H. Farmer, *The World and God: A Study of Prayer, Providence and Miracle in Christian Experience* (London: Nisbet, 1936), 73.

18 Barth writes, "If the question what God can do forces theology to be humble, the question what is commanded of us forces it to concrete obedience. God may speak to us through Russian Communism, a flute concerto, a blossoming shrub, or a dead dog. We do well to listen to Him if He really does." Karl Barth, *Church Dogmatics*, vol. 1, pt. 1, *The Doctrine of*

the Word of God (Edinburgh: T&T Clark, 1975), 55. We need to take care to attend to both halves of this quotation.
19 See further Hart, *Faith Thinking*.
20 John Henry Newman, *An Essay in Aid of a Grammar of Assent* (London, 1870).
21 Rom 4:3.

Chapter 2

1 See, e.g., Mark 4:30; Luke 13:20.
2 See further the entry on "Imagination" in Kevin Vanhoozer, ed., *Dictionary for Theological Interpretation of the Bible* (Grand Rapids, MI: Baker Academic, 2005), 321–23.
3 Exod 4:22–23 NASB.
4 Exod 6:7; Ezek 36:28; Jer 7:23; 31:33.
5 See Tom Wright, *The Lord and His Prayer* (London: SPCK, 2012), 14–16.
6 See Wright, 13.
7 Exod 15:11.
8 Pss 95:4–5; 104; 134:3.
9 Isa 43:10.
10 Isa 43:13.
11 Mark 10:42–45.
12 Luke 1:37 TPT (emphasis added).
13 Bird, *Christians Ought to Believe*, 67.
14 C. S. Lewis, *The Problem of Pain* (London: Geoffrey Bles, 1940), 16.
15 This point is sometimes overlooked in the perfectly reasonable observation that the image of God as Father may be damaging rather than helpful for individuals whose experiences of their own human fathers have been painful or traumatic ones. The point is well made, and it may well lead to pastoral discretion being exercised as regards the use of the image in certain circumstances. But we cannot afford to miss the force of the point made above in relation to images of human power. Following the scriptural lead and calling God our "Father" does not endorse or leave unchallenged *any* understanding or experience of human fatherhood and actually affords more rather than less in the way of resources to deconstruct, judge, and redeem the worst abuses of both the language and the relationship of which it speaks. One significant danger of simply avoiding the language, in fact, is that this same critical and redemptive cauterizing involved in its application

to God is evaded, and the opportunity for healing language and experience alike left unattended to.

16 C. E. B. Cranfield, *The Apostles' Creed: A Faith to Live By* (Edinburgh: T&T Clark, 1993), 15.
17 Rom 13:1–2.
18 Ps 104:29–30.
19 The image of a celebration, banquet, or party, we should not forget, is central to Jesus's teaching about the kingdom of God and about God's joyful response to the salvation of those who were lost.
20 Neil Postman, *Amusing Ourselves to Death: Public Discourse in the Age of Show Business* (London: Methuen, 1987).
21 Charles Dickens, *Hard Times: For These Times*, ch. 6.
22 Matt 13:35 WEB.
23 Exod 24:17.
24 Exod 33:20.
25 Exod 34:29–33.
26 Hab 2:14.
27 A detailed and accessible commentary can be found in the relevant sections of Terence Fretheim, *Exodus* (Louisville, KY: Westminster John Knox, 1991).
28 John 1:14 (emphasis added). The NRSV has, "lived among us." The Greek verb *eskēnōsen*, though, can mean "pitched his tent," a resonance that, given the context and the accompanying reference to God's glory, should not be lost on anyone familiar with the Old Testament story. Here, John is telling us, God has at last come to dwell in our midst directly and bodily, fitting out our own humanity as his tabernacle or temple.
29 Mal 3:1.
30 Saint Augustine, *Confessions*, trans. Henry Chadwick (Oxford: Oxford University Press, 1991), 3.
31 Cranfield, *Apostles' Creed*, 18.
32 See, for instance, the helpful account in Cameron Wybrow, *The Bible, Baconianism, and Mastery over Nature: The Old Testament and Its Modern Misreading* (New York: Peter Lang, 1991).
33 Gen 1:26–27.
34 What follows is indebted to arguments developed in Richard Bauckham, *The Bible and Ecology: Rediscovering the Community of Creation* (Waco, TX: Baylor University Press, 2010).
35 Gen 1:26–28.
36 Bauckham, 49–54.

37 John Maddox, *What Remains to Be Discovered* (New York: Free Press, 1999), quoted in Bauckham, *Bible and Ecology*, 46.

Chapter 3

1 For details, see, for instance, Matt Thorne, *Prince* (London: Faber & Faber, 2012), chs. 24–26.
2 The personal anecdote is contained in N. T. Wright, "Jesus and the Identity of God," *Ex Auditu* 14 (1998): 44. I owe familiarity with it, though, to its inclusion in Bird, *Christians Ought to Believe*, 74.
3 See, e.g., P. T. Forsyth, *The Work of Christ* (Eugene, OR: Wipf & Stock, 2001).
4 On this important distinction, see chapter 2.
5 See, for instance, John Goldingay, *Old Testament Theology*, vol. 1, *Israel's Gospel* (Downers Grove, IL: IVP Academic, 2003), 15.
6 See John 1:41.
7 Matt 11:3.
8 Cranfield, *Faith to Live By*, 22.
9 Gal 4:4–5.
10 See, e.g., Exod 4:22; 2 Sam 7:12–14; 1 Chr 17:13; Ps 2:7; Hos 11:1.
11 John 1:14, 18; 3:16 NASB.
12 Col 1:13–16.
13 John 1:1–3, 14–18.
14 The Nicene Creed says,

> *I believe . . . in one Lord Jesus Christ,*
> *the only-begotten Son of God,*
> *eternally begotten of the Father,*
> *God from God, Light from Light*
> *true God from true God,*
> *begotten, not made,*
> *of one substance with the Father.*

15 See esp. Richard Bauckham, *Jesus and the God of Israel* (Milton Keynes, UK: Paternoster, 2008), ch. 1.
16 The Second Temple period was between the rebuilding of the Jerusalem temple in the late sixth century BCE and its destruction by the Romans in 70 CE.
17 By "identity" here, he intends the sort of personal identity or self-continuity by reference to which, as we say, we are able precisely to "identify" someone

or specify who they are, differentiating them clearly from others in the process. See Bauckham, *God of Israel*, 6n5.
18 Bauckham, 11.
19 Col 1:16–17.
20 Acts 2:33–35; Eph 1:21–22; Heb 1:2–4, 7.
21 Matt 2:11; 28:9, 17; Luke 24:52; John 5:21–23; Phil 2:9–11; Rev 5:12–14. Bauckham notes that while other figures (angels and servants of God of various sorts) were certainly thought to exercise power and authority on God's behalf and by God's permission within certain specific spheres of influence (just as human rulers do), none were ever pictured as seated on the divine throne itself, and the way the New Testament uses such imagery places heavy emphasis on Jesus being qualitatively quite distinct from such angelic rulers themselves and established in a "higher" position such that all things (i.e., all created things, including angels) are "under his feet" and must serve and worship him. See, e.g., Heb 1:1–8; Eph 1:20–22. "The point is," Bauckham writes, "that Jesus now shares precisely God's exaltation and sovereignty over every angelic power." Bauckham, 24.
22 Phil 2:9–10.
23 See Bauckham, 24–25.
24 The same idea is found in Hebrews 1:4, where "the name which he has inherited" and which is so superior to cast even angels and their names in the shade can only be the name of God itself.
25 See, e.g., Rom 10:9; 1 Cor 12:3; Phil 2:11.
26 Thomas F. Torrance, *The Mediation of Christ* (Edinburgh: T&T Clark, 1992), 59.
27 Torrance, 59.
28 Torrance, 59–60.
29 Gal 4:5–6.
30 John 20:28.
31 1 Cor 6:20.

Chapter 4

1 Luke 1:35.
2 Matt 1:18.
3 Matt 1:19.
4 John 6:41–46.
5 See, in this passage alone, John 6:27, 32, 37, 40, 44–46, 57.

6 Emphasis added. The Greek phrase actually means "the offspring of fornication [*porneia*]."
7 In this light, the question put to Jesus in John 8:19 also gains an additional layer of significance: "They said to him 'Where is your Father?' " Not so much an inquiry about the geography of heaven, perhaps, as another leering insinuation about the character of Jesus's mother and the quality of his Jewish bloodline.
8 This claim is recorded by the Christian theologian Origen (184–253 CE) in his polemical work *Against Celsus* 1:2.
9 John 1:12–13.
10 John 3:3.
11 John 1:13, "born, not of blood or of the will of the flesh or of the will of man."
12 Gal 4:4 (emphasis added).
13 Cranfield, *Faith to Live By*, 27.
14 See, e.g., Luke 2:33.
15 Although the Gospels were written with the whole church in mind rather than as niche religious products, they do have their distinctive characteristics, and it is widely recognized that Matthew shows particular concern to emphasize the essential Jewishness of Jesus and his fulfillment of the Old Testament's history of promise. In this regard and in relation to the above, for instance, it is interesting to notice the words of the angel to Joseph in Matt 1:20, identifying him explicitly as a "son of David."
16 Matt 1:22–23.
17 Isa 7:3 KJV.
18 C. S. Lewis, *Miracles* (1947; London: Fontana, 1960), 50–51.
19 Cranfield, *Faith to Live By*, 28.
20 Luke 1:34–37.
21 This suggestion is handled helpfully, I think, by C. S. Lewis, who, as a scholar of literature, was better placed than most theologians to judge the parallels and differences between pagan myths and the Christian story. The Divine Light, according to John 1:9, gives light to everyone. It is unsurprising, therefore, Lewis opines, if in the great literatures of humankind, we find fleeting glimpses of truths which nonetheless lie way beyond the vision or understanding of their authors or the cultures from which they issue and only make proper sense when viewed in the full light of the truths they have glimpsed. Such myths, where we find them, he suggests, are "like dim dreams or premonitions. . . . It is like

watching something come into focus." C. S. Lewis, "Is Theology Poetry?," in *Essay Collection: Faith, Christianity and the Church*, ed. Lesley Walmsley (London: HarperCollins, 2000), 16.
22 Lewis, *Miracles*, 142.
23 Isa 43:19 ESV.

Chapter 5

1 David Day, *This Jesus* (Leicester, UK: IVP, 1980), 74.
2 Cranfield, *Faith to Live By*, 32.
3 Alister McGrath, *I Believe: Exploring the Apostles' Creed* (Downers Grove, IL: IVP, 1997), 55–56.
4 See Barth, *Dogmatics in Outline*, 101.
5 See P. T. Forsyth, *The Justification of God: Lectures for War-Time on a Christian Theodicy*, 1st ed. (London: Duckworth, 1916), 152.
6 John 19:30.
7 Mark 15:34; Matt 27:46.
8 Matt 3:17 KJV.
9 An informative and helpful, if taxing, account is contained in Martin Hengel, *Crucifixion: In the Ancient World and the Folly of the Message of the Cross* (Minneapolis: Fortress, 1977).
10 Bird, *Christians Ought to Believe*, 112–13.
11 Bird, 113.
12 See John 19:31–36. Breaking victims' legs meant that they could not use them any longer to prop themselves up and so avoid the "dead weight" of their bodies compressing their lungs. Most would die shortly afterward from asphyxiation. From John's account, it is clear that this is what happened to those crucified with Jesus but was not necessary in Jesus's own case. He was already dead.
13 Lewis, *Mere Christianity*, 47, 53.
14 Lewis, 53–58.
15 On the larger topic of the imaginative nature of our talk about the atonement, see further Colin Gunton, *The Actuality of Atonement: A Study of Metaphor, Rationality and the Christian Tradition* (Edinburgh: T&T Clark, 1988).
16 See, e.g., Rom 6:5–6; Gal 2:20; 6:5.
17 Ps 139:7–8.

Chapter 6

1. See, helpfully, the comments on the place of death in modern Western societies in Jürgen Moltmann, *The Coming of God: Christian Eschatology* (London: SCM, 1996), 54–57.
2. David Jenkins was the bishop of Durham from 1984 to 1994. The comment was made in a radio debate on BBC Radio 4's *Poles Apart* program in October 1984.
3. 1 Cor 15:44.
4. Popular uses of *spiritual* and *spirituality* (and, of course, *spiritualism*) in our own culture can thus be highly misleading if we read them blithely back into the New Testament. On Paul's use of *pneumatikos*, see, e.g., Gordon D. Fee, *God's Empowering Presence: The Holy Spirit in the Letters of Paul* (Peabody, MA: Hendrickson, 1994), 28–29.
5. C. S. Lewis, *The Weight of Glory and Other Addresses* (London: Geoffrey Bles, 1949).
6. See chapter 12.
7. 1 Cor 15:4 NET.
8. See chapter 6.
9. An exhaustive account may be found in N. T. Wright, *The Resurrection of the Son of God* (London: SPCK, 2003), 85–206. As Wright demonstrates, in the Old Testament itself, while the idea of bodily resurrection is undoubtedly present, it is, "to put it at its strongest, deeply asleep, only to be woken by echoes from later times and texts" (85), gathering weight and definition only in the period between the Testaments. Among the most obvious and influential Old Testament allusions to the idea, he addresses texts such as Hos 6:1–2; Isa 26:13–19; Ezek 37:1–14; and Dan 12:2–3.
10. John 20:1–18.
11. John 20:8.
12. John 20:9–10.
13. Tom Wright, *Surprised by Hope* (London: SPCK, 2007), 51.
14. Mark 8:31.
15. Mark 9:10.
16. 1 Cor 1:23.
17. John 11:23.
18. John 11:24.
19. John 11:25–27 (emphasis added).
20. Isa 43:19; 65:17; Rev 21:5.
21. N. T. Wright, *Resurrection*, 197–206.

22 1 Cor 15:26.
23 Wright, *Surprised by Hope*, 86–87.
24 *Guerrilla theater* is a suggestive phrase coined by Amos Wilder to refer to the "performance" of the Christian story by the church's presence on the stage of the world. Amos Wilder, *Theopoetic* (Philadelphia: Fortress, 1976), 28.
25 Acts 2:32, 36.
26 A penetrating account of the methods, accomplishments, and limitations of history as an intellectual discipline may be found in R. G. Collingwood, *The Idea of History* (Oxford: Oxford University Press, 1946).
27 Wright, *Surprised by Hope*, 74.
28 1 Cor 15:23.
29 On the use and abuse of this in principle helpful distinction, see chapter 10.

Chapter 7

1 Luke 24:51; Acts 1:9.
2 So, e.g., John 3:13; 20:17; Eph 4:10.
3 Acts 1:2; 1 Tim 3:16.
4 John 14:2, 28.
5 1 Pet 3:22.
6 Luke 24:53.
7 Matt 28:20.
8 See John 16:7.
9 In *Philosophical Fragments*, Kierkegaard's pseudonymous author, Johannes Climacus, suggests that the true contemporary of Christ is not the *historical* contemporary but the person who, through faith, is able to relate personally to the figure of Jesus. On the other hand, despite actual historical proximity to Jesus, "a contemporary may for all that be a non-contemporary," lacking faith and incapable of such a relationship and response. The material conditions alone do not constitute genuine contemporaneity at all. Søren Kierkegaard, *Philosophical Fragments* (1844; Plano, TX: Jovian, 2017), 61.
10 See John 1:14; 1 John 1:1.
11 This is not to suggest, of course, that God cannot and does not deal with people in all sorts of different ways. It is simply to affirm the Christian conviction that it is in Jesus that God has acted decisively to draw creation (and humankind as part of it) to its promised end and that it is in Jesus that we see both God and God's redemptive engagement with our humanity bodied forth in the world. So while we cannot deal here with the question of precisely how God may engage with those who, for whatever

reason, have not heard and responded to the good news, we can and must say at least that God has already dealt with the humanity that is theirs just as surely as it is ours by regenerating it in the life, death, and resurrection of Jesus for us—and since the resultant new humanity is Jesus-shaped, so too is our sharing in it bound finally to be, no matter who we are. If salvation is sharing in Jesus's Spirit-filled relationship with his heavenly Father in a creation renewed by love, then embracing and enjoying it cannot involve seeking it in "spiritual" experiences or practices that by their nature are at odds with or present themselves as alternatives to it.

12 Luke 24:52–53.
13 Heb 6:19–20.
14 See chapter 2.
15 E.g., Matt 11:27; John 3:35; Phil 3:21; Col 3:20; Heb 1:2–3.
16 Bauckham, *God of Israel*, 163–64.
17 John 1:3; 1 Cor 8:6; Col 1:16–17.
18 John 5:21–23; Phil 2:9–11; Rev 5:12–14.
19 Bauckham, 7–11.
20 Heb 1:3–9.
21 Heb 6:19–20.
22 Gen 2:1–3. On the divine name Yahweh, see chapter 2. This, of course, is "the name [Jesus] has inherited," according to Heb 1:4.
23 E.g., Rom 10:9; 1 Cor 12:3; 2 Cor 4:5; Phil 2:11.
24 John 15:19; 17:14–16; 18:36.
25 Stanley Hauerwas and William H. Willimon, *Resident Aliens: Life in the Christian Colony* (Nashville: Abingdon, 1989).
26 Wright, *Surprised by Hope*, 111.
27 Phil 3:20.
28 Col 3:1–2.
29 See Heb 8–9. On this, see the rich and very accessible treatment in James B. Torrance, *Worship, Community and the Triune God of Grace* (Carlisle, UK: Paternoster, 1996).
30 Luke 3:22.

Chapter 8

1 For a helpful theological reflection on this, linking the liturgical "repetition" involved in weekly eucharistic celebration to elements of musical repetition in the Western tradition, see Jeremy Begbie, *Theology, Music and Time* (Cambridge: Cambridge University Press, 2000), 155–75.

2   Matt 28:20.
3   First Corinthians itself is among the earliest New Testament writings, usually dated early in the fifth decade of the first century—that is, just twenty years or so after the crucifixion and resurrection of Jesus. Anything odd cropping up as already too well established in the church's life to require comment is thus likely to be very early indeed. Corinth was a multicultural Greek trading hub at the heart of a Mediterranean dominated by the demands of the Roman Empire.
4   See, for instance, Anthony C. Thiselton, *The First Epistle to the Corinthians* (Grand Rapids, MI: Eerdmans, 2000), 1347–52.
5   Wright, *Surprised by Hope*, 140. I am pleased to acknowledge my substantial debt in this section to Wright's discussion of the subject in chapter 8 of his book and to recommend that readers interested in pursuing the subject further seek the book out if they are not already familiar with it.
6   1 John 2:28; 3:2.
7   Col 3:1, 4.
8   Wright, 147.
9   Wright, 148–49.
10 Dan 7:13.
11 See 1 Thess 1:6; 2:14; and the whole of 1 Thess 3.
12 Jer 31:33; Ezek 36:26; see also 2 Cor 3:3.
13 Ps 98:4, 7–9.

Chapter 9

1   In reality, of course, this popular image of the scientist itself falls far short of reality—science's best practitioners being anything but dispassionate and "verification" in the laboratory being far more complex than the merely descriptive process it is sometimes taken to be. Even white coats are not compulsory. See chapters 1 and 10. See further Hart, *Faith Thinking*, 44–64.
2   So, for instance, the BBC TV serial *Doctor Who*'s Cybermen (making their first appearance in 1966), the German pop group Kraftwerk's album *The Man-Machine* (1978), Ridley Scott's movie *Blade Runner* (1982), the antics of Bender the robot in the animated series *Futurama* (1999), and the "Agents" in the Wachowskis' *Matrix* trilogy (1999–2021), among many others, all reflect the mesmerizing capacity of questions regarding the apparently fragile boundaries between our humanity and robotic replications of it. Serious grappling with the issue dates back at least as far

as the publication in December 1950 of Isaac Asimov's fix-up SF novel about "positronic" androids, *I, Robot*, and is to be found alive and kicking, for instance, in Ian McEwan's most recent novel, *Machines like Me* (2019).

3 As the Victorian poet and professor of literature George MacDonald reminds us, it is through the ministry and mediation of metaphor and other imaginative tropes alone that our talk (and thereby our articulate thought) about anything lying beyond the reach of our senses is possible, borrowing and relying, as it does and must, from the vocabulary and the grammar of the flesh. Such poetic borrowings and allusions are embedded as fossils in the sediment of our languages, despite the fact that, as we traverse language's contemporary surfaces with confidence, we generally remain ignorant or forgetful of their vital yet fragile contribution to all "hard edged" (*sic*) discourse. See George MacDonald, "The Imagination, Its Functions and Its Culture," in *A Dish of Orts: Chiefly Papers on the Imagination, and on Shakespeare* (Whitehorn, CA: Johannsen, 1997).

4 On the "imaginaries" and "liturgies" of contemporary public life in the West, see the works of philosopher Charles Taylor and theologian James K. A. Smith cited in chapter 10.

5 See chapter 1.

6 John 4:24.

7 Hos 5:12.

8 Cf. William Shakespeare, *Hamlet*, act 3, scene 4, line 109. Joseph Priestley notes that for many classical authors, "air," like ether, fire, and light, was considered an instance of "incorporeity" or "attenuated matter." Joseph Priestley, *Disquisitions Relating to Matter and Spirit*, vol. 1 (Birmingham, UK: J. Johnson, 1782), 212.

9 Nick Moore, *Mindful Thoughts for Cyclists: Finding Balance on Two Wheels* (Brighton, UK: Leaping Hare, 2017), 17.

10 On this point, see further Trevor Hart, *In Him Was Life: The Person and Work of Christ* (Waco, TX: Baylor University Press, 2019), 309–36.

11 William Shakespeare, *A Midsummer Night's Dream*, act 5, scene 1, line 14; cf. line 16.

12 The process of "intercision" imagined in Philip Pullman's *His Dark Materials* trilogy, whereby a person's "daemon" (soul) may be separated from their body but only at risk of serious damage and most likely the death of both, captures the gist of this antidualist claim. See, e.g., Philip Pullman, *Northern Lights* (London: Scholastic Children's, 1995), 266–80.

But Pullman's imagining of daemons as discrete embodied (animal) forms tends inevitably to suggest that a clean surgical "cut" between the body and the soul, while difficult to accomplish, is nonetheless possible in principle and with sufficiently sophisticated tools, as though their mode of conjunction were analogous to the umbilical cord of a newborn. The coinherence between nonmaterial and material realities that I have in mind, though, is more analogous to the way in which one substance may, in its natural state, be wholly suffused by another from which it nonetheless remains perfectly distinguishable; or the way in which two distinct dimensions of something arise together in the actual existence of the thing, such that to erase one would necessarily be to threaten or imperil the other; or the way in which quite different levels of description of the same thing or event may and must be offered if we are to give a full account of it, neither of which may properly claim to be the "truth" of the matter, and the absence of either of which would leave any report of its "reality" lacking.

13 As the text of the ancient fourth-century Latin hymn known as the *Te Deum* affirms, this same God "did not abhor the virgin's womb" or, therefore, the life of flesh and blood, sinew, slime, and shit in which the incarnation necessarily implicated and continues to implicate God. Readers understandably offended by the use of the word *shit* here may only now, perhaps, have grasped the genuinely shocking nature and extent of the gospel claim that in Jesus, God "takes flesh." On the implications of this claim for our appreciation of the nature of religious and theological language more widely, cf. Hart, *In Him Was Life*.

14 Lewis, *Mere Christianity*, 62.

15 Lewis, 88.

16 A successful metaphor, theologian Sallie McFague suggests, indicates only the slightest thread of similarity between two dissimilar objects so that its use is, initially, always surprising, striking, and remarkable, generating imaginative tension which remains even when the connection is grasped and the metaphor's "fittingness" appreciated. Sallie McFague, *Metaphorical Theology: Models of God in Religious Language* (Philadelphia: Fortress, 1982), 12, 15. Metaphor, Nelson Goodman insists (metaphorically), involves "an affair between a predicate with a past and an object that yields while protesting," the conjunction between them being risqué, unseemly, and "contra-indicated." Nelson Goodman, *Languages of Art: An Approach to a Theory of Symbols* (London: Oxford University Press, 1969), 68.

17 I am presuming in all this, of course, that the "Achilles" in question is a hero of Greek myth and not in fact an imaginatively named specimen of the species *Panthera leo* to be seen conveniently at the local safari park. Context, as they say, is everything.

18 See Paul Ricoeur, *The Rule of Metaphor: Multi-disciplinary Studies of the Creation of Meaning in Language* (London: Routledge, 1978), 224, where Ricoeur cites the exordium to many fairy tales, "It was and it was not." Here, he suggests, "is contained *in nuce* all that can be said about metaphorical truth."

19 For this and many other illuminating examples, see George Lakoff and Mark Johnson, *Metaphors We Live By* (Chicago: University of Chicago Press, 1980), 92 passim.

20 Images taken respectively from the poems "Overlap" and "Undertones" in Micheal O'Siadhail's collection *Tongues* (Tarset, UK: Bloodaxe, 2010), 26–27.

21 See McFague, *Metaphorical Theology*, 13.

22 Aquinas, *Summa Theologiae* 1a.13, 5, in Herbert McCabe O. P., ed., *St. Thomas Aquinas Summa Theologiae*, vol. 3, *Knowing and Naming God* (London: Blackfriars, 1964), 63. The observation arises as the premise for one of the arguments *in contrarium*, but Aquinas's *responsio* endorses it as a ground for rejecting univocal predication while denying that complete equivocation is the only alternative to be reckoned with. See McCabe, *St. Thomas Aquinas Summa Theologiae*, 67.

23 Janet Soskice, *Metaphor and Religious Language* (Oxford: Clarendon, 1985), 64–65.

24 For Christians, this trust is rooted substantially in the belief that God has appropriated not just our flesh and blood but our language and has sanctioned the use of certain images, words, and forms of speech as "fit" to speak appropriately of God's own character and behavior. The task of discerning the mysterious scope of the "it is" and the "it is not" in such use is, in one sense, precisely the task of the theologian.

25 See, e.g., Isa 55:8–9; Hos 11:9. The sin of idolatry, into which Israel falls repeatedly and fatally in the story told by the Old Testament, involves precisely the dangerous elision of this essential difference between God and everything else that exists (even other putative "gods"), ascribing the prerogatives of creaturely reality to God and God's unique prerogatives to creatures in a manner that, if not corrected, leads (and always will lead) to religious, moral, and political-economic disaster.

26 All these are, we might say, biblically sanctioned, but not all, of course, are given equal weight or significance by the pattern of their use in Scripture or in subsequent theological and liturgical development of them. That is precisely where discrimination is called for in our engagement with God through our engagement with the text.

27 For a helpful, highly readable, and authoritative account not just of biblical materials but of the Christian doctrine of the Holy Spirit as a whole, see Gary D. Badcock, *Light of Truth and Fire of Love: A Theology of the Holy Spirit* (Grand Rapids, MI: Eerdmans, 1997). I am glad to acknowledge my grateful debt to this book in what follows.

28 See chapter 3.

29 Gen 2:7. Cf., too, Job 33:4: "The spirit of God has made me, and the breath of the Almighty gives me life."

30 In due course, as we have already seen and will see again, this connection will be picked up in the New Testament's insistence that when God's Word "takes flesh," it is precisely as the "anointed one"—that is, the one whose humanity is unique in both the manner and the extent of its involvement with the Spirit of God.

31 Gen 1:3, 6, 9, 11, 14, and so on (emphasis added).

32 Ps 33:6.

33 See, for instance, Irenaeus of Lyons, *Against Heresies*, 4.20.1; 5.1.3. For further discussion of this image, see Hart, *Making Good*, 59–63; and Eric Osborne, *Irenaeus of Lyons* (Cambridge: Cambridge University Press, 2001), 89–93.

34 See 1 Sam 10:1–13; 19:18–24.

35 See 1 Kgs 18:12.

36 Amos 7:12–15.

37 The Babylonian exile is dated to the late seventh / early sixth century BCE, and "preexilic" prophets are thus generally identified as those who were active prior to this in the period of the divided monarchy (i.e., in the southern and northern territories of Judah and Israel, respectively) and after whom biblical books are named. In practice, this includes the larger number: Jonah, Joel, Amos, Hosea, Isaiah, Micah, Nahum, Zephaniah, Habakkuk, and Jeremiah.

38 See, e.g., Neh 9:30; Ezek 2:2, 12–17.

39 See Zech 7:12.

40 According to the later doctrine of God as "Trinity," while each of the three "persons" in God (the Father, Son, and Spirit) is distinct and has a

distinct sphere of prerogative in God's engagement with the world, each is nonetheless fully participant in the one "nature" of God so that each person "coinheres" and is present to and "known" in, with, and under our encounters with the others. Thus the fourth-century "Cappadocian" theologian Gregory of Nazianzus writes, "No sooner do I conceive of the One than I am illumined by the splendour of the Three; no sooner do I distinguish them than I am carried back to the One." Gregory of Nazianzus, *Oration 40*, in *Nicene and Post-Nicene Fathers*, 2nd ser., vol. 7, ed. Philip Schaff and Henry Wace (Buffalo: Christian Literature Publishing, 1894), http://www.newadvent.org/fathers/310240.htm. This claim of classical Christian theology (the so-called perichoretic penetration of divine persons by virtue of their "consubstantiality") is, however, no mere conceit of authors steeped in philosophical learning. Its roots are to be identified clearly enough in the patterns of biblical teaching about the Father and the Son, the Son and the Spirit, and as here, the Spirit and the Word. Indeed, the doctrine of the Trinity as such is best thought of precisely as an attempt to interrogate and then articulate in intellectually robust form the wider shape of God's dealings with the world as narrated in Scripture and to make sense of what we must say on the basis of this about God per se.

41 Num 27:18.
42 Judg 6:34–7:14.
43 Judg 11:29–33.
44 Judg 14:5–6; 15:14–17.
45 Alasdair I. C. Heron, *The Holy Spirit* (Philadelphia: Westminster, 1983), 12, 13.
46 Gen 41:38–39.
47 See, e.g., Exod 31:3; Job 32:8–9; Wis 9:17. Perhaps it is not too farfetched to observe that it is by the blowing of a powerful *wind* that God eventually *speaks* to Job, granting him wisdom regarding, if not complete "understanding" of, innocent suffering in God's world. See Job 38:1; 40:6.
48 This is the emphasis helpfully foregrounded in Jürgen Moltmann, *The Spirit of Life: A Universal Affirmation* (London: SCM, 1992). The church's failure to acknowledge the Spirit's presence and activity wherever life, truth, goodness, beauty, and so on are to be found is a function of the lack of an adequate doctrine of creation. And yet what counts as "life," "truth," "goodness," and "beauty" is, from a theological perspective, to be ascertained in the light of Christ and not otherwise. And the reality

of sin and evil in God's world means that the Spirit cannot, without further qualification, be identified behind what humans sometimes judge to belong within these categories but will exist in critical (and finally redemptive) tension with them.

49 Lev 11:44–45; 19:2. The notion of "holiness" as we find it in Scripture is complex. Perhaps the most helpful way of thinking about it is to remember that the adjective *holy* applies to God first and foremost and to God's creatures only insofar as they reflect, correspond to, or "fit" with God's character, as they were and are intended to. Creaturely holiness thus involves all those qualities of existence that are fit to be offered to God in response to God's love and fit to share in God's glory as God dwells in creation's midst. This includes moral or ethical qualities in God's human creatures, but other things too (objects, places, seasons, and so on) can be spoken of as "holy." One might simply say, perhaps, that whatever is conformed completely to the character of God by the renewing agency of God's Spirit (the *Holy* Spirit) is "holy," and that holiness will thus be the overarching quality of the new, redeemed creation of God.

50 Isa 43:14–21; 55:1–11; 65:17–25.
51 Ezek 36:26–28; Exod 6:7; Jer 32:38–41.
52 Mal 3:1; Exod 25:8; 29:45–46; Lev 26:11–12. See chapter 2.
53 Luke 3:22.
54 1 Sam 16:6–7.
55 1 Sam 16:13; see also, e.g., 1 Sam 10:1, 6; 1 Kgs 1:32–35, 38–40.
56 Karl Barth, *Church Dogmatics*, vol. 3, pt. 1 (Edinburgh: T&T Clark, 1958), 94–229.
57 "Instruments of the covenant" is a phrase coined helpfully by Walther Eichrodt, *Theology of the Old Testament*, vol. 1 (London: SCM, 1961), 289–456.
58 Isa 11:2–3.
59 Isa 61:1–2 NRSVA.
60 Isa 44:1–6; Ezek 36:22–28.
61 Joel 2:28.
62 Exod 33:11; Deut 34:10.
63 Num 11:29.
64 The familiar phrase generally translated as "new testament" (Gr. *kaine diatheke*) means "new covenant."
65 Luke 1:35; John 1:13. As we have already observed, a well-attested variant reading of this verse in the Greek text makes Jesus rather than believers the

grammatical subject, and so of a "birth from above" that, in a manner both analogous and directly linked to that "rebirth" experienced by believers, is from the outset the work of the Spirit. See chapter 4.

66 Mark 1:9–11; John 1:32–33.
67 Luke 10:21.
68 Luke 4:1–14; Matt 12:28.
69 Luke 4:14–19; John 3:2. "Apart from the presence of God" is an allusion to God's Spirit and directly to Jesus's teaching about being born, by the Spirit's work, "from above."
70 John 19:34; Heb 9:14. While the combination of blood and water may well be physiologically apt and so an index of eyewitness testimony behind the Johannine account (see, e.g., Cahleen Shrier, "The Science of the Crucifixion," AZUSA Pacific University, accessed September 19, 2019, https://www.apu.edu/articles/15657/), it is widely accepted that water here, as often in Jesus's teaching and elsewhere, is a symbol of the Spirit being poured out. See, e.g., Badcock, *Light of Truth*, 32. Cf. John 3:5, 8; 4:10–14, 21–26; 7:37–39; 1 John 5:6–8.
71 Rom 8:11.
72 Matt 10:20.
73 Gal 4:6.
74 Mark 1:9–11.
75 See, e.g., Luke 4:14–15.
76 Despite the habitual use of masculine forms to refer to the Spirit in English translations of Scripture, the gender of the relevant noun is neuter in Greek (*to pneuma*) and feminine in Hebrew and Aramaic (*ruach/ruacha*). In today's theological context, there are all sorts of good reasons for sometimes imagining the Spirit, as I choose to here, in terms of feminine rather than masculine imagery. God, of course, is no more female than male, but the use of the impersonal neuter pronoun *it* hardly seems appropriate to refer to a mode of God's being (i.e., a way in which God is God) that is undeniably "personal," albeit more "anonymous" than the "persons" we know, respectively, as the Father and the Son. On this latter point, see helpfully Tom Smail, *The Giving Gift: The Holy Spirit in Person* (London: Hodder & Stoughton, 1988), 30–55.
77 John 19:30.
78 Cf. Luke 23:46, "Father, into your hands I commit my spirit!" (ESV).
79 On this, see helpfully Smail, *Giving Gift*, 144–65.
80 1 Cor 15:45.

81 Rom 9:3–8; Gal 3:24–29; Heb 8:6–13.
82 1 Cor 20–22; Col 1:15–18.
83 John 20:22. Notice again here the interplay between images of breath, spirit, and (eternal) life and the tacit allusion to Gen 2:7.
84 John 7:39; 19:28–30, 33–35. In John's Gospel, Christ is spoken of as "lifted up" and "glorified," paradoxically, in his betrayal and execution. See John 3:14–16; 12:28–33; 13:31–32.
85 Smail, *Giving Gift*, 200. For those interested, I have argued at length elsewhere that just such a "give-and-take" also lies at the heart of creation itself, being the form in our most thoroughly human relationships and interactions with and within the world. See Hart, *Making Good*.
86 1 Cor 3:16–17; Rom 8:26–27.
87 Exod 3:4, 13–14; 19:23; Lev 11:44–45; Pss 22:1–5; 29:1; 111:1–9; Isa 6:3.
88 2 Kgs 19:22; Ps 78:41; Isa 1:4; 31:1; 47:4; 54:5; Jer 50:29; 51:5.
89 2 Cor 3:17.
90 Smail, *Giving Gift*, 32–44.
91 Yves Congar, *I Believe in the Holy Spirit*, vol. 3 (New York: Crossroad Herder, 1997), 5.
92 J. I. Packer, *Keep in Step with the Spirit* (Leicester, UK: IVP, 1984), 66.
93 "Through your Holy Spirit you call us to new birth in a creation restored by love." *Scottish Liturgy 1982* (Edinburgh: General Synod of the Scottish Episcopal Church, 1996), 9.
94 Rev 21:1–4.
95 Rev 21:22–25.
96 Rom 8:9.
97 1 Cor 6:19.
98 See, for what follows (with a certain amount of editorial license), 1 Cor 3:16; 6:19; and Eph 2:21–22; 4:30.
99 Gal 5:25.
100 Acts 19:2.
101 Acts 19:2 (emphasis added).
102 See page 200 above.
103 John 3:3–9.
104 1 John 4:12.

Chapter 10

1. See Karina Martinez-Carter, "8 of Our Favorite Ridiculously Long German Words," *The Week*, June 10, 2013, accessed January 2, 2019, https://theweek.com/articles/463500/8-favorite-ridiculously-long-german-words.
2. Anthony Newton Flew, *Jesus and His Church: A Study of the Idea of Ecclesia in the New Testament* (Carlisle, UK: Paternoster, 1998), x.
3. For further instances, see, amusingly, Joe Varadi, "A Playful Rant on Verbing," Writing Cooperative, September 23, 2017, https://writingcooperative.com/a-playful-rant-on-verbing-b1fbd2f073dd; and Joe Varadi, "A Playful Praise of Nouning," Writing Cooperative, October 6, 2017, https://writingcooperative.com/a-playful-praise-of-nouning-8ed9b8515d4c.
4. Lesslie Newbigin, *The Gospel in a Pluralist Society* (London: SPCK, 1989), 227, 224. As will be apparent, this chapter owes a significant debt to Newbigin's thought, which remains, more than twenty years after his death, altogether less familiar among thinking Christians than it deserves to be.
5. See, e.g., Richard Bauckham and Trevor Hart, *Hope against Hope: Christian Eschatology at the Turn of the Millennium* (London: Darton, Longman & Todd, 1999), 10–20.
6. Ironically, this history of Christian malfeasance and malpractice serves precisely to confirm rather than contradict the basic diagnosis and prescription of that same gospel as regards the human condition in which we all share.
7. Newbigin, *Pluralist Society*, 223. In 1938, as the "civilized," intellectually advanced nations of the world were bracing themselves for yet another devastating military conflagration, Jacques Maritain published a study of human action informed by the rich vision of the medieval Christian theologian Thomas Aquinas. It was entitled, provocatively, *True Humanism* (London: Geoffrey Bles, 1938).
8. 1 Cor 1:18.
9. Newbigin, *Pluralist Society*, 222. See also Newbigin, chs. 1–4 and 17. On these same themes, see further Hart, *Faith Thinking*.
10. See, e.g., Hart, *Faith Thinking*, 11–14.
11. See Hart, ch. 3.
12. Polanyi, *Personal Knowledge*.
13. Hart, *Faith Thinking*, 53. See Polanyi, *Personal Knowledge*, 272–79.
14. Polanyi, *Personal Knowledge*, 300–316. A belief invested with "universal intent" (i.e., believed to be a truth to which all should subscribe), Polanyi

notes, is one the act of believing in which compels us to behave "as we must" in the light of it, whereas a truth conceded as "private" leaves us, strictly speaking, free to do as we choose. See Polanyi, 308–9.
15 Newbigin, *Pluralist Society*, 222.
16 See, e.g., Charles Taylor, *Modern Social Imaginaries* (Durham, NC: Duke University Press, 2004).
17 The metaphor of the wider culture possessing and shaping its citizens through their participation in "liturgies" is developed to helpful effect by James K. A. Smith. See, e.g., James K. A. Smith, *Desiring the Kingdom: Worship, Worldview, and Cultural Formation* (Grand Rapids, MI: Baker Academic, 2009). Smith's work provides a rich, nuanced account of how "believing" in anything is a multifaceted matter and how knowing a truth involves the heart, the imagination, and the body as well as the mind. An accessible starting point is James K. A. Smith, *You Are What You Love: The Spiritual Power of Habit* (Grand Rapids, MI: Brazos, 2016).
18 Newbigin, *Pluralist Society*, 222.
19 Newbigin, 226.
20 See, e.g., Karl Barth, *Church Dogmatics*, vol. 2, pt. 2 (Edinburgh: T&T Clark, 1957), 195–305.
21 Isa 6:9–10.
22 Newbigin, *Pluralist Society*, 232.
23 John 8:32 NKJV.
24 Polanyi refers to scientific communities as "communities of verifiers" in precisely this sense—i.e., groups whose shared commitment to certain beliefs and ways of thinking about and dealing with reality are reinforced by their mutual testimony to the perceived fruitfulness and "truth" of results which confirm their hypotheses and theories. In structural terms, precisely the same is true of any human community of knowers in their encounters with reality.
25 Newbigin, *Pluralist Society*, 227.
26 Newbigin, 222.
27 Newbigin, 227.

Chapter 11

1 Among those referred to in this chapter, see, for instance, L. Gregory Jones, *Embodying Forgiveness: A Theological Analysis* (Grand Rapids, MI: Eerdmans, 1995); Jacques Derrida, *On Cosmopolitanism and Forgiveness* (London: Routledge, 2001); David Konstan, *Before Forgiveness: The Origins*

of a Moral Idea (Cambridge: Cambridge University Press, 2010); and Martha Nussbaum, *Anger and Forgiveness: Resentment, Generosity, Justice* (New York: Oxford University Press, 2016).

2 Jeffrie Murphy, *Getting Even: Forgiveness and Its Limits* (New York: Oxford University Press, 2003), viii; cited in Nussbaum, *Anger and Forgiveness*, 10.

3 "Dieu me pardonnera, c'est son métier." The same statement is commonly but seemingly mistakenly attributed to Voltaire.

4 This concern lay at the heart of Dietrich Bonhoeffer's distinction between "cheap" and "costly" notions of grace. See Dietrich Bonhoeffer, *The Cost of Discipleship* (London: SCM, 1959), 35–47.

5 Jürgen Moltmann, *God in Creation: An Ecological Doctrine of Creation* (London: SCM, 1985), 72–93. Moltmann's focus in this passage is actually upon the sense in which it may be said that it is "natural" for God to *create* rather than to forgive, but as his discussion in the same chapter makes quite clear, he sees the two things as inseparably linked in the purposes of God, and the same fundamental issues (about the nature of God's "freedom" to act in various ways) apply to each context.

6 See, for instance, P. T. Forsyth, *God the Holy Father* (London: Independent, 1957), 3–27.

7 Lev 20:26.

8 Lev 20:26; 1 Pet 1:15–16. Cf. Matt 5:48.

9 Exod 6:7; Lev 26:12; Jer 30:22; Ezek 36:28.

10 Jones, *Embodying Forgiveness*, 207.

11 See, e.g., pages 39–40, 47–48, 109–11 above.

12 See Jones, *Embodying Forgiveness*, 207.

13 John 14:9.

14 John 14:9 NKJV (emphasis added).

15 Luke 23:34.

16 Hannah Arendt, *The Human Condition*, 2nd ed. (1958; Chicago: University of Chicago Press, 2018), 240–42.

17 See, e.g., Matt 6:14–15; 16:27; Mark 2:5–12; 11:35; Luke 7:47–50.

18 The same question is posed by the disciples in the miracle of the calming of the storm. Authority over the forces of nature and turbulent waters that evoked the chaos out of which creation itself was summoned in the beginning was again something associated directly with God's unique role and power as the creator of heaven and earth. See, e.g., Mark 4:39–41; cf. Gen 1:1–2; Job 38:10; Ps 18:16–19; 29:1–4, 10–11; 77:16–20; 107:23–32; Prov 8:29; Jer 5:22.

19 Phil 2:7.
20 See, e.g., Mark 2:10.
21 Matt 13:37, 41–42; 18:11; 24:30; 25:31–32; Mark 10:32; 14:62; Luke 9:26–27; Acts 7:54–57; Rev 1:12–13. Elsewhere, the phrase is used by Jesus seemingly by way of self-reference ("I") but again to refer to things radically particular to himself rather than common to human beings in general, including his passion and crucifixion and his resurrection. See, e.g., Mark 9:31; 14:21.
22 Konstan, *Before Forgiveness*, 115.
23 Matt 6:12; 18:15–35.
24 On this, see further, for instance, the helpful and accessible treatment in Torrance, *Mediation of Christ*, 26–42.
25 So, e.g., as C. S. Lewis observes, "if God's moral judgment differs from ours so that our 'black' may be His 'white,' we can mean nothing by calling Him good; for to say 'God is good,' while asserting that His goodness is wholly different than ours, is really only to say 'God is we know not what.' And an utterly unknown quality in God cannot give us moral grounds for loving or obeying Him. If He is not (in our sense) 'good' we shall obey, if at all, only through fear—and should be equally ready to obey an omnipotent Fiend." The idea that our creaturely notion of goodness can have absolutely no purchase on God at all, therefore, Lewis concludes, "may turn Christianity into a form of devil-worship." C. S. Lewis, *The Problem of Pain* (London: Fount Paperbacks, 1977), 25.
26 See pages 73, 187–99 above.
27 Philosopher Martha Nussbaum disentangles these three distinct relational contexts in which the category of forgiveness is widely, if not always appropriately or helpfully, deployed in today's world. See Nussbaum, *Anger and Forgiveness*, 7–9 passim.
28 See, for instance, Nussbaum, 76. It is on these grounds that Nussbaum finally concludes "forgiveness," even in its best human versions, to be less obviously a virtue in our human dealings with one another than is typically supposed. Better still, she argues, would be a moral disposition that did not react with anger in the first place and had no need, therefore, deliberately to waive or forego it.
29 Derrida, *On Cosmopolitanism*, 55.
30 Derrida, 27–28.
31 Derrida, 42.
32 Derrida, 55.

33 It is common enough in the sphere of metaphor generally, and therefore in the case of metaphors related to the divine atonement too, for there to be a clash between the logic or various "entailments" of distinct metaphors used to speak of the same thing. My point here is not that different metaphors may *not* clash without necessarily provoking concern about their value as instruments suited to the disclosure of truth but simply to observe that these particular two metaphors actually *do not* clash in the way that they have sometimes been held to. The wider issue is treated in a helpful and accessible manner in George Lakoff and Mark Johnson, *Metaphors We Live By* (Chicago: University of Chicago Press, 1980).

34 Charles L. Griswold, *Forgiveness: A Philosophical Exploration* (Cambridge: Cambridge University Press, 2007).

35 Nussbaum, *Anger and Forgiveness*, 57.

36 Nussbaum, 57.

37 See, e.g., Matt 6:14–15; Luke 17:3–4. Cf. Acts 3:19.

38 Tertullian, *On Penitence*; and Tertullian, *On Purity*.

39 For a fuller consideration of Tertullian's thought, see Hart, *In Him Was Life*, 117–29.

40 See further Hart, 115–49.

41 Nussbaum, *Anger and Forgiveness*, 68.

42 Eph 2:8–9.

43 See Torrance, *Triune God*, 44. The distinction between "legal" (we might better catch the connotation by saying "legalistic") and "evangelical" forms of repentance is one used already by major Reformers such as Martin Bucer and John Calvin (see, for instance, Calvin's discussion of repentance in his *Institutes of the Christian Religion* 4.3) but is further refined and reaches its most precise form in the eighteenth century and the writings of the so-called Marrow Men in Scotland. Insistence on this distinction and the pastorally disastrous consequences of failing to draw it remains central to this theological tradition, within which Torrance stands.

44 Derrida, *On Cosmopolitanism*, 34–35.

45 Derrida, 32.

46 Konstan, *Before Forgiveness*, 21.

47 "Tout comprendre, c'est tout pardonner." The proverb is of unknown origin, despite multiple ascriptions of it. Tolstoy cites it in *War and Peace*, vol. 1, pt. 1 (1868), ch. 28.

48 Derrida, *On Cosmopolitanism*, 48–50.

49 Derrida, 49.

50 Derrida, 34; Nussbaum, *Anger and Forgiveness*, 12. It is interesting to note that among "secular" theorists on this topic, it is precisely two thinkers steeped inevitably and thoroughly by virtue of their upbringing in the milieu of Jewish texts and practices who are driven to this radical account of forgiveness as either utterly gratuitous or fatally compromised.
51 Derrida, *On Cosmopolitanism*, 39.
52 Rom 5:8.
53 Rom 5:10.
54 Rom 5:8; cf. 1 John 4:10, 16.
55 1 John 4:7–12.
56 Nussbaum, *Anger and Forgiveness*, 12.
57 Nussbaum, 12–13.
58 Luke 15:20.
59 Luke 15:19.
60 Nussbaum, 80. Cf. Luke 15:11–24.
61 Nussbaum, *Anger and Forgiveness*, 81.
62 See, e.g., William B. Irvine, *A Guide to the Good Life: The Ancient Art of Stoic Joy* (New York: Oxford University Press, 2009); Massimo Pigliucci, *How to Be a Stoic: Ancient Wisdom for Modern Living* (London: Rider, 2017); and Jonas Salzgeber, *The Little Book of Stoicism: Timeless Wisdom to Gain Resilience, Confidence, and Calmness* (self-pub., 2019).
63 Ichiro Kishimi and Fumitake Koga, *The Courage to Be Disliked: How to Free Yourself, Change Your Life and Achieve Real Happiness* (London: Allen & Unwin, 2018), 15–18.
64 We are familiar these days with the notion of "emotional intelligence" (the capacity to recognize and respond appropriately to emotions in ourselves and others) but mostly tend still to think of emotion itself as belonging in an entirely different category from the operations of our intellect or "reason," perhaps even thinking of it as intrinsically nonrational or even *ir*rational in its operations. That our "feelings," or emotional responses, to a state of affairs can be not just "rational" (utterly appropriate to the reality confronting us) but sometimes altogether more reliable guides to the nature of a circumstance than the more detached deliverances of purported "cool reason" is the compelling argument of Scots philosopher John Macmurray's *Reason and Emotion* (London: Faber & Faber, 1961).
65 See, e.g., Forsyth, *God the Holy Father*, 3–19.
66 Acts 2:38 NLT.
67 Luke 11:4 NLT.

68 Arendt, *Human Condition*, 240–43.
69 Matt 10:8.
70 Derrida, *On Cosmopolitanism*, 39, 45.
71 *Scottish Liturgy* (Edinburgh: General Synod of the Scottish Episcopal Church, 1982), 6; and 1 Cor 15:28.

Chapter 12

1 See Wright, *Surprised by Hope*, 25, 52, 206.
2 So, for instance, Charlotte Elliott's classic "Just as I Am, without One Plea" petitions God that she may be granted opportunity to prove God's boundless love "here for a season, then above," while the authors of "Come Gracious Spirit, Heavenly Dove" implore God to "lead us to heav'n that we may share / fullness of joy for ever there." Among numerous Christmas carols guilty of perpetuating this misapprehension, especially notable is William Chatterton Dix's "As with Gladness Men of Old," the fourth verse of which urges Jesus to "keep us in the narrow way" so that "when earthly things are past," he can "bring our souls at last" to the "heav'nly country," where we shall sing alleluias to him forever, a sentiment echoed directly in the theologically dreadful "Away in a Manger" and its familiar plea that the Lord would "fit us for heaven to live with thee there." Meanwhile, the Collect for Ascension Day is surely misleading in its request that "we in heart and mind may also ascend and with him continually dwell," not least when compounded by the following Sunday's "exalt us to the place where our Saviour Christ is gone before" (i.e., "your kingdom in heaven").
3 Phil 1:21 ESV.
4 Wright, *Surprised by Hope*, 25–27.
5 Dante Alighieri, *The Comedy of Dante Alighieri the Florentine*, 3 vols., trans. Dorothy L. Sayers with Barbara Reynolds (London: Penguin Classics, 1949–62).
6 Dante's near-contemporary Giotto di Bondone, for instance, painted a series of remarkable frescoes in the Scrovegni Chapel in Padua, including a depiction on the west wall of the Last Judgment and its presumed sorting of humankind into the categories of those saved and lost, respectively. While the former are to be seen joining the ranks of the saints in midair, the latter are being dragged down to hell by demons while enduring punishments just as terrible as anything imagined by Dante in his *Inferno*. Since this particular fresco is the last thing one sees on departing the building through the west door, this is no doubt intended by the artist as a

salutary reminder to the congregation of the importance of decisions made and actions undertaken in the world to which they are returning.

7 Wright, *Surprised by Hope*, 26.
8 Compare, e.g., Matt 5:3 with Luke 6:20 or Matt 13:31–32 with Mark 4:30–32.
9 Matt 6:10.
10 *Scottish Liturgy* (1982), 6.
11 This is a refrain familiar from Henry Francis Lyte's hymn "Praise, My Soul, the King of Heaven."
12 Hab 2:14.
13 2 Cor 5:2–5.
14 Grey Town is variously interpreted as hell or purgatory but seemingly serves the function of either, depending on whether one remains there.
15 See C. S. Lewis, *The Great Divorce: A Dream* (London: Geoffrey Bles, 1946), 13–29.
16 See, for instance, Iain McGilchrist, *The Master and His Emissary: The Divided Brain and the Making of the Western World*, new expanded ed. (New Haven, CT: Yale University Press, 2019); and Mark Johnson, *The Meaning of the Body: Aesthetics of Human Understanding* (Chicago: University of Chicago Press, 2007).
17 See Johnson, *Meaning of the Body*, 12.
18 Gen 3:19. See also Gen 2:7; Eccl 3:19–20; Ps 104:29. Such verses serve at least to show that the idea of our bodies as "stardust," temporary configurations of atoms with both long pasts and futures that are unlikely to involve us ever again, is not a peculiarly modern one, and it seems obvious that biblical imaginings of a future "general resurrection" would have had to reckon already with the implications of their contemporary versions of it.
19 See, e.g., Isa 65:17; 66:22; Rev 21:5. Emphasis on the qualitatively new, unprecedented action of God in this regard is a particular theme of Isa 44–66, and the prophet makes a deliberate use of the Hebrew term *bara'*, reserved in the Bible more widely for the unique prerogative and action of God as creator. The apostle Paul draws on this same theme in his use of the phrase "new creation" to refer to the phase of God's redemptive activity that begins decisively with the appearance of Christ—its "first fruits" (2 Cor 5:17; Gal 6:15).
20 Matt 22:28: "In the resurrection, then, whose wife of the seven will she be? For all of them had married her."

21 See Bauckham and Hart, *Hope against Hope*, 127–32.
22 *Out of nothing* is a technical theological phrase deployed classically to indicate that God's original creative act was unconstrained by the existence and characteristics of any given materials or any agents or forces apart from God himself, the donation of existence itself being part and parcel of God's summoning of "all things" into being in the form of a world. Before this gracious decision and act (though since creaturely time was itself part of the gift, we can use terms such as *before* only metaphorically, having no other way of expressing ourselves meaningfully on the point), there was only God, and creation was thus a self-limiting act on God's part, granting something existence and "making room" for its existence alongside himself.
23 Mic 4:1–4.
24 Isa 25:6; Matt 26:27–29; Luke 14:12–24. See also, e.g., Exod 24:11; Job 36:16; Ps 23:5; Isa 55:1–2; Joel 2:24–26; Luke 15:22–32; John 2:1–11; Rev 19:9.
25 Bauckham and Hart, *Hope against Hope*, 100.
26 Bauckham and Hart, 100.
27 Bauckham and Hart, 99.
28 Rev 21:4; Isa 25:7–8.
29 Bauckham and Hart, 77–80.
30 Matt 19:26.
31 See pages 133–34, 274 above.
32 Bauckham and Hart, *Hope against Hope*, 201–10.
33 See page 8 above.

SELECTED BIBLIOGRAPHY

Alighieri, Dante. *The Comedy of Dante Alighieri the Florentine*. Cantica 1, *Hell*; Cantica 2, *Purgatory*; Cantica 3, *Paradise*. Translated by Dorothy L. Sayers. London: Penguin Classics, 1949, 1955, 1962 [with Barbara Reynolds].

Arendt, Hannah. *The Human Condition*. 2nd ed. Chicago: University of Chicago Press, 2018.

Augustine. *Confessions*. Translated by Henry Chadwick. Oxford: Oxford University Press, 1991.

Badcock, Gary D. *Light of Truth and Fire of Love: A Theology of the Holy Spirit*. Grand Rapids, MI: Eerdmans, 1997.

Barth, Karl. *Church Dogmatics*. Vol. 1, bk. 1, *The Doctrine of the Word of God*. Edinburgh: T&T Clark, 1975.

———. *Church Dogmatics*. Vol. 2, bk. 2, *The Doctrine of God*. Edinburgh: T&T Clark, 1957.

———. *Church Dogmatics*. Vol. 3, bk. 1, *The Doctrine of Creation*. Edinburgh: T&T Clark, 1958.

———. *Dogmatics in Outline*. London: SCM, 1949.

Bauckham, Richard. *The Bible and Ecology: Rediscovering the Community of Creation*. Waco, TX: Baylor University Press, 2010.

———. *Jesus and the God of Israel*. Milton Keynes, UK: Paternoster, 2008.

Bauckham, Richard, and Trevor Hart. *Hope against Hope: Christian Eschatology at the Turn of the Millennium*. Grand Rapids, MI: Eerdmans, 1999.

Begbie, Jeremy. *Theology, Music and Time*. Cambridge: Cambridge University Press, 2000.

Bird, Michael F. *What Christians Ought to Believe: An Introduction to Christian Doctrine through the Apostles' Creed*. Grand Rapids, MI: Zondervan, 2016.

Bonhoeffer, Dietrich. *The Cost of Discipleship*. London: SCM, 1959.

Collingwood, R. G. *The Idea of History*. Oxford: Oxford University Press, 1946.

Congar, Yves. *I Believe in the Holy Spirit*. Vol. 3. New York: Crossroad Herder, 1997.

Cranfield, C. E. B. *The Apostles' Creed: A Faith to Live By*. Edinburgh: T&T Clark, 1993.

Day, David. *This Jesus*. Leicester, UK: IVP, 1980.
Derrida, Jacques. *On Cosmopolitanism and Forgiveness*. London: Routledge, 2001.
Eichrodt, Walther. *Theology of the Old Testament*. Vol. 1. London: SCM, 1961.
Farmer, H. H. *The World and God: A Study of Prayer, Providence and Miracle in Christian Experience*. London: Nisbet, 1936.
Fee, Gordon D. *God's Empowering Presence: The Holy Spirit in the Letters of Paul*. Peabody, MA: Hendrickson, 1994.
Flew, Anthony Newton. *Jesus and His Church: A Study of the Idea of Ecclesia in the New Testament*. Carlisle, UK: Paternoster, 1998.
Forsyth, P. T. *God the Holy Father*. London: Independent, 1957.
———. *The Justification of God: Lectures for War-Time on a Christian Theodicy*. 1st ed. London: Duckworth, 1916.
———. *The Work of Christ*. Eugene, OR: Wipf & Stock, 2001.
Fretheim, Terence. *Exodus*. Louisville, KY: Westminster John Knox, 1991.
Goldingay, John. *Old Testament Theology*. Vol. 1, *Israel's Gospel*. Downers Grove, IL: IVP Academic, 2003.
Goodman, Nelson. *Languages of Art: An Approach to a Theory of Symbols*. London: Oxford University Press, 1969.
Griswold, Charles L. *Forgiveness: A Philosophical Exploration*. Cambridge: Cambridge University Press, 2007.
Gunton, Colin. *The Actuality of Atonement: A Study of Metaphor, Rationality and the Christian Tradition*. Edinburgh: T&T Clark, 1988.
Hart, Trevor. *Faith Thinking: The Dynamics of Christian Theology*. 2nd ed. Eugene, OR: Cascade, 2020.
———. *In Him Was Life: The Person and Work of Christ*. Waco, TX: Baylor University Press, 2019.
———. *Making Good: Creation, Creativity, and Artistry*. Waco, TX: Baylor University Press, 2014.
Hauerwas, Stanley, and William H. Willimon. *Resident Aliens: Life in the Christian Colony*. Nashville: Abingdon, 1989.
Hengel, Martin. *Crucifixion: In the Ancient World and the Folly of the Message of the Cross*. Minneapolis: Fortress, 1977.
Heron, Alasdair I. C. *The Holy Spirit*. Philadelphia: Westminster, 1983.
Irvine, William B. *A Guide to the Good Life: The Ancient Art of Stoic Joy*. New York: Oxford University Press, 2009.
Johnson, Mark. *The Meaning of the Body: Aesthetics of Human Understanding*. Chicago: University of Chicago Press, 2007.

Jones, L. Gregory. *Embodying Forgiveness: A Theological Analysis*. Grand Rapids, MI: Eerdmans, 1995.

Kierkegaard, Søren. *Philosophical Fragments*. Plano, TX: Jovian, 2017.

Kishimi, Ichiro, and Fumitake Koga. *The Courage to Be Disliked: How to Free Yourself, Change Your Life and Achieve Real Happiness*. London: Allen & Unwin, 2018.

Konstan, David. *Before Forgiveness: The Origins of a Moral Idea*. Cambridge: Cambridge University Press, 2010.

Lakoff, George, and Mark Johnson. *Metaphors We Live By*. Chicago: University of Chicago Press, 1980.

Lash, Nicholas. *The Beginning and End of "Religion."* Cambridge: Cambridge University Press, 1996.

Lewis, C. S. *The Great Divorce: A Dream*. London: Geoffrey Bles, 1946.

———. "Is Theology Poetry?" In *Essay Collection: Faith, Christianity and the Church*, edited by Lesley Walmsley, 10–21. London: HarperCollins, 2000.

———. *Mere Christianity*. London: Collins, 1952.

———. *Miracles*. London: Fontana, 1960.

———. *The Problem of Pain*. London: Geoffrey Bles, 1940.

———. *The Problem of Pain*. London: Fount Paperbacks, 1977.

———. *The Weight of Glory and Other Addresses*. London: Geoffrey Bles, 1949.

Mackie, J. L. *Ethics: Inventing Right and Wrong*. London: Penguin, 1971.

Macmurray, John. *Reason and Emotion*. London: Faber & Faber, 1961.

Maritain, Jacques. *True Humanism*. London: Geoffrey Bles, 1938.

McCabe, Herbert, ed. *St. Thomas Aquinas Summa Theologiae*. Vol. 3, *Knowing and Naming God*. London: Blackfriars in conjunction with Eyre and Spottiswoode, 1964.

McFague, Sallie. *Metaphorical Theology: Models of God in Religious Language*. Philadelphia: Fortress, 1982.

McGilchrist, Iain. *The Master and His Emissary: The Divided Brain and the Making of the Western World*. New expanded ed. New Haven: Yale University Press, 2019.

McGrath, Alister. *I Believe: Exploring the Apostles' Creed*. Downers Grove, IL: IVP, 1997.

Moltmann, Jürgen. *The Coming of God: Christian Eschatology*. London: SCM, 1996.

———. *God in Creation: An Ecological Doctrine of Creation*. London: SCM, 1985.

———. *The Spirit of Life: A Universal Affirmation*. London: SCM, 1992.
Moore, Nick. *Mindful Thoughts for Cyclists: Finding Balance on Two Wheels*. Brighton, UK: Leaping Hare, 2017.
Murphy, Jeffrie. *Getting Even: Forgiveness and Its Limits*. New York: Oxford University Press, 2003.
Newbigin, Lesslie. *The Gospel in a Pluralist Society*. London: SPCK, 1989.
Newman, John Henry. *An Essay in Aid of a Grammar of Assent*. London, 1870.
Nussbaum, Martha. *Anger and Forgiveness: Resentment, Generosity, Justice*. New York: Oxford University Press, 2016.
Osborne, Eric. *Irenaeus of Lyons*. Cambridge: Cambridge University Press, 2001.
O'Siadhail, Micheal. *Tongues*. Tarset, UK: Bloodaxe, 2010.
Packer, J. I. *Keep in Step with the Spirit*. Leicester, UK: IVP, 1984.
Pigliucci, Massimo. *How to Be a Stoic: Ancient Wisdom for Modern Living*. London: Rider, 2017.
Polanyi, Michael. *Personal Knowledge*. London: Routledge & Kegan Paul, 1958.
Postman, Neil. *Amusing Ourselves to Death: Public Discourse in the Age of Show Business*. London: Methuen, 1987.
Priestley, Joseph. *Disquisitions Relating to Matter and Spirit*. Vol. 1. Birmingham, UK: J. Johnson, 1782.
Pullman, Philip. *Northern Lights*. London: Scholastic Children's, 1995.
Ricoeur, Paul. *The Rule of Metaphor: Multi-disciplinary Studies of the Creation of Meaning in Language*. London: Routledge & Kegan Paul, 1978.
Rollins, Peter. *How (Not) to Speak of God*. London: SPCK, 2006.
Salzgeber, Jonas. *The Little Book of Stoicism: Timeless Wisdom to Gain Resilience, Confidence, and Calmness*. Self-published, 2019.
Scott, Drusilla. *Everyman Revived: The Common Sense of Michael Polanyi*. Lewes, UK: Book Guild, 1985.
Smail, Tom. *The Giving Gift: The Holy Spirit in Person*. London: Hodder & Stoughton, 1988.
Smith, James K. A. *Desiring the Kingdom: Worship, Worldview, and Cultural Formation*. Grand Rapids, MI: Baker Academic, 2009.
———. *You Are What You Love: The Spiritual Power of Habit*. Grand Rapids, MI: Brazos, 2016.
Soskice, Janet. *Metaphor and Religious Language*. Oxford: Clarendon, 1985.
Taylor, Charles. *Modern Social Imaginaries*. Durham, NC: Duke University Press, 2004.

Thiselton, Anthony C. *The First Epistle to the Corinthians*. Grand Rapids, MI: Eerdmans, 2000.
Thorne, Matt. *Prince*. London: Faber & Faber, 2012.
Torrance, James B. *Worship, Community and the Triune God of Grace*. Carlisle, UK: Paternoster, 1996.
Torrance, Thomas F. *The Mediation of Christ*. 2nd ed. Edinburgh: T&T Clark, 1992.
———. *Theology in Reconstruction*. London: SCM, 1965.
Vanhoozer, Kevin, ed. *Dictionary for Theological Interpretation of the Bible*. Grand Rapids, MI: Baker Academic, 2005.
Wilder, Amos. *Theopoetic*. Philadelphia: Fortress, 1976.
Wolterstorff, Nicholas. *Divine Discourse: Philosophical Reflections on the Claim That God Speaks*. Cambridge: Cambridge University Press, 1995.
Wright, N. T. *The Resurrection of the Son of God*. London: SPCK, 2003.
Wright, Tom. *The Lord and His Prayer*. London: SPCK, 2012.
———. *Surprised by Hope*. London: SPCK, 2007.
Wybrow, Cameron. *The Bible, Baconianism, and Mastery over Nature: The Old Testament and Its Modern Misreading*. New York: Peter Lang, 1991.

INDEX

Adler, Alfred, 266
Alighieri, Dante, 157, 278, 280, 325nn5–6
Anselm, 30–31
Aquinas, Thomas, 185, 313n22, 319n7
Arendt, Hannah, 240–42, 272, 321n16, 325n68
Asimov, Isaac, 311n2
Augustine, 59, 299n1, 302n30

Badcock, Gary, 314n27, 317n70
Barth, Karl, 30, 102, 193, 226, 299n3, 300n18, 301n18, 306n4, 316n56, 320n20
Bauckham, Richard, 63, 77, 149–50, 302n34, 302n36, 303n15, 304nn17–18, 304n21, 304n23, 309n16, 309n19, 319n5, 327n21
Begbie, Jeremy, 309n1
Bird, Michael F., 298n12, 301n13, 303n2, 306nn10–11
Bonhoeffer, Dietrich, 321n4
Bucer, Martin, 323n43

Calvin, John, 323n43
Carroll, Lewis, 299n7
Chadwick, Henry, 302n30
Collingwood, R. G., 308n26
Congar, Yves, 198, 318n91
Cranfield, C. E. B., 302n16, 302n31, 303n8, 305n13, 305n19, 306n2

Day, David, 306n1
Derrida, Jacques, 250–51, 259, 261, 262, 273, 320n1, 322nn29–32, 323nn44–45, 323nn48–49, 324nn50–51, 325n70
Dickens, Charles, 55, 302n21
Dix, William Chatterton, 325n2

Eichrodt, Walther, 316n57
Elliott, Charlotte, 325n2
Epictetus, 266

Farmer, H. H., 300n17
Fee, Gordon, 307n4
Flew, Anthony Newton, 319n2
Forsyth, P. T., 70, 103, 237, 269–70, 303n3, 306n5, 321n6, 324n65
Fretheim, Terence, 302n27

Giotto di Bondone, 157, 325n6
Goldingay, John, 303n5
Goodman, Nelson, 312n16
Griswold, Charles, 252–53, 254, 258, 259, 260, 323n34
Gunton, Colin, 306n15

Hart, Trevor, 297n4, 299n14, 300n15, 301n19, 310n1, 311n10, 312n13, 314n33, 318n85, 319n5, 319nn9–11, 319n13, 323nn39–40, 327n21, 327nn25–27, 327n29, 327n32

Hauerwas, Stanley, 152, 309n25
Heine, Heinrich, 236
Hengel, Martin, 306n9
Heron, Alasdair, 190, 315n45

Irenaeus of Lyons, 314n33
Irvine, William B., 324n62

Jenkins, David, 119, 307n2
Jerome, 1
Johnson, Mark, 313n19, 323n33, 326nn16–17
Jones, L. Gregory, 238, 239, 320n1, 321n10, 321n12

Kierkegaard, Søren, 144, 308n9
Kishimi, Ichiro, 324n63
Koga, Fumitake, 324n63
Konstan, David, 242–43, 320n1, 322n22, 323n46

Lakoff, George, 313n19, 323n33
Lash, Nicholas, 300n13
Lewis, C. S., 4, 9, 16, 48, 94, 108, 111, 121, 184, 282–83, 298n6, 299n6, 301n14, 305n18, 305n21, 306nn21–22, 306nn13–14, 307n5, 312nn14–15, 322n25, 326n15
Luther, Martin, 129, 256
Lyte, Henry Francis, 326n11

MacDonald, George, 311n3
Mackie, J. L., 300n14
Macmurray, John, 324n64
Maddox, John, 303n37
Marcion, 69
Marcus Aurelius, 266

Maritain, Jacques, 319n7
Martinez-Carter, Karina, 319n1
McEwan, Ian, 311n2
McFague, Sallie, 312n16, 313n21
McGrath, Alister, 306n3
Moltmann, Jürgen, 237, 307n1, 315n48, 321n5
Moore, Nick, 311n
Murphy, Jeffrie, 321n2

Nazianzus, Gregory, 315n40
Newbigin, Lesslie, 215, 221, 225, 227, 231, 233, 319n4, 319n7, 319n9, 320n15, 320nn18–19, 320n22, 320nn25–27
Newman, John Henry, 31–32, 301n20
Nussbaum, Martha, 252–54, 262, 264–65, 267, 268, 269, 321n1, 322nn27–28, 323nn35–36, 323n41, 324n50, 324nn56–57, 324nn60–61

Origen, 305n8
Osborne, Eric, 314n33
O'Siadhail, Micheal, 313n20

Packer, J. I., 318n92
Pigliucci, Massimo, 324n62
Plato, 61
Polanyi, Michael, 219–21, 300n11, 319n12, 319n14, 320n14, 320n24
Postman, Neil, 55, 302n20
Priestley, Joseph, 311n8
Pullman, Philip, 311n12, 312n12

Reynolds, Barbara, 325n5
Ricoeur, Paul, 185, 313n18
Rollins, Peter, 300n10

Salzgeber, Jonas, 324n62
Sayers, Dorothy L., 325n5
Scott, Drusilla, 300n11
Seneca, 266
Shakespeare, William, 88, 182, 311n8
Shrier, Cahleen, 316n70
Smail, Tom, 3, 17n76, 317n79, 318n85, 318n90
Smith, James K. A., 311n4, 320n17
Soskice, Janet, 186, 313n23
Spielberg, Steven, 57
Spurgeon, Charles, 203, 205

Taylor, Charles, 222, 311n4, 320n16
Tertullian, 253–54, 256, 323nn38–39
Thiselton, Anthony C., 310n4
Thorne, Matt, 303n1
Tolstoy, Leo, 323n47

Torrance, J. B., 258, 271, 309n29, 323n43
Torrance, T. F., 80, 299, 304nn26–28, 322n24
Twain, Mark, 209

Vanhoozer, Kevin, 301n2
Varadi, Joe, 319n3
Vincent of Lérins, 297n3
Voltaire, 321n3

Wilder, Amos, 308n24
Willimon, William, 152, 309n25
Wolterstorff, Nicholas, 300n16
Wright, N. T., 68, 128, 136, 152, 164–69, 278, 279, 301nn5–6, 303n2, 307n9, 307n13, 307n21, 308n23, 308n27, 309n26, 310n5, 310nn8–9, 325n1, 325n4, 326n7
Wybrow, Cameron, 302n32